William Morris
Textiles

Caricature of William Morris giving a lecture on weaving. A pencil drawing by Edward Burne-Jones c. 1880.

William Morris Textiles

LINDA PARRY

A Studio Book   The Viking Press   New York

To Don

PICTURE SOURCES

Illustrations in this book are reproduced by kind permission of the following: Academy
Editions, London, 116 *top*; Author's collection, 109 *left*; Badisches Landesmuseum
Karlsruhe, 118; Berger Collection, Sanford and Helen, 44; Birmingham Museum and
Art Gallery, back cover, 38, 51 *below*, 52, 60 *above*, 119 *below*; Castle Howard collection,
22–3, 60 *below*, 86; Castle Museum, Norwich, 113; Cecil Higgins Museum, Bedford, 34;
Hampshire County Museum Service, 124; *Country Life*, 141; Cranbrook Academy of
Art, USA, 35; Harland and Wolff Ltd, 129; Johnson, R.W.A., 49; Kersting, A.F.,
142; Los Angeles County Museum, 72 *left*; Metropolitan Museum of Art, New York,
121; Musées Royaux D'Art et D'Histoire, Brussels, 122; National Gallery of South
Africa, 112; National Gallery of Victoria, Australia, 25; National Monuments Record,
London, 80, 81, 144; National Portrait Gallery, London, 33, 174, National Trust,
London, 26 *below*, 143; Private collection, 14 & 39 (Sally Chappell), 31, 88, 90, 93, 94,
96, 98 *left* (S. Francis), 99 (Sally Chappell), 105 *right*, 109 *right*, 111 *above right*, 127, 138,
140; Public Record Office, London, 18, 76; Royal Scottish Museum, 21 *above*; St Bride
Printing Library, London, 132; Sherratt, Heather, 28; Society of Antiquaries, London,
12, 13, 63 (Sally Chappell), 101; State Library of South Australia, 145; Stead McAlpin
& Co. Ltd, 37 *above* (Sally Chappell); University of Newcastle Upon Tyne, 137; Victoria
and Albert Museum, London, front cover, 19, 20, 21 *below*, 24, 26, *above*, 27, 30, 34, 37
bottom, 42, 44, 46, 53, 54, 55, 57, 59, 62, 65, 66 *right*, 67, 72 *right*, 75, 82, 84, 91, 92, 93
below, 95, 108, 109, 111, 115, 119 *above*, 123, (photos, 19, 24, 26, 30, 54, 55, 59, 62, 95,
115, 123, taken by Sally Chappell; 91 & 115 *right* taken by Pip Barnard); Victorian
Society, London, 139; Walker Art Gallery, Liverpool, 109 *centre*; Weidenfeld &
Nicolson, 43, 46, 47, 51, 79, 83, 87, 105 *below*, 133, 134, 136, (photos 53, 46, 47, 51, 133,
134 taken by Sally Chappell; 79, 83, 87, 105, 136 taken by Pip Barnard); Whiteway,
Michael, 104; Whitworth Art Gallery, Manchester, 50; William Morris Gallery,
Walthamstow, frontispiece, half title, 56, 61, 66 *left*, 69, 70, 71, 93 *above*, 107, 110, 116
above.

Copyright © 1983 by Linda Parry
All rights reserved

First published in the United States of America in 1983
by The Viking Press (A Studio Book)
625 Madison Avenue, New York, N.Y. 10022
Published simultaneously in Canada by
Penguin Books Canada Limited

First published by George Weidenfeld & Nicolson Ltd, London, 1983

Library of Congress Cataloging in Publication Data
Parry, Linda
    Willaim Morris textiles.
    (A Studio book)
    Includes index.
    1. Morris, William, 1834–1896.   2. Textile
fabrics—England—History—19th century.
I. Title.
NK 8898.M67P37   747.22   82–70184
ISBN 0–670–77075–2 (cloth)   AACR2
ISBN 0–670–77074–4 (paper)

Printed and bound in Italy by L.E.G.O., Vicenza

Contents

Introduction

Throughout history textiles have been used to insulate and decorate the home and clothe the body but they have never been as popular as they are today. People are not only anxious to have well designed modern textiles and carpets around them but they are also becoming interested in collecting textiles popular in their parents' and grandparents' day. Nothing gives a quicker or more lasting example of period and style as fabric; it is portable, can be stored in a small area and with a minimum of care keeps its texture and pattern.

With this new awareness of historical textiles, both as collectors' items and as source material for modern design, one nineteenth-century designer and manufacturer, William Morris, comes to mind instantly as the single most important figure in British textile production. It was Morris who designed many of the textiles available in the shops today and it is thanks to the reproduction of his designs and admiration of his methods of work throughout the late nineteenth century that the standards of textile design and manufacture have improved from the printed dog-roses of mid Victorian design to what we see today. As a designer and manufacturer he was unique both in the context of Victorian traditions and the wider study of textile history. A pattern-maker of genius, he explored techniques in order to get the best from his designs in colour, composition and texture. He revived long forgotten techniques of dyeing, printing and weaving and, in his own workshops, revitalized medieval traditions of the designer-craftsman. He restored the status and self respect of the textile designer, printer and weaver, sunk in the doldrums of the Industrial Revolution.

Little is known of any early interest that William Morris may have had in textiles. His own childhood and education was one of Victorian middle-class normality and it is likely that the furnishings in his parents' homes in Walthamstow and Woodford, both south of London, conformed to conservative nineteenth-century taste. This was characterized by realistic floral designs for printed cottons and richly coloured reproductions of eighteenth-century patterns for woven silk damasks. The latter were much favoured for the curtains and upholstery of the well-to-do household then, as now. Morris's father, who died in 1847, when Morris was just thirteen years of age, made money from investments in copper mining and neither Morris's home life nor education at the newly opened Marlborough School show any evidence of or encouragement for his later skills. All of his formative years were spent in the south of England, far removed from the 'dark satanic mills' of the north, where, from the early years of the nineteenth century England's cotton and woollen industries had developed in the towns of Lancashire and Yorkshire.

Gaining a place to read Theology at Exeter College, Oxford did little to change Morris's isolation from the ravages of the Industrial Revolution but his early ambition to found a new monastic order was soon forgotten when, with friends from Pembroke College, he first discovered the delights of English Literature, particularly the work of poets such as Milton, Tennyson and Kingsley which encouraged him to start composing verse himself. By this time he was already forming his own ideas on design and decoration. It is said that on a family trip, some years earlier in 1851, to see the Great Exhibition displayed in Joseph Paxton's Crystal Palace in Hyde Park, London, he refused to enter, having some inkling of the over-mechanized and over-decorated exhibits inside. It is interesting to note that the earliest known studio photograph taken of Morris in Oxford at the age of twenty-three shows him sitting at a table, his arms resting on a cloth of printed felt. Decorated in the so-called 'Elizabethan' style, the piece would not have looked out of place in the Crystal Palace, and one is tempted to guess at the colours used, maroon and gold perhaps, or was it bottle-green?

Concurrent with his interest in secular literature, Morris developed a passion for all things medieval. His interest was not confined to gothic architecture and decoration, however, and he began, what his biographer J.M. Mackail described as, 'a prodigious assimilation of Medieval chronicles and romances'. This pre-occupation was to stay with him throughout his life. He was not an innovator in admiring the gothic style and, in fact, turned to it later than many of his contemporaries. The Catholic Emancipation Act of 1829 marked a renewal of interest in Church furnishings and led by the teachings and writings of the architect A.W.N. Pugin (1812–1852) the architectural style most admired and copied was European gothic. Morris went up to Oxford in the midst of this new religious fervour and must have come into personal contact with the teachings of the two main religio-intellectual groups active at the time, the Oxford Movement and the Cambridge Camden Society. However, Morris's own interest in medieval gothic was developed not so much from the puritanical, uncompromising ideas of Pugin but from the writings of John Ruskin, the critic, art patron and amateur watercolourist, and in particular, Ruskin's chapter 'Of the Nature of Gothic' from the second volume of *The Stones of Venice*. This was published in 1853 while Morris was in his first year at Oxford. Encouraged by this, Morris spent his first long vacation travelling in France and the Low Countries viewing the cathedrals and art collections available to the public. He must have seen many tapestries hanging in the cathedrals of Amiens, Beauvais and Chartres, and his obvious interest in oriental carpets and medieval tapestries, when he returned to Britain, showed the great impact the visit had had on him. His great friend and fellow Exeter College student, Edward Burne-Jones, accompanied him to the Continent the following year. Morris showed him all the treasures he had discovered on the previous visit with additional visits to the Louvre and Musée de Cluny in Paris. It was on the last night of the holiday, while walking on the quay at Le Havre that the two determined to abandon any ideas they had previously of entering the Church, to quit their studies as soon as they could, and 'begin a life of art'. Burne-Jones as a painter and Morris an architect.

After obtaining a pass degree from Exeter College in 1856 Morris entered the offices of George Edmund Street, a leading gothic-revival architect. His interest in architecture stayed with him throughout his life but his training was cut short for within a year he had joined Burne-Jones in rooms in Red Lion Square in London with the intention of pursuing a career as a designer. It is clear that during the first two years' tenancy, the two experimented with all forms of decoration and made a number of items of furniture and other artefacts for their own use. It was not until the year of his marriage in 1860, when he moved into his first home, the Red House, Bexleyheath, that his first textiles – embroideries of medieval-inspired female figures – were conceived by Morris. At this point he began to produce objects on a commercial basis and in 1861, together with seven friends he founded the firm of Morris, Marshall, Faulkner and Company. Morris's reasons for turning to commercial manufacture were explained by him some years later, in 1883, '[I] got a friend [Philip Webb, who he had met in Street's Oxford office] to build me a house very medieval in spirit in which I lived for 5 years, and set myself decorating it, we found ... that all the minor arts were in a state of complete degradation especially in England, and accordingly in 1861 with the conceited courage of a young man I set myself to reforming all that.'

Morris was not the first of his circle of friends to consider textiles as a technique worthy of consideration and design. By 1861 Ford Madox Brown and Dante Gabriel Rossetti, both founder members of the firm, were supplying manufacturers with repeating designs. William Holman Hunt had been brought up close to the textile industry, his father being manager of a cotton warehouse and he had in his youth worked in Richard Cobden's calico-printing design studio in London. By the middle of the nineteenth century textile designing was gaining a respectable status despite the anonymity insisted on by manufacturers competing one against another which was the rule at the various International Exhibitions of the period. As late as 1878, at the Paris

International Exhibition, Thomas Wardle who had been printing designs for Morris in the absence of his own workshops, displayed a number of these patterns under his own name in the Indian section, many of his own products having been imported from the East. Only when various well-respected architects began designing textiles for the churches they had built, did such denigration of the industrial artist begin to diminish. Pugin also made secular designs for textiles for his own home, which were commercially produced through the firms of Crace of London and Hardman of Birmingham. The geometric structure of Pugin's patterns based on an architectural format was developed to a greater extent by Owen Jones (1809–1874) with his silk designs for the Spitalfields firm founded by Benjamin Warner. These were taken in part from illustrations from his two influential books *Plans, Elevations, Sections and Details of the Alhambra*, published in 1842 and *The Grammar of Ornament* (1856). Both of these publications and a number of others published in the 1850s and 1860s became prime source material for freelance designers and manufacturers' design studios throughout Britain. Commercial textiles available to Morris in 1860 for the furnishing of the Red House, therefore fell into two diverse groups. Those inspired by architecture, repeating the various geometric and linear forms seen on stone and metal, and the stock-in-trade designs of super-realistic floral patterns dyed with the new bright aniline dyes showing roses, lilac, convolvulus, hydrangeas and lilies in a three-dimensional way that had not been possible before. Morris used both geometric repeats and natural forms in all his designs but the results were completely different from those seen before.

The reason for Morris's success as a designer can be attributed to four factors. Firstly, he insisted on learning the various modern and ancient techniques associated with textiles before he started to design so that he was fully aware of the benefits and limitations available. He became one of the most knowledgeable textile historians of his generation, and utilized this experience of tried traditional patterns and techniques in his own work, and, finally, he had knowledge, understanding and a deep love of all natural things – flowers, trees, insects, animals and birds – and used these motifs with authority gained from observing nature at first hand. More important than these practical considerations was his 'heaven-sent gift', as his daughter May referred to it, an ability to see design in mass and not in line and to create numerous successful original designs in swift succession with little apparent effort.

Morris was, in personality and appearance, the opposite of his carefully controlled, immaculate and balanced textile designs. Whereas he was a perfectionist in the preparation and manufacture of all his fabrics, he cared little for his own appearance which was scruffy and unkempt. He wore his hair unfashionably long and bushy, not in any attempt to appear bohemian, but because he had neither the time nor the patience to have it cut. He wore a flat and very battered soft hat, a worn suit of blue serge and indigo-dyed shirts of a brighter blue. In later years he carried a huge walking stick.

Morris possessed an explosive temper which friends found, at times, a most endearing trait, knowing when to avoid or to encourage the discussion of controversial topics. His genial face betrayed not only a great sense of fun but was marked with a deep compassion for mankind, who he believed 'to be roof and crown of things'. His interest in his fellow man transcended all class and social barriers although he could not help this involvement, on his side, being of an intellectual nature. Wilfrid Scawen Blunt, himself a great admirer of the opposite sex, remembered Morris as a man who would talk in precisely the same tone 'to a pretty woman as to a journeyman carpenter – that is to say, he would be interested if she had anything interesting to tell him but for not a moment longer'. To go into society was a torture to Morris and he never took pains to conceal it, although he enjoyed good food and wine and the company of friends. He was, however, happiest when hard at work (preferably of a manual nature) and is said to have carried out the tasks of ten men single-handed. This must have greatly contributed to his early death at the age of sixty-two. His own enthusiasm and willingness to work alongside his employees in the Morris & Co. workshops helped create an atmosphere of well-being, and Merton Abbey, the firm's workshop opened in 1882, was described as 'a colossal kindergarten for adults'.

Whereas Morris began to design and manufacture textiles only for his own use, and saw this chiefly as an exalted pastime, he was not averse to making money when this manufacture took on a commercial form. In his advice to the Commission for Technical Instruction in 1882 he wrote 'On the whole one must suppose that beauty is a marketable quality and that the better the work is all round both as a work of art and in its technique the most likely it is to find favour with the public.' It is this pioneering attitude that provides Morris's great inspiration to industry today and whereas it has become fashionable nowadays to question Morris's contribution to the history of twentieth-century design few can deny that he improved both the standard of products and conditions of manufacture.

As the owner of a factory and employer of workmen, Morris's own political beliefs are also questioned, but he explained his own socialism very clearly and to repudiate his critics this must be quoted in full:

There are some Socialists who do not think that the problem of the organisation of life and necessary labour can be dealt with by a huge national centralisation, working by a kind of magic for which no one feels himself responsible; that on the contrary it will be necessary for the unit of administration to be small enough for every citizen to feel himself responsible for its detail and be interested in them; that individual men cannot shuffle off the business of life on the shoulders of abstraction called the State, but must deal with it in conscious association with each other; that variety of life is as much the aim of true communism as equality of condition, and that nothing but an union of these two will bring real freedom.

He had tried, in his own company, to adopt profit-sharing for the workers, but as most of the journeymen were on piece-work this was not possible. Managers and under managers did, however, share in the profits and workmen's wages were higher than the average; an opportunity giving 'less to the capitalist' Morris believed. His insistence on good quality raw materials, almost obsolete natural dyes and time consuming hand processing for all his textiles meant that they were very expensive and it grieved him that his products were exclusive only to those who could afford them. However there could be no lowering of standards as the high quality of design and finish was the very essence of Morris's work and subsequently ensured his success.

This book is not intended to be yet another biography of Morris but looks rather more closely at one specific aspect of his life and that of others who contributed to the firm's manufacture of textiles. It is hoped that it will bury a number of previous misconceptions about fabric manufacture once and for all and that it will also stimulate new theories which may become the controversies of the future. Morris's reputation has, after all, vastly outgrown his own humble ambitions:

I have tried to produce goods which should be genuine as far as their mere substances are concerned, and should have on that account the primary beauty in them which belongs to naturally treated substances; have tried, for instance, to make woollen substances as woollen as possible, cotton as cottony as possible, and so on; have used only the dyes which are natural and simple, because they produce beauty almost without the intervention of art; all this is quite apart from the design in the stuffs or what not. On that head it has been, chiefly because of the social difficulties, almost impossible to do more than to ensure the *designer* (mostly myself) some pleasure in his art by getting him to understand the qualities of materials and the happy chances of processes.

Embroidery

I do not hope to be great at all in anything but perhaps
I may reasonably hope to be happy in my work. [1]

With these words Morris broke the news to his mother that he was not, as had been expected, to enter the Church on finishing his studies at Exeter College, Oxford. Instead, on the morning of 21 January 1856, he started as articled apprentice in the Beaumont Street, Oxford office of the architect George Edmund Street (1824–81) whom he had previously met at the Oxford Plainsong Society. At this time Street had run his own office for only seven years but was already a church architect of high esteem. An advocate of gothic-revivalist styles and a believer in Tractarianism (a re-awakening of interest in the decoration, pomp and regalia of religious ceremony), Street designed churches not as empty buildings but as receptacles for furniture and furnishings of his own taste and often his own design. Embroidery became a crucial part of these furnishings and altar frontals from his designs were worked initially by Jones and Willis, a leading ecclesiastical outfitters and, from 1854, by a small but influential group, the Ladies Ecclesiastical Embroidery Society. Founded jointly by Street's sister and Miss Agnes Blencowe, the Society produced some of the finest church embroideries of the nineteenth century from designs by many leading designers and architects.

Although Morris stayed in Street's office for only nine months his time there was extremely happy. Morris had a great deal of admiration for Street himself and the daily companionship of a new friend, Philip Webb (1831–1915), who went on to become one of the leading domestic architects of his day. Impressions formed whilst working here were to influence Morris for many years but this introduction to textile design and to embroidery in particular was to have a profound effect on his career. Influenced not only by design practices adopted in the studio and by the patterns of the finished embroideries, Morris absorbed Street's own preferences as to how and why such work should be carried out.

In the autumn of 1856 Morris and Street travelled together to the Low Countries and Morris must have been particularly interested to hear his companion's opinions on the historic textile collections he had already encountered in cathedrals and museums during his earlier college vacations. It is easy to assess Street's views on textiles from his writings and lectures, especially his influential book *Ecclesiastical Embroidery*, written with Agnes Blencowe in 1848, and his published lecture 'On Medieval Embroidery' given before the Durham Architectural Society and printed in *The Ecclesiologist* magazine for 1863. This lecture is the most revealing statement of his ideas and subsequently those of the young Morris. Condemning the nineteenth-century vogue for thick, brightly coloured, woollen canvas embroidery he states,

Is it possible for anyone to feel any joy in the contemplation of the work in which so many ladies pretend to find pleasure — that contemptible system of cross-stitch work, which requires no sense, no thought, hardly any manual dexterity on the part of the worker; and which, be the worker good, bad or indifferent, produces the same hard formal absence of good results?

Instead he advocates the study of existing medieval embroideries, especially those pieces worked in England and known as *opus anglicanum*; from a period when English work led the world. 'Undertake works which may exhibit the industry, the intellect and the good taste of the worker … The furniture of our homes, our curtains, tablecloths, napkins and the like, may all be decorated in the way I have shown that old works were adorned'.

Street's own embroidery designs show essentially late medieval motifs of stylized pomegranates, artichokes and thistles worked in silk and gold thread and often applied to dark or richly coloured background cloths, usually velvet. This new use of old patterns was innovatory in the mid nineteenth century although it was to form the basis of what has now become traditional ecclesiastical design. It made a great impact on Morris, and one of his earliest artistic works and his only known oil painting, worked in 1859, shows a typical design of powdered motifs in a portrait of Jane Burden as *La Belle Iseult*. To the left of the canvas can be seen a blue table-cloth embroidered with thistle motifs, this even has the form of an altar frontal and may have been copied directly from one of Street's own works. It also has great similarities of pattern to a later altar frontal designed for St Michael's Church, Scarborough.

In the late summer of 1856 Street's office moved to London and within a short time Morris had realized that he was unable to achieve the skills of draughtsmanship expected of him. Encouraged by Dante Gabriel Rossetti, now a firm friend, with the words 'if any man has poetry in him he should paint it',[2] he left Street's office abandoning any ambitions to become an architect.

He began to paint but his talents as a designer were now becoming far more obvious. Early in 1857 Morris moved into 17 Red Lion Square with Edward Burne-Jones and for the next two years the two cultivated the ritual bohemian life of designer and artist. Their artistic experiments introduced them to many media and decorative techniques and, as well as carving, stained glass designing and clay modelling, Morris now tried embroidery. Realizing that to design for any technique a fundamental knowledge of its process is required, he had a wooden embroidery frame made, copied from an old example, and had some worsted woollen embroidery yarns dyed for him by an elderly French dyer whom he had contacted locally.

Morris's biographer, J.W. Mackail describes how, in his tireless efforts to learn the technique, 'He worked at this till he had mastered the principle of laying and radiating the stitches so as to cover the ground closely and smoothly.' It is to this determination and patience that Morris owed most for his skills and success as a textile designer; without the knowledge gained from this initial learning process his designs would simply show the superficial prettiness present in the flat patterns of many of his contemporaries. Morris's first embroideries sought to bring to life his own idea of the British medieval interior and, in the absence of existing examples, the type of wall hangings that would have been used. Forsaking the silks and metal threads with which he had already become familiar through Street's ecclesiastical work, he chose wool as a background fabric and for the embroidery yarns to gain the effects he wanted. His chosen technique, 'laying and couching' is a difficult method to use successfully without previous needlework practice, and the additional aggravation of working in wool, with its tendency to shred and knot, must have made it a most trying exercise but one from which Morris learned a great deal about the technique of embroidery.

Morris's first known embroidery is a contradiction both in technique and colour to what Mackail tells us however. Worked in 1857, it depicts a repeated design of birds and fruit trees surmounted by his motto 'If I can'.[3] The technique is not surface couching but a series of irregular long and short stitches randomly placed which form a stiff cloth of similar texture and weight to woven tapestry. Embroidered with thick, brightly coloured aniline-dyed crewel wools (those most readily available in needlework shops at that time), the design has a charming naivity enhanced now by its faded colours[4] and hopelessly stylized birds. In comparison the trees are elegantly worked and their raised fruit provide relief to the densely textured surface. Besides being the only example showing this primitive technique and the use of chemical dyestuffs, it is also the only known embroidery to have been worked by William Morris alone, for having mastered the technique to his own satisfaction he soon felt that he could teach others the stitches he favoured and leave them to work the embroideries from his designs.

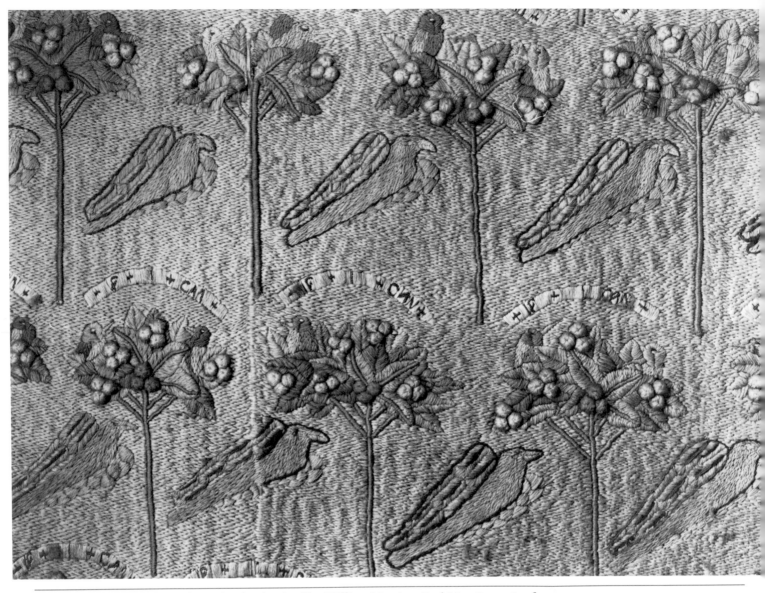

Woollen hanging IF I CAN, *designed and embroidered by William Morris at Red Lion Square in 1857.*

The nearest available person was the maid 'Red Lion Mary', later to become Mrs Mary Nicholson. A lady of timid nature she was quickly dragooned into Morris's employ and was frequently made to bring her frame into the studio to work under his direction. Unfortunately, none of these pieces survive.

Morris's skills as a designer were by the late 1850s becoming recognized; Rossetti had already described him as 'unrivalled among moderns in all illumination and work of that kind' and in 1857 John Ruskin, much to Morris's satisfaction, recommended him to the Keeper of Manuscripts at the British Museum as an illustrator 'as great as any thirteenth century draughtsman'. This comparison must have been particularly gratifying to

Morris who had already steeped himself in the literature of the period and admired every aspect of medieval culture. No other Morris embroideries exist for the period 1857–9 and other art forms must be referred to in order to judge his own stylistic development for this crucial period. Preliminary studies for the Oxford Union murals (1857) and early furniture painted with Burne-Jones and other friends at Red Lion Square, show a very individual use of medieval design with repeating patterns of stylized floral motifs (sunflowers and daisies in particular) juxtaposed to create a patchwork of colour and form. The control of such complex arrangements of design was to prove one of Morris's greatest skills when he later turned to printed textiles.

In 1857 while working on the decoration of the Oxford Union, Morris met and fell in love with a local stableman's daughter, Jane Burden, and their subsequent marriage, on 26 April 1859, gave Morris his greatest excuse for commissioning the building of a new house and, finding no suitable furnishings commercially available, for designing all the interior decoration and fittings. The Red House built on land purchased by Morris in Bexleyheath was designed by Philip Webb with wall decorations, furniture and furnishings all provided by Morris and his friends. Georgiana Burne-Jones's description of the house, made soon after her first visit, conveys a great deal. 'It was not a large house', she said, 'but purpose and proportion had been so skillfully observed in its design to arrange for all reasonable demands and leave the impression of ample space everywhere.'[5] The interior decorations, however, were to say the least, eccentric to the unaccustomed eye. 'The total effect was strange and barbaric to Victorian sensibility', wrote William Bell-Scott a friend of Rossetti's and fellow Pre-Raphaelite associate, 'and the adornment had a novel, not to say, startling character, but if one had been told that it was the south sea island style of thing one could have believed such to be the case, so bizarre was the execution.' But what were these bizarre furnishings? Having taught his wife Janey and her sister Elizabeth (Bessie) Burden to embroider in wools in the method he favoured he designed two schemes to be worked in embroidery for the house; a set of panels for the drawing room depicting female figures and some curtains with repeating floral designs for the master bedroom. The curtains, made of dyed indigo blue woollen serge, which Janey had found by chance in a London shop shows rows of daisy clumps in couched yellow, red and white wool. The design derived from a Froissart manuscript in the British Museum and was used a number of times, notably in designs for glazed tiles and wallpaper.

The drawing room panels were much more adventurous and original in design but (through inexperience or lack of labour) remain incomplete today. The embroideries were intended to form a narrative border around the walls. They were designed to be embroidered on to plain linen and then cut out and applied to a heavy silk velvet background in much the same manner as late medieval and early Tudor

Hangings, designed in 1860 for the Red House, embroidered in wools on serge by Janey Morris and friends.

embroideries. The eight existing panels thought to be part of this scheme[6] all depict famous historical female characters and were originally intended to be divided, one from another, with fruit and other types of symbolic trees. Although based on Chaucer's poem *Legend of Good Women*, the characters do not correspond to those listed and it is likely that Morris himself confidently selected his own heroines. Chaucer is the main influence, however, as the daisy, which is much admired in the prologue to Chaucer's poem, is evident in the background and foreground of the three finished panels (illus. p. 22) (made into a screen for the Earl of Carlisle in 1887 still remaining in the Howard family).[7] Three further panels identified as St Catherine, Isoude and Penelope are now at Kelmscott Manor. The St Catherine embroidery,[8] which is the only panel to retain its tree, has been applied to velvet in the form of a curtain whereas the other two are exhibited in their unfinished state. Three other partially worked embroideries are also associated with the Red House frieze. One shows a fruit tree, the others depict a garlanded female figure, probably Eve (the nearest Morris ever came to conceiving a design with a naked female figure in it) and an unidentified classical heroine. The latter is particularly interesting as it shows that the design was first sketched out in water-colours on the background holland material in preparation for the embroidery. Associated with the Burne-Jones family, this panel may have been worked by Georgiana Burne-Jones who had already been taught by Morris 'what stitches to use and how to place them'.[9]

The idea of domestic embroidered friezes was also adopted by the Burne-Jones family. In 1863 Edward Burne-Jones used Chaucer's 'Legend' as the literary

Unfinished panel, designed in 1861 for the Red House. Embroidered in crewel wools and couched gold thread.

source for a two-tiered scheme designed for John Ruskin and intended to be worked by his wife Georgiana, female relatives and pupils of a girls' school at Winnington Hall, Cheshire, run by Miss Bell, a friend of Ruskin. The existing preliminary drawing[10] identifies which figures were to be allotted to each embroideress. The scheme was abandoned before any embroidery was initiated but the designs were not wasted and were used for stained glass at a later date. In the same year, a plan for a similarly arranged double row of embroidered figures – this time based on the Arthurian legend – was drawn by Burne-Jones for his own home at 62 Great Russell Street. Four of these panels, which depict *Launcelot, Arthur*[11], *Merlin* and *Morgan le Fay*, were all worked by Georgiana and still exist. These panels are approximately half the size of the Red House embroideries and they suffer aesthetically from the embroideress's lack of practical experience, direction and technical knowledge. When confining herself to less ambitious projects Georgiana Burne-Jones's embroidery shows her own great charm and modesty and a jacket made by her for Morris of indigo dyed linen with linen embroidery (now in the Victoria and Albert Museum) shows a design based on Balkan peasant work, a much more suitable vehicle for her talents. Her own admiration for Jane Morris, who she described as an 'exquisite needlewoman'[12] showed none of the jealousy sometimes associated with young women often in each other's company and Georgiana was soon to recognize her own capabilities and never again to attempt embroidery of such scale.

The informal atmosphere at the Red House, where friends often stayed with the Morrises – the ladies embroidering, the men painting and playing bowls – contributed greatly, both in terms of industry and comradeship, to the success of the artefacts being made there. The idea of taking commercial advantage of such arrangements was finalized on 11 April 1861 with the foundation of the firm Morris, Marshall, Faulkner and Company. The founder members – Morris, Burne-Jones, Webb, Rossetti, Ford Madox Brown, Charles Faulkner and Peter Paul Marshall (with Arthur Hughes resigning soon after the formation) – each invested a small amount of capital with an unsecured loan of £100 from Morris's mother. It was agreed that Morris as manager should receive £150 per annum and Faulkner a small sum as book-keeper. Each designer was to be paid for the designs he produced for the firm, which in the case of the newly married Burne-Jones occasionally meant payment in kind of blue and green serge for use in his own home in Great Russell Street.

Morris never used the background fabrics and embroidery yarns available from London shops after his first attempt, but went direct to Yorkshire manufacturers for the ready woven and dyed woollen serges he had chosen to work his early embroideries upon. These provided not only interesting textures and weights for his hangings but their colours, because of the nature of the wool itself, were subtle and subdued, positive but not brash. Indigo blue, a dye of infinitely varying tones and hues was to become Morris's favourite and it was by selecting heavy dark woollen fabrics for his early embroideries that he first developed his taste for the dark backgrounds which were to become his trademark.

With the advent of chemical aniline dyes, supplies of worsted embroidery threads in natural colours became extremely difficult to obtain and very soon Morris was dyeing hanks of wool in the firm's first premises at 8 Red Lion Square and at 26 Queen Square where they moved in 1865. From this time all Morris's embroideries were worked in yarns dyed specifically by, or for, the firm, although a letter from Henry Holiday to his wife Catherine in September 1877 describes Morris's approval of some Pearsall's 'warm mellowy colours'. It is doubtful that Mrs Holiday ever used yarns from Pearsall's (then a shop in Cheapside, London) since a small surviving collection of silks from her own workbox consist of Morris silks.

The first embroideries produced by the firm were worked by relatives and friends, notably by Jane Morris and her sister Bessie, Georgiana Burne-Jones, Lucy and Kate Faulkner (sisters of the firm's book-keeper) and Mrs George Campfield, wife of the company foreman. A circular promoting the early products of the firm mentions 'embroidery of all kinds', and on 19 April 1861 Morris wrote to his old tutor, Rev. F.G. Guy 'In about a month we shall have some things to show in these rooms, painted cabinets, embroidery and all the rest of it.' As Morris goes on to ask the names of clergymen he might invite to see the products it is clear that some of these were of an ecclesiastical nature. Everyone busied themselves in the embroidery of these woollen hangings and 'The workshop became such a whirlpool of industry that sucked in everyone who came near them'[13]. Rossetti described the goings-on with more humorous insight. 'Top has taken to worsted work',[14] he wrote.

The first opportunity for publicizing the products of the firm came in 1862 at the International Exhibition held in South Kensington. Exhibiting in the Medieval Section, the firm displayed furniture, stained glass and embroideries, erroneously referred to as 'tapestries'. It is not known exactly what items of embroidery were shown but their various descriptions suggest embroidered woollen hangings of the type worked for the Red House. *The Clerical Journal* described them as 'quaintly pleasing reproductions'[15] without practical use, and *The Ecclesiologist* was equally unimpressed. Having described the firm's furniture as 'preposterous', the stained glass as 'pseudo-grotesque' they went on to say 'Messrs. Morris, Marshall, and Co., have produced some most antique-looking tapestry hangings, which are effective in colour but of rude manufacture, and (we fancy) not at all economical.' By judging domestic exhibits in ecclesiastical terms, it is not surprising that the critics came to these opinions. Despite these notices, the firm's debut was successful; they won two gold medals for faithfulness to medieval traditions, sold £150 worth of goods and gained a number of orders.

Church Embroidery

G.F. Bodley, (1827–1907) a leading architect, impressed with the objects exhibited, commissioned the decoration and furnishing of a few of his own, newly designed churches, including St Michael's Brighton, All Saints Cambridge, All Saints Selsley in Gloucestershire and St Martin's on the Hill Scarborough. St Martin's still possesses three items which date from this period; an altar frontal with a repeating design of pomegranates and sunflowers in silk and couched gold thread on a dark red velvet ground and two silk embroidered borders of chequered design which almost certainly decorated riddel posts.[16] Because of their boldness and stylistic confidence it is likely that the borders are the work of Philip Webb; the altar frontal, on the other hand, is probably by Morris. The flat-headed sunflower and pomegranate motifs worked in alternating rows are close to his domestic work of the same period, especially the *Daisy* and *If I Can* pieces and an embroidered hanging of repeating sunflowers now at Kelmscott Manor and probably made for the Red House.

Morris and Philip Webb provided all the early designs for church embroidery and orders received included frontals for churches in Clapham, London, Llandaff in Wales and Busbridge Church, Godalming, Surrey.[17] Webb's own accounts[18] list two for the 1860s but only the *Lamb and Flag*, worked by Bessie Burden in 1868 for the restoration of Llandaff Cathedral, is known to exist. Comparing embroideries designed by Webb and Morris one is immediately struck by Webb's superior draughtsmanship but Morris's ingenuity in devising repeating designs and his ability to retain a fresh, light effect of colour and line make Webb's work, when embroidered, look heavy and over-worked. Webb's preliminary designs are very beautiful however, and their precise instructions to the embroideress concerning colour and measurement show his professional skills to perfection. (illus. p. 19)

Although it is likely that a number of churches ordering stained glass windows from the firm also commissioned embroidered furnishings this is now difficult to prove in the absence of identifiable surviving examples. Textiles fade and wear and even in

ecclesiastical circles, fashions change comparatively quickly. Many church embroideries available both from the early firm and from Morris and Company were advertised in two late catalogues *Church Decoration* (*c.* 1910) and *Embroidery Work* (*c.* 1912) and it is clear that this provided an important part of the firm's business into the twentieth century, competing with such esteemed companies as Watts and Co. of London and Hardmans of Birmingham. Morris and Co. were chosen in 1910 to embroider the altar hangings for Westminster Abbey for the coronation of George V and Queen Mary. The background chosen was not a Morris fabric but a silk damask woven by the St Edmundsbury Weavers, a comparatively new company, indicating that the embroidery section of Morris and Company was flourishing when other products were not so popular. By the early twentieth century the firm's catalogues were advertising plain and embroidered vestments and cloth 'made in accordance with the standards set forth by the Ornaments Rubric of the Church of England' with complete communion sets from 18s, dalmatics of blue silk at £9, frontals from £10 10s and much more. With the exception of two frontals worked in the 1890s for All Saints Wilden in Worcestershire (designed by Morris in about 1893 and worked by Georgiana Burne-Jones and two of her sisters) and the Rochester and Southwark Deaconess House (designed by Webb 1898-9 and

Altar frontal. St Martin's Church, Scarborough. Embroidered in silks and gold thread on velvet at a cost of £28.

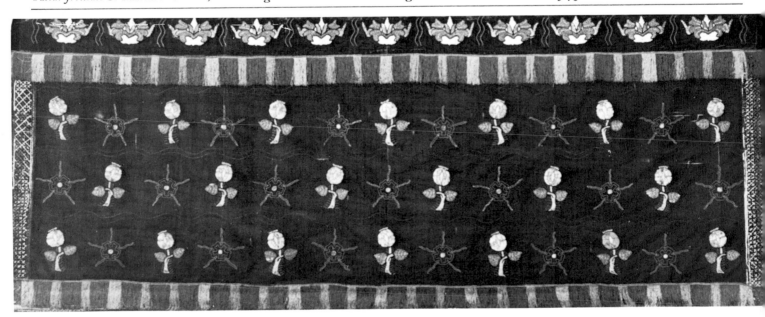

embroidered by May Morris), all other late ecclesiastical embroideries show a singular lack of artistic merit and even early twentieth-century figurative designs for banners, although well drawn show none of the Pre-Raphaelite characteristics made famous by the firm's stained glass and popular in ecclesiastical art at the time. Many early designs were re-sold however and the Busbridge Church frontal design originally made in 1870 appears in both catalogues listing embroidery.

Morris & Co.

In 1874 Rossetti and Ford Madox Brown decided to leave the firm and its demise became inevitable. Burne-Jones, Faulkner and Webb made no claims on the business at this point but Rossetti, Marshall and Madox Brown all required a return on their shares, a costly business now that orders were increasing. The success of the company owed as much to the efficiency and imagination of the firm's first two business managers as to the work produced. George Warrington Taylor ran the business from March 1865 until his untimely death in February 1870, and without his gentle bullying of Morris, it is unlikely that the firm would have adopted certain commercial practices and have expanded to the extent it did. George Wardle who succeeded him, was equally successful in administration and also took an active part in the artistic side of production graphing out working drawings amongst other things. Wardle was an established draughtsman and Morris, Marshall, Faulkner & Co. had purchased a number of drawings from him before his appointment. These drawings (of which a number are now in the Victoria and Albert Museum) were made in country churches throughout England, they show repeating designs taken from medieval decorations; tiles, wall-paintings, carved rood screens and bench ends. Wardle worked for the firm for twenty years and was there to assist Morris in the reorganization when Morris, Marshall, Faulkner & Co. was finally dissolved and the firm was reborn as Morris and Company on 25 March 1875, under Morris's sole management and proprietorship.

The embroideries designed by Morris in the 1870s showed more sophistication than before; the designs no longer imitated medieval hangings and it is interesting to note that they ceased to be known by the firm, or subsequently the public, as 'tapestries'. Embroidery techniques were exploited for the first time and the embroideress, whether amateur or working for Morris and Company, was encouraged to take some part in the creation of the embroidery she worked on by selecting the colours or the stitches. Two main influences affected the development of Morris's mature style at this period. One, which started in 1875, was the long working association with the silk dyer Thomas Wardle (the brother of Morris's manager) at his dyeworks in Leek in Staffordshire, the aims of both men being to resurrect old recipes and techniques using vegetable dyestuffs. Wardle clearly benefited from this co-operation and his own printed textiles show the strong influence of Morris in their patterns and colour schemes. Besides acquiring the facilities with which to experiment with dyes and to produce his early printed textiles, Morris profited in less tangible ways. In business matters Wardle was considerably more experienced than Morris and Morris learnt a great deal from working at Leek which was to prove of commercial benefit when he opened his factory at Merton Abbey in 1881. Wardle began to print Morris and Company designs in 1875 but before long he had registered his own designs, and was selling panels printed in outline for embroideries, based very closely on Morris's patterns.[19] This plagiarized yet ingenious enterprise was noted by Morris and subsequently many of his own embroidery patterns became more commercially attractive and he was also to adopt the printed embroidery 'kit' for sale by his own firm.

The second influence, which was of greater aesthetic value, was Morris's increasing interest in historical textiles and his frequent visits to the South Kensington Museum (now the Victoria and Albert Museum), which he claimed to have 'Used . . . as much as any man living',[20] show in the development of his own pattern making. Visiting the museum for his own pleasure and subsequently for the benefit of the collections,[21] he had the opportunity to examine items of many different periods and cultures and his artistic interests expanded from the narrow confines of medievalism. His fascination with the technicalities of textile manufacture shows in his 1870s embroidery designs for the firm, all of which have repeating designs of single and interlocking motifs. Out

Printed panel, sold by Thomas Wardle for embroidery. The design shows the strong influence of Morris patterns.

of this study of historical textiles Morris created a totally individual style for his embroideries, using the motifs he had seen in antique fabrics – stylized pomegranates and artichokes in particular – for repeating designs. From the mid 1870s a special feature of the firm's production were large hangings of horizontally and vertically repeating floral forms. His involvement in block-printing and weaving from 1875 also accounts for Morris's interest in the art of repeating motifs although the patterns seen in these embroidered hangings are derived from sixteenth- and seventeenth-century embroideries, woven velvets and silks from Persia, Turkey and Italy. Their format, often showing wide patterned borders at the top and bottom edge of the hangings, are a feature of cushion and couch covers from Turkey, now known as 'Broussa velvets' from the area in which they were first made. Although late seventeenth-century English crewel-work embroideries are always cited as the main historical source for Morris's own needlework and it is indeed clear that he was attracted by the technique of wool embroidery on a heavy cotton backing, stylistically only one of his designs, *The Vine* of 1879, shows the characteristic meandering branch and tree forms of traditional crewel-work. This type of design was adopted for use in later Morris & Co. hangings by May Morris and Henry Dearle, although the technique employed owed nothing to the seventeenth-century originals.

In the nineteenth century, the habit of collecting textiles was not nearly as rare as it is today and Morris, along with many contemporary artists and designers,[22]

had a number of pieces of embroidery which, Jane Morris tells us, would be unpicked from time to time to discover the way in which they were made. It is from this awareness and appreciation of embroidery technique that Morris developed his own favourite stitches; those which would provide the effects he sought. Raised embroidery techniques were seldom used in his designs and those stitches most favoured – darning, running, long and short, satin and stem stitches – merely follow and accentuate the lines of the design, they never make distracting patterns by themselves.

The increasing popularity of Morris embroideries in the 1870s is shown by the large number of commissions for wall-hangings received by the firm. These were often ordered on recommendation by the clients of Philip Webb for the walls of newly built houses and most of the embroideries were worked by the ladies of the household. The first commission of this type was from the Yorkshire industrialist, Sir Isaac Lowthian Bell, for his house, Rounton Grange, Northallerton in Yorkshire, which was designed and built by Webb in 1872–6. Using the theme of Chaucer's *Romaunt de la Rose* (a literary progression from the earlier *Good Women* to which the poet refers in this poem), the scheme was realized in five panels,[23] Burne-Jones supplying the composition and individual figure drawings and Morris the background and other decoration. The embroideries were worked in silks, wools and gold thread on a linen ground by Lady Bell and her daughters Florence and Ada Phoebe and these show great skill and patience. The combined design

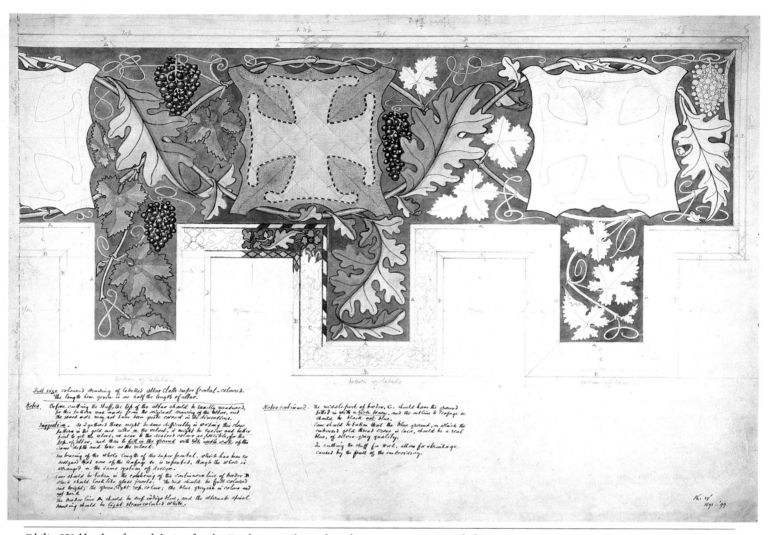

Philip Webb, altar frontal design for the Rochester and Southwark Deaconess House, 1898–9.

efforts of Burne-Jones and Morris were to be used in other designs for embroideries, notably in panels worked for the Royal School of Art Needlework, and subsequently for tapestry cartoons.

By the mid 1870s the firm was expanding fast and both the designs and finished pieces of embroidery were reaching a far wider market. Morris became a leading figure in the movement to break the grip of mechanically worked canvas embroidery and to introduce new techniques and designs and he was one of the first designers to be associated with the Royal School of Art Needlework. Founded in 1872, the Royal School was the most celebrated of a number of embroidery groups and societies set up at the time and by using designs by many leading designers of the day it succeeded in its ambition 'to restore Ornamental Needlework for secular purposes to the high place it once held among decorative arts'. Morris and Burne-Jones jointly produced three figurative designs for the school; *Poesia, Musica* and *The Musicians*, which were embroidered in sepia wools in outline stitches on natural coloured cotton grounds[24] and examples of Morris/Burne-Jones designs were exhibited in the Royal School of Art Needlework's section at the Philadelphia Centennial Exhibition of 1876 where they made a great impression. The school continued to use a number of designs by Morris, for example *Pomona* originally designed as a tapestry in 1885, *Honeysuckle* from a printed linen design and *Myrtle* later used for wallpaper. The Leek Embroidery Society, founded in 1879 by Mrs Thomas (later Lady) Wardle, also used Morris designs as a basis for embroidery, especially the silks printed by her husband's works for Morris & Co. between 1875 and 1878.

Apart from the large hangings of the 1870s, a few

THE MUSICIANS, *designed by Burne-Jones and Morris* c. 1875. *Embroidered by the Royal School of Art Needlework.*

small personal objects designed by Morris for his family and friends are still extant, they include an embroidered evening bag for Jane worked in coloured silks on a blue ribbed silk ground and two embroidered velvet bell-pulls made by Jane for her friend Mrs Edward Wormald to use in her new home, Woodcote at Carshalton in Surrey. The bag and one of the bell-pulls are now in the Victoria and Albert Museum.

The last vestiges of Morris's medieval-inspired designs for embroideries can be seen in two curtains designed for Mrs Alexander Ionides and worked by her and female relatives.[25] Although the motifs used show the influence of what can now be identified as sixteenth-century cut

velvets, these would have been to a nineteenth-century medievalist part of the same period and style, since the Middle Ages was taken to embrace a much greater period of time then than is acceptable today. These curtains which stylistically date from the mid 1870s[26] are worked in outline embroidery and are very similar in pattern to *Honeycomb* registered for Kidderminster carpet in February 1876 and for woven fabric (illus. p. 24). Mrs Ionides was to become a great patron of Morris & Co. some years later in the furnishing of her home, 1 Holland Park, and a number of embroidered items were purchased from the firm.[27]

The most popular Morris embroidery design of the late

Panel of Leek embroidery. Coloured silks worked over Morris BLUEBELL *printed silk, c. 1880.*

Detail of ARTICHOKE *hanging. Part of a set designed in 1877 for Ada Godman. Worked in wool on a linen ground.*

1870s and the early 1880s was the *Artichoke*; commissioned by Ada Phoebe Godman (*neé* Bell) as wall hangings for her own Philip Webb designed Northallerton home, Smeaton Manor. Her diary describes her anxious wait for the design, its eventual delivery by train on Friday, 31 August 1877 and her subsequent tracing of it on to linen. The task she set herself was enormous and an existing Paul Bramley pencil drawing shows Mrs Godman at her frame as late as 1900. A number of panels were worked in wool on linen to hang around the walls of one room, and the three now in public collections (the William Morris Gallery, Walthamstow, the Victoria and Albert Museum and the Fitzwilliam Museum, Cambridge) all show variations in the arrangement of colour and application of the main repeating artichoke motifs, a practice adopted, no doubt, to break the monotony of the work and to help maintain enthusiasm. This design was used more than once and did not, as with other commissions, remain the copyright of the original client. A very fine silk version was worked later by Margaret Beale, a fine needlewoman and Morris admirer (illus. p. 26). Friends of the Ionides family, the Beales also commissioned Philip Webb to build a house for them at Standen in East Sussex, and many of the interior furnishings were supplied by Morris & Co. Mrs Beale was also responsible for embroidering one of Morris's finest early hangings, a repeating design of lotus blossom worked in silks, in shades of peach and brown on a dark ground. Thought to have been completed between 1875 and 1880, this panel and a working drawing for it are part of the fine collection of large Morris embroidered hangings and designs now in the Victoria and Albert Museum.

The circle of ladies embroidering for Morris & Co. had, by the mid 1870s expanded considerably from the cosy groups of friends and relatives involved in the Red House work in the 1860s. A number of professionals were now employed in work under the direction of Janey with increasing interest being taken in this side of the firm by May (Mary), Morris's youngest daughter. Both May and Jenny (Jane Alice), her eldest sister, began embroidering from an early age and Henry James, describing a visit made to Queen Square in 1869, mentions Morris being assisted in 'tapestry' by his wife and little girls, when they were just eight and seven years

Three panels depicting female heroines, designed for the Red House c. 1861 and made into a screen, 1889.

respectively. Jenny, who in some respects was the most intellectually promising of the two girls, developed epilepsy in her teens and from that point led the life of an invalid. Although those pieces which she is known to have embroidered show fine workmanship, her involvement in the firm's productions was limited. Morris's sister-in-law, Bessie Burden (or 'Bessy' as Morris always spelled it in his letters), was a keen and experienced needlewoman and worked not only for Morris & Co., but for other designers and other organizations. She worked for a time as instructor at the Royal School of Art Needlework and is known to have applied for a post of craft examiner to the Board of Education. She was also responsible for at least one embroidery design, *Bayleaf*, sold by Morris & Co. Her involvement both as embroideress and as a supervisor of outworkers at the firm continued despite Morris's own dislike of her, brought on early in his marriage by Bessie's constant attendance at his home. Bessie, however, does not appear to be the only annoyance caused to Morris by this section of the firm's work, and his letters to Janey in March 1876 show his frustration. 'The embroidery ladies gave me such a turn this morning. I thought I should have been both walked and talked off my legs.'[28] The outworkers were no less trouble, it seems, for in December 1877 he wrote:

Miss Marshall writes bothering; says that she only got 13/- for 8 days work at Bessy's and so was obliged to give up working there: of course, she lies, but she clearly didn't intend working there: am I to give her more than £2 for the table-cover (less the floss silk) which she has just sent in? She says you gave her that for it and had done an eighth yourself.

Such seemingly trivial annoyances must have contributed towards Morris's eagerness to hand over the management of this side of the firm some years later.

No such pettiness or unprofessional conduct enters into Morris's dealings with his favourite and most proficient embroideress Catherine Holiday, wife of the painter and stained glass designer Henry Holiday. A lady of immense skills she had very definite views on design and her own work and all her negotiations with Morris were always conducted on an equal footing. Morris produced a number of designs specifically for her to work and although he made suggestions as to the technique and the colour in which they should be worked, she

One of two hangings designed by Morris, 1875. Embroidered in wool on cotton by Mrs Alexander Ionides and relatives.

herself contributed a great deal to the final decision and consequently the results are quite unlike Morris's other embroideries. Morris's letters to Catherine Holiday[29] concerning details of particular pieces, show a great deal of respect for her as a women and a craftsman and, even when trying to deter her from certain courses of action or persuade her against her will, his manner is to cajole rather than demand. 'I am quite delighted with the success of the door-hanging ... I know you don't like doing repetitions but this is such a beautiful thing that I should think it a great pity if there were not more than one of it in the world.' His admiration for her work is well documented and a letter from Henry Holiday to his wife describes his views, 'He says you are the only person he has ever met whose work is as good as the old. Miss Burden is all very well but she doesn't know how to put her stitches together like this.' When writing to May in March 1878, he had to check his admiring description of a new Holiday embroidery recently sent to the shop 'or I shall rouse jealousy'.[30] Constant commercial considerations worried Morris and his aesthetic appraisals of work were often tempered by the pieces' financial worth. Realizing the high standards of Catherine Holiday's work and the time taken to complete each piece he was concerned that she might price herself out of the market. Keeping only 10 per cent of the price of work sold through the firm (a generous token considering that the background and embroidery yarns were supplied) he repeatedly warned her that the high prices she demanded (£100 or £150 for a bedcover or hanging) could mean that items remained unsold.

Designs made for Catherine Holiday are quite different to those prepared for other clients to complete at home; they show greater pattern details and often have more complex gradation of colours. The earliest known example attributed to Catherine Holiday and worked about 1876 in silk on linen for the Earl of Southampton[31] shows a central design of a radiating sunflower in shades of yellow and gold on an indigo dyed blue linen ground. Mrs Holiday's later embroideries show more directional patterns, many made presumably as portières. An example in the Metropolitan Museum, New York shows a growth of curving leaves issuing from the centre base of the design, the leaves are peppered with carnations, peonies and other flowers in silk on a satin ground. Another example shows a design centred on a large 'aesthetic' bowl of flowers, this was designed by Henry Holiday for his wife (and bears both their signatures) but an existing working drawing in the collection of the Victoria and Albert Museum bequeathed by May Morris points to it having been drawn out in the Morris & Co. workshops. The attribution of a designer for Mrs Holiday's embroideries is often difficult as her own personal style is heavily stamped on each piece. Her own independence from Morris & Co. is also evident; as early as 1879 she was asking Morris to sell her work, through the firm, in America but Morris's reply was less than encouraging, 'I should explain that we have only an agency over there; neither have we ever sent any embroideries on sale because of the enormous customs duties would raise the price more than the risk of selling them would be worth.' Undeterred Catherine Holiday made her own investigations and

Panel embroidered in silk by Catherine Holiday. Designed by Henry Holiday, drawn out in the Morris workshops.

proceeded to sell to the U.S. independently.

In 1881 Morris and Company received their second commission from St James's Palace in London. Having worked on the decoration and furnishing of the Armoury and Tapestry Room in 1866–7 they were now asked to decorate the Blue Room and Throne Room. Morris

Trial for embroidered pelmet for St James's Palace, 1881. Silk appliqué and couched cord on ST JAMES *damask.*

designed a woven silk damask, the *St James's*, especially for the curtains of the Blue Room and a set of appliqué embroidered pelmets were made for these showing a simple, stylized design of pomegranates and foliage in pink, gold and green silk with couched silk braid. A padded interlining gives the motifs a raised appearance and this, together with the wine coloured background, make the pelmets look suitably luxurious and regal. The pelmet designs are not typical of Morris's contemporary domestic embroideries but are an integral part of the more conventionally accepted designs for the rest of the St James's decorations comprising wall and ceiling paintings chiefly in dark green, maroon, white and gold leaf paint. A plan showing the proposed arrangement of curtains and pelmets in the room is now in the Victoria and Albert Museum.

The 1880s saw a complete change in Morris's embroidery designs with much more complex patterns arranged not in rows of horizontal and vertical repeats as before, but, as in hand-knotted carpets, with the design arranged around a central motif with borders around the edges. Morris's preoccupation with carpets at the time is shown in the composition of these designs, in which each

ARTICHOKE *hanging, designed by Morris in 1877. One of a pair embroidered by Mrs Margaret Beale and daughters.*

ACANTHUS *hanging, designed by Morris* c. 1880. *This small version was embroidered by Morris & Co.*

Four cushion cover or fire-screen panels sold by Morris & Co. (A) FLOWERPOT, *(B)* ROSE WREATH, *(C)* CLANFIELD, *(D)* ROSEBUSH.

quarter is a mirror image of the other. This classical format could be used for bed-hangings and wall-hangings as the pattern had no definite direction. Early examples of this type of design were worked to show much of the background fabric, whereas later pieces had the surface completely worked in silk embroidery stitches in a manner also favoured at this time by the Royal School of Art Needlework.

The success of particular Morris embroidery designs is shown in the many repeats and adaptations of individual designs made in the firm's workshops by employee outworkers and by clients at home. From the late 1870s,

Morris had given less and less time to this side of the firm being more involved in the production of carpets and printed and woven textiles so fewer designs were available. These later 'carpet' patterns are therefore rare although they often exist in a number of forms. *The Acanthus* bed-hanging, one of the most popular, exists in four versions.[32] Two similar examples show the design worked in wool and in silk on a linen ground, another is in silk on a blue flannel ground and a fourth, worked as a small wall-hanging, shows approximately a quarter of the design with silk embroidery covering the entire surface (illus. p. 27). A coloured working drawing is in the collection of the Victoria and Albert Museum.

For commercial reasons and because Morris now had little time to devote to embroidery his last designs for this technique, drawn between 1878 and 1885, are for cushion covers and firescreen panels. These provided an opportunity for many more people to acquire designs, their price (especially if bought in kit form) being much cheaper than for the wall-hangings, bed-covers and portières, and these small panels became the financial mainstay of this section of the business. The designs were available in three different stages of completion; as background fabric marked with the design to be embroidered entirely at home, with the embroidery already started as a guide,[33] or, if desired, all the work would be done in the Morris & Co. workshops. The firm would also, if required, transfer their designs on to clients' own background fabric and, in the 1890s, they were willing to draw the clients' own designs out for them and prepare these for embroidery. It is very difficult to single out these smaller items which are definitely the work of William Morris from the large number of designs and existing samples. One of the earliest the *Flowerpot* is taken directly from the design of two samples of seventeenth-century Italian lacis work acquired by the Victoria and Albert Museum in 1875, at a time when Morris would have seen them soon after acquisition.[34] The successful format of the design, starting as it does from the centre bottom and working up and out in a flurry of stems, leaves and flowers, was repeated in all the most succesful later cushion cover designs including the *Rose and Olive,* the *Rosebush,* the *Apple Tree,* the *Clanfield* and *Honeysuckle.* Judging from their date of execution, some of these examples could not be the work

of Morris and even *Flowerpot* itself has a stiffness uncharacteristic of his work. Many pieces exhibited at the Arts and Crafts exhibitions from 1888 simply compound the confusion as a large proportion of items exhibited by individual embroideresses, and in some cases by the firm itself, are described as 'Morris work' or being 'from designs by William Morris' when this was not the case. Confusion is caused by the nineteenth-century habit of using William Morris and Morris & Co. as synonymous titles. Even Henry Dearle and May Morris, the true designers of many of the items, did not correct the myth, believing, presumably for business reasons, that such association with the firm's founder could only be advantageous, clients being more anxious to own Morris's own work than that of an assistant however good, as Morris was already a legendary figure.

In 1885 Morris handed over the management of the embroidery section of the firm to his daughter May who was then twenty-three years old. She had by this time considerable experience of embroidery technique and had already designed some embroideries. All new designs from this time were produced by her and John Henry Dearle, Morris's assistant, who on Morris's death in 1896 became Art Director of the firm. Other designers occasionally supplied single designs to the firm and many were put into production in the twentieth century, particularly after 1910, but few of these designers are known by name and usually only by their initials. Many of Morris's designs continued to be used but often these were adapted, added to or otherwise altered to suit clients. The *Vine* portière, designed in 1878, changed many times[35] and became the basic pattern for later standard products of the firm, including May Morris's *Acanthus* portière, illustrated in the catalogue *Embroidery Work* (c. 1912). A number of Morris's designs for other media — wallpaper and printed textiles in particular — were also adapted for embroidery at the end of the nineteenth century. A working drawing for *Trellis,* adapted from the wallpaper is now in the Victoria and Albert Museum and this and a number of other similarly adapted panels including *Fruit* and *Convolvulus* were worked as cushion covers by ladies of the Beale family and can now be seen at Standen in Sussex.

It is unlikely that Henry Dearle produced any embroidery designs before the late 1880s when he began to establish himself as a designer for the firm and produced his first repeating textile designs. Although this early work is imitative of Morris's own, his later mature style, as seen particularly in a series of large portières worked on *Oak* silk damask, show a high degree of skill both in the drawing of animals and birds and in the general composition. For a man whose only artistic training was undertaken as an apprentice at Merton Abbey, these present a considerable achievement. Dearle also designed a series of panels showing fruit trees and flower shrubs and these were made up into portières and as long panels for two, three and fourfold screens. Worked in silk and usually embroidered over the entire surface of the background these panels were set into Morris and Company wooden screens and sold as items of furniture. Many of these screen designs show the distinctive handling of May Morris and may have been adapted from larger designs. Although all of Dearle's identifiable designs are for large objects some smaller panels and cushion covers may also be his work, indeed those showing small fruit trees and flower shrubs are very similar to his contemporary wallpaper designs, especially *The Orchard* published in the *Art Journal* in 1906. A collection of late Morris & Co. designs and samples of embroidery are now owned by the William Morris Society and the Trustees of Kelmscott House and examples of Dearle's pencil designs show a sensitivity and refinement in drawing not always present in Morris's own textile designs.[36]

Portière designed by Henry Dearle c. 1890. Embroidered on to Oak *silk by Mrs Battye.*

May Morris (1862–1939)

May Morris's talents have long been underestimated and she has, for too long, lived in the shadow of her father. Her choice, to work in the same techniques and mannerisms of design initially perfected by her father, make it difficult to judge her work objectively without constant reference to Morris's own work, although in many respects she was able to surmount these obstacles and her own artistic output compares favourably with many of her own contemporaries, male and female alike.[37]

She had little formal education and spent less than three years at Notting Hill High School, which she attended from September 1873 to April 1876. Her childhood spent at home was not without literary pursuit however and the first indication of her artistic leanings was a home-magazine written with her sister Jenny, Margaret and Philip Burne-Jones and their young cousin 'Ruddie' Kipling. The book was called *The Scribbler* and was 'printed by Messrs Morris & Co (Junior) and published by them . . . NB No connection with a firm of the same name in Oxford Street.' In 1876 Jenny was diagnosed as an epileptic, an illness she was to suffer badly from for the rest of her life, and what promised to be a fine academic career (she had just passed the Cantab. Junior Examination) came to an end. Little is known of the severity of her epilepsy but from this time little more is ever written of her. William and Jane Morris's letters merely hint at their sadness but clearly the household was badly affected and May, in particular, must have experienced one of the saddest and most neglected periods of her life. Her increasing interest in the technique and design of embroidery is clear and her father encouraged her talents in this direction. After attending the South Kensington School of Design to further her studies in the craft, she took charge of the embroidery section of Morris & Co.

It is not known what form May's management took in the early years although she was never to become involved either in book keeping or financial affairs of any kind (apart from estimates) as this side of the business was controlled by the shop manager of 449 Oxford Street, the firm's retail outlet until 1917. In June 1890 she married Henry Halliday Sparling,[38] then Secretary of the Socialist League, and took a lease on 8 Hammersmith Terrace, London, not far from her parents' home at Kelmscott House, Hammersmith. From this time the embroideresses worked in May's drawing room under her supervision. Many of the girls were recruited from local schools and one in particular, Ellen Mary Wright, thought herself extremely lucky at the age of seventeen to be trained and employed by such an illustrious establishment.[39] Her only previous experience of needlework had been at school, involving the traditional exercises of patching, darning and dressmaking, all useful practices for future wives and mothers. When she first went to Hammersmith Terrace in 1891 she was the youngest of a number of assistants, the most experienced being Lily, sister of poet W.B.Yeats, who worked for Morris and Co. from 1886 to 1894. Other assistants included Maude Deacon, Stephanie Popianopolos (known as 'Mrs Stefan'), Mrs Emery (the actress Florence Farr), Mary de Morgan, sister of the potter, and Mrs George Jack,[40] wife of the firm's chief furniture designer. Ellen Wright's sister Fanny Isobel joined the firm some years later when the embroidery section had already moved to 449 Oxford Street. The embroideresses wore white cotton overalls for work and each completed a full day with a break for lunch which they were permitted to eat in Mrs Sparling's dining room. Each morning, at Hammersmith Terrace, they were visited by William Morris, who would stroll along from Kelmscott House to see how they all were. May was, by all accounts,

One of two embroidered panels, designed and embroidered by May Morris c.1895.

a kind and helpful employer much concerned with the welfare of the staff. Each year she would invite them and their families to a garden party given on Boat Race day, which would be watched from the end of the garden and each year would give them small presents. This habit lasted throughout her life and Ellen Wright received skeins of gold thread from her for many Christmases, long after she had left her employ. Wages were also higher than the average and were usually calculated on the experience and skills of the particular embroideress.[41] In working one hanging three embroideresses earned a total of £23 0s 6d, Lily Yeats earned £3 7s 6d for two and a half weeks' work, Maude Deacon, £12 5s 0d for fourteen weeks' work and Ellen Wright £7 8s 0d for eight weeks. This, together with the time taken for drawing out, pricking the pattern, and transferring it on to cloth was how the eventual price was calculated.

Orders taken in the shop were chosen from displayed samples, special exhibitions and from photos of completed work. From 1909 the firm's illustrated catalogues brought in postal sales. Those concerned with embroidery were then relayed to May and a book covering the years 1892–6 lists orders, designs, time taken and dates of delivery of finished embroideries.[42] The embroideresses worked from designs drawn (usually by George Wardle) on to greased paper. These were then pounced or carbon traced onto background fabric although in a few cases the working drawing itself was supplied to the customer.[43] In the 1890s the cost of a cushion cover panel traced on to Manchester cloth was 4s, 5s if the client wished to use her own fabric, a few shillings were added if the embroidery was started as a guide. For a finished embroidery, the cost ranged from 14s for a *Flowerpot* cushion cover to £9 charged to Mrs Theodosia Middlemore for the *Fruit Garden* portière which was ordered on 4 April 1893 and delivered on 16 May of the same year.[44] The day-book from which these details come is a veritable who's who of fashionable London households, although a number of items embroidered 'for stock' show that direct retail purchases were available to more lowly shoppers. The most prolific clients for the period 1892–6 were Lady Trevelyan, Mrs Ambrose Ralli, Mrs Battye, Mrs Hudson and Mrs Barr-Smith who ordered thirty-seven items between them. Mrs Hudson, who moved into a new house in 1893 ordered twelve separate articles, all with embroidery started, for her lady companion, Helena Wolfe, to complete for her.

Much of the success of Morris and Co. embroidery in the late nineteenth and early twentieth century must be attributed to May's hard work designing, embroidering and supervising the work, first at Hammersmith Terrace, then, in a purely advisory role from 1896, at 449 Oxford Street and some years later at Kelmscott Manor. Her own finest designs for the firm were for large scale items such as wall-hangings, portières and screens. A number of sets of bed-hangings were also designed by her and one set, based on the *Trellis* wallpaper was embroidered by Lily Yeats, Maude Deacon, Ellen Wright and herself, between 1891 and 1894: these can be seen at Kelmscott Manor. A number of special designs for wall-hangings show trees laden with blossom or fruit with inscriptions often of her father's poetry. *June* a long embroidered frieze is now in the collection of the William Morris Gallery, Walthamstow, another showing a tree with rose entwined bark has recently been discovered at Bateman's, Rudyard Kipling's home in Sussex. The Walthamstow collection also owns a panel designed for the Battye family incorporating the family's arms. *The Fruit Garden* and *The Orchard* (near identical designs with different inscriptions) show the height of May Morris's skills and the use of satin stitches in overlapping leaves of the trees give a marvellously shimmering silky texture, an effect described by George Bernard Shaw, a great admirer, as 'glowing fruit-forests'. Many later designs show complex designs of birds and foliage (illus. p. 31).

Like her father, May Morris was interested in embroidery technique and with experience she became much more of an expert than he ever professed to be. Her first publication 'Chain stitch embroidery' in the *Hobby Horse* for January 1888 (No.9) was illustrated with one of her embroidered screen designs. In 1892 she contributed a chapter on 'Embroidery' for A.H.Mackmurdo's book *Plain Handicrafts* and the following year published her Arts and Crafts essays and the first of a series of articles on ecclesiastical embroidery for the *Building News*. Her most authoritative work on the subject of embroidery, her book *Decorative Needlework*, published in 1893, is both a history book and a technical manual and by quoting from the past she encouraged the reader, either designer or embroiderer, to learn by example. Although not totally original in text, as similar ideas had already appeared in L.Higgin's *Handbook of Embroidery* published in 1880 by the Royal School of Art Needlework, her great love of craft is evident. May was to publish a number of other articles on textiles including 'Coptic Textiles. Illustrated from the collection in the South Kensington Museum' for the *Architectural Review*, 1894, and articles on *opus anglicanum* for the *Burlington Magazine*, 1905.

Morris & Co. Embroideresses

May Morris embroidering at Hammersmith Terrace.

Fanny Isobel Wright.

Maud Deacon.

Jenny Morris.

Lily Yeats.

Ellen Mary Wright.

Two panels from a fourfold screen, designed c. 1885 *showing poppy patterns.*

Surprisingly, with such a busy public life, May pursued an active private life and also found time to passionately involve herself in politics. She designed and made many embroideries for herself but these are often, mistakenly, thought to be part of the firm's output. Her earliest known embroideries were banners for the Socialist League, founded by her father in 1884, but, due no doubt to wear and tear, these no longer exist. By the late 1880s she had developed a great interest in the art of book-binding and her greatest embroidered example, for William Morris's *Love is Enough* was started in 1888. She took two years to complete it, studying historic bindings in the British Museum for inspiration.'The *Love is Enough* has grown very dear to me', she wrote to F.S.Ellis, the publisher, 'and yet I am extremely glad to have it finished.'[45] Undeterred she completed a number of other bindings and no less than six were still at Kelmscott Manor on her death.

As well as embroidering from her own designs May

also tutored privately and from 1888 advertisements featured in the *Hobby Horse* offered 'private lessons in embroidery, particulars on application'. May is known to have had at least one small exhibition in her own right of 'Embroidery, jewelry and bookbinding' with her friend Katherine Adams at 33 Hertford Street, Mayfair, in March 1905 and various exhibits at later Arts and Crafts exhibitions at home and abroad were of her own and not the firm's work. She also collaborated with contemporary designers on special commissions such as the two pairs of gloves, one for a child, the other for ecclesiastical use, both designed by Charles Ricketts, which are now in the Victoria and Albert Museum. One of her greatest deeds was the foundation in 1907 of the Women's Guild of Art (of which much has still to be discovered). Described as a 'centre and a bond for the woman who were doing decorative work and all the various crafts represented at the time' fellow members include many of the leading craftswomen of the day. The various members often worked on specific projects together including a lady's bedroom designed and furnished by the Guild for the 1916 Arts and Crafts Exhibition 'in which elaboration and luxury have been purposely avoided'. May Morris embroidered a set of bed-hangings with designs of birds and foliage, with Mary Newill and pupils of Birmingham School of Art. These were later displayed at the Detroit Society of Arts and Crafts Exhibition of British Arts and Crafts 1920–1 from which they were purchased by George Booth for his own home at Cranbrook, Michigan. May Morris's influence within the Guild of Art cannot be underestimated and when on her death plans were made for a memorial meeting of the Guild, tributes came from many leading Fabians, literary and artistic figures.

If May Morris's various publications and her embroidery work are not recognized today as they were in her own lifetime, nonetheless, the influence of her teaching has spanned the generations. She became a visiting advisor to the embroidery classes of Miss Maggie Briggs at the Central School of Arts and Crafts in 1897, taking a more direct teaching role from 1899 until 1905 with the classes of Ellen Wright her former pupil who, in turn, taught other leading twentieth-century needle-women, notably Mrs Archibald Christie. From 1905–7 she was 'visitor' to the school. She lectured on

Part of a set of bed-hangings designed by May Morris and embroidered by May, Mary Newill and pupils.

being there',[46] and one girl was trained to help fill in the backgrounds of May's larger embroideries. Her last years sound pleasant and peaceful and even after the death of Jenny in 1935 she made no attempt to move back to London, preferring the company of her companion of many years, Miss Lobb,[47] and occasional visits from friends. A description by Una Fielding of such visits hints at the industry of May and reveals the respect of a close friend.

> Then in the garden in the afternoons we used to sew and read and I often had a sleep, but I don't think she ever did. If she had been tired, perhaps making a design in a really serious piece of work, she would do some knitting. I would awake after a while and there she was still busy . . . but never seemed to rest until she actually went to bed.[48]

Late embroidery work by Morris & Co.

Because of other commitments, May Morris's role in the firm diminished after 1910 and although she continued to embroider commercial items after her move to Kelmscott Manor, her administrative involvement ceased. Embroidery was continued at 449 Oxford Street and later, from 1917, at George Street, Hanover Square, but designs with titles such as *Arcadia*, *Chippendale* and *Lyndon* show a tendency to follow the fashion of the day and indicate that the firm's search for commercialization had involved the adoption of Edwardian tastes.

Many of these later designs, which include prestigious orders for the coronation, and investiture thrones in 1911,[49] were poorly constructed, often by unknown hands, although the technical excellence of the embroidery was maintained. By 1925 the technique most favoured by the firm was cross-stitch canvas work—that most reviled by Morris—and the firm's last catalogue advertised fire-screens of galleons in full sail and 'Jacobean' canvases 'adapted . . . for seat coverings' – a far cry from Morris's own designs and a misunderstanding of his views on the potential of the technique: 'It is not worth doing unless it is either very copious and rich, or very delicate – or both. For such an art nothing patchy or scrappy, or half-starved, should be done: there is no excuse for doing anything which is not strikingly beautiful.'[50] Advice which is still as relevant today as it was in 1888.

embroidery to a number of British art schools, particularly Birmingham, Manchester and Leicester and from winter 1909 to spring 1910 she completed a lecture tour of the U.S.

In 1914 Jane Morris died and from this time May spent her time as Jenny's new guardian, between Hammersmith Terrace and Kelmscott Manor. In 1916 she became the President of the Kelmscott Women's Institute, spending more and more time in the country and in 1923 she sold the lease on her London home. She enjoyed the life of lady squire and loved to deliver presents at Christmas to the village children. She continued to embroider and encourage all around her to do the same, 'The girls employed to do housework [at Kelmscott Manor] developed a capacity for needlework just by

Printed Textiles

Soon after the foundation of Morris, Marshall, Faulkner and Co., Morris was shrewd enough to realize that if the firm was to be established as successful house decorators and furnishers, then he would have to undertake the design and manufacture of more commercial furnishings than had previously been attempted. Patterned textiles in particular were needed for use on walls, at windows and as loose covers and upholstery on furniture.

Already equipped with an innate ability to draw, without effort, commercially feasible and attractive repeating designs, Morris became excited at the prospect of improving upon techniques employed in contemporary Victorian factories. Abhorring the products, atmosphere and working conditions of existing foreign and British manufactures (often the result of the race for technological supremacy initiated by the Industrial Revolution) he spent the next twenty years realizing his own ambitions in the field.

In 1865 the firm moved from their premises in Red Lion Square to 26 Queen Square, Bloomsbury and a twenty-one year lease, at an annual rent of £52 10s 0d was signed by all members of the firm. This became the firm's headquarters for the next sixteen years; for most of that time acting as both a manufacturing and a retailing outlet.[1] The house not only held the firm's offices and showroom (on the ground floor), a principal and smaller subsidiary workshops (shortly expanded into premises at Ormond Yard close by) but also became the home of the Morris Family – William, Janey, Jenny and May – who moved into London from the Red House the same year.[2] Consequently space was at a premium.

As early as 1862 Morris produced his first three commercial repeating designs, for wallpapers. These patterns – *Daisy*, *Fruit* and *Trellis* – were inspired not only by the medieval motifs he admired and included in earlier embroideries but also by the trailing roses, fruit trees and flowers in his garden at the Red House. Morris's interest in gardening and his knowledge of horticulture and botany were major factors in the success of his own floral designs. There was a gap of six years before any further wallpapers appeared and these, with names such as *Venetian*, *Indian* and *Queen Anne* show derivative designs based on historic styles. Morris's first textile design *Jasmine and Trellis* is of the same period but is quite different in design, and looks back to the earlier floral patterns in subject matter, colour and simplified repeat. Although this was Morris's first original textile design, it was not the first pattern to be printed commercially for the firm. In 1868 Morris approached Thomas Clarkson of the Bannister Hall Print Works near Preston in Lancashire[3] to inquire if any of the sets of wood-blocks used for their earlier products were still available.[4] Morris had already decided that to achieve the effects he wished for his own printed textiles, the ancient technique of block-printing must be used in preference to engraved rollers which, by the mid-nineteenth century, had been adopted by most of the leading commercial textile manufacturers. The blocks Morris chose were for designs first printed at Bannister Hall between 1830 and 1835. George Wardle remembered 'the processes of printing the patterns were not yet forgotten though long since superceded by modern styles . . . After a few trials the best of these patterns were reproduced in the original colourings and they took their places as novelties when exhibited in "the shop".'[5] May Morris described the textiles, 'These were on a white ground and several of them were copied from the pleasant old-fashioned shiny

Pattern book of Bannister Hall printed cottons. This 1830 sample is similar to those chosen by Morris.

("calendered") chintzes. I remember two Chinese rose patterns, large and small and a pretty open "Coiling Trail" pattern.'[6] A sample of the *Small Stem* pattern recently acquired by the Victoria and Albert Museum has an early Queen Square selvedge mark[7] and is obviously one of the two Chinese rose patterns; the other being the similarly named *Large Stem*. *Coiling Trail* has always retained its original name.[8]

Although the 'original colourings' were achieved for these prints synthetic dyes were used in their manufacture. *Jasmine and Trellis* was also printed by Clarkson using the same dyes but the sludgy greens, yellows and browns (an unusual palette for Morris) reproduced well and he found the results satisfactory.[9] The discovery and introduction into the trade of chemical dyestuffs had quite a revolutionary effect on nineteenth-century textile production. A number of colours were available in the

SMALL STEM, *1830s design adopted by Morris and block-printed on to wool by Thomas Clarkson.*

37

earlier part of the century – Prussian blue, cochineal pink, antimony orange, manganese bronze and alizarin red – to name the most popular, but it was with the discovery of a mauve by Perkins in 1856, and subsequently other colours, that aniline dyes, as they were known, flooded the market. All were extremely bright in tone and few colours were not available. The expanding commercialization and competition amongst international dyeing industries bitterly challenged not only traditional processing in Britain but throughout the world. Natural plant and animal dyestuffs, many of which came from abroad, became less easy to obtain and import into Britain and many of the techniques associated with these dyes were abandoned and eventually forgotten. To the manufacturer, the advantages of these new dyestuffs were threefold; they were cheaper, quicker and easier to use, and provided colours and tones not seen before. They also dried more quickly thus facilitating the use of engraved rollers for printing. The disadvantages were great as not only were the colours garish and totally unnatural but they were fugitive, bleeding when washed and fading quickly, often completely changing colour in the process.

For some years Morris had considered dyeing his own embroidery yarns as colours produced by contractors, in England and France, had not always pleased him. In 1872 the Morris family acquired Horrington House in Chiswick Lane and moved from Queen Square. This gave him the opportunity he was waiting for. George Wardle noted that:

The conversion of the house in Queen Square into offices, workshops and showroom seemed almost a desecration, but I do not think Mr. Morris felt the change very much. He was rather elated by the prospect of getting out of it a little dye shop. This was established in the basement in the old scullery (with its coppers) and larder, while the kitchen was turned into a drying ground, under the care of the caretaker.[10]

At first Morris used aniline dyes being the most readily available but chose 'tones which were deep and rather neutral than crude. Being of deep full tone they would be able to give up something to light and air and still have something left for the purchaser.'[11] Realizing that the colours, and shades of fading that he admired in historical textiles, tapestries, silks and velvets were all

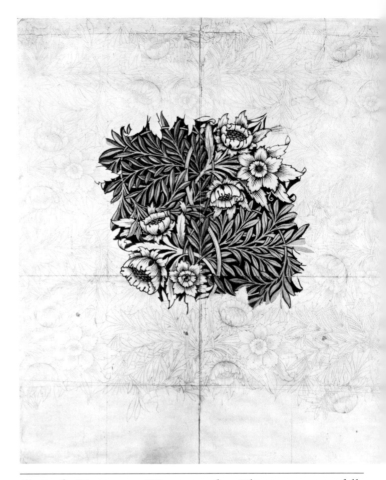

Design for TULIP AND WILLOW, *1873. This was not successfully printed on to fabric by indigo discharge until 1883.*

produced by vegetable and animal dyestuffs, Morris began to read as much as he could find on the subject.

Morris's next textile design was *Tulip and Willow* printed by Clarkson and registered by the Lancashire firm on 30 December 1873. Morris was horrified with the results. The design, which has a dark blue ground, and was intended for discharge printing was surface block-printed and was spoilt by the use of Prussian blue instead of the more subtle grey-blue shades of indigo which Morris had intended. The dominating colour scheme of dark blue contrasted with scarlet red in Morris's patterns first appeared in 1859, when, moving into the Red House, the only usable fabrics Morris found were Turkey red cottons and dark blue serge, and he continued to use this colour scheme throughout his career, even where there were no restrictions either on the dyes or fabrics available.[12] Morris's preoccupation with bright primary colours was completely out of pace with mid-Victorian fashions, which demanded complicated multi-coloured floral patterns on white ground for printed fabrics[13] and heavy, dark, rich tones for woven velvets and silks. Popular colours included plum, maroon, magenta, olive green, rust, cobalt and ultramarine blue and black. Morris soon began to hate aniline dyes and their properties: 'It must, I suppose, be considered a negative virtue in the new dyes that they are as fugitive as the older ones are stable.' He was no less savage when discussing the effects he believed they were having on industry and design as a whole:

It must be enough to say that their discovery while conferring the greatest honour on the abstract science of chemistry, and while doing a great service to capitalists in their hunt after profits has terribly injured the art of dyeing, and for the general public has nearly destroyed it as an art. Henceforward there is an absolute divorce between the *commercial process* and the *art* of dyeing. Anyone wanting to produce dyed textiles with any artistic quality in them must entirely forego the modern and commercial methods in favour of those which are at least as old as Pliny, who speaks of them as being old in his time.[14]

The search for and attainment of the dyeing technique and subsequently the colours he sought (and for these there could be no compromise) is a fascinating story which can be traced, step by step, through his own correspondence.[15] These letters give far more information about Morris than simply his preference for colours, however. At times they show an uncompromising, penny-pinching, dictatorial tyrant but also a man of intelligence, dedication and determination. Surprisingly, a shrewd business mind is also evident, a characteristic Morris is seldom credited with.

Dyeing

Until recently it has not been possible to state, with certainty, which of the many dyeing manuals available in 1870 Morris used to learn the techniques he employed himself. He does mention a number of authors and treatises in his letters but often this is in the form of criticism, so it must be assumed that these were not followed. Lists of books from his own library show the collection of a bibliophile rather than a technician. He owned a copy of Giovanni Ventura Roseto's *Plictho de*

PRINTERS NOTES, *dated from 1883 and written by Morris. This page gives a bibliography of dyeing manuals used.*

larte de tentori (published in Venice in 1540) the first book written specifically on the art of dyeing, and a number of 'Herbals' but these were kept for their intrinsic beauty rather than their texts. For instance John Gerard's *Herball or Generall Historie of Plants* of which Morris owned two editions, printed in 1597 and 1636 (the latter given to him as a boy), was used as reference for plants and plant dye properties but as there are no recipes printed, it can have been of little further use. A small notebook in Morris's handwriting has recently been found, called 'Printers

Notes' and dated 1883. It was started, presumably, to chronicle the technical details of dyeing and printing which Morris wished his own workmen to follow at the newly opened Merton Abbey Works. The notes are brief and sketchy and many sections are left incomplete. There is, however, a bibliography for the dyeing section listing seven authors whose writings were used by him.[16] The period of tinctorial research covered by these articles and books is over one hundred years, the earliest being the treatise *sur les toiles Peintes* published under the pseudonym 'Monsieur Quarelles' in Amsterdam (not Antwerp as listed by Morris) in 1760. The latest lists the findings of Underwood as published in the *Textile Colourist* magazine published in Manchester in 1876–7. The book most consistently referred to throughout the notes is Persoz's *L'impression des Tissus* published in Paris in 1846, whose recipes he quotes for a number of dyes including indigo, for which Morris compares the work of Persoz and Underwood with Napier from *A Manual of the art of dyeing* (published in London in 1853). Always open to new ideas, Morris also noted suggestions from his own workmen and, under the heading 'Buffs', which records the recipe used at Merton Abbey in August 1883, he has added 'May 18. 1885 Kenyon has been accustomed to raise the dolly as follows'. It is difficult at times to comprehend how Morris was capable of the most complex chemistry or the minutest delicate detail often necessary in dyeing, but his unruly (not to say scruffy) appearance and deliberate unscientific attitude to life and art denied his true capabilities.

From 1872 Morris conducted dyeing experiments in Queen Square with the help of John Smith, the errand boy from the glass-painter's shop. He soon realized however that he possessed neither the facilities nor the industrial experience needed to develop this side of manufacture. The coppers at Queen Square were adequate to cope with the wools and silks needed to complete the firm's embroidery patterns but his ambitions were now expanding and dyes required to print cloth and dye yarns for woven fabrics and carpets were needed in large quantities. On George Wardle's suggestion Morris approached his brother Thomas Wardle (1831–1909) who had recently (in 1870) set himself up as an independent silk dyer and printer, and silk and calico finisher in the Hencroft Dye Works in Leek, Staf-

fordshire. The Wardle family were already accomplished in this art as Joshua, father of George and Thomas, was a leading Leek silk dyer in the 1830s and 1840s, having previously been employed in the silk industry of Macclesfield in Cheshire. Joshua used all the most common natural dyestuffs in his own factory[17] and it is sad to note that just over thirty years later, the techniques that he employed were so redundant that Wardle and Morris found difficulty in beginning the most rudimentary processes. The search for a successful method of printing patterns with woad and indigo blue dye (indigo providing the better colour) occupied the printed cotton industry for much of the eighteenth century and the discovery of 'china-blue' and 'pencil-blue' techniques by British manufacturers contributed to their own superiority in the market in the first quarter of the nineteenth century. The tradition was strong but short lived. By the 1830s the use of blue in the production of green (by overprinting with yellow) was made redundant with the discovery of a solid arsenic green and by the introduction of aniline dyes in the late 1850s the complicated and exacting processes of indigo and woad were abandoned in the printing trade although retained in some quarters for the piece dyeing of woollen lengths, in particular.

Morris found Wardle 'full of interest in the revived methods which he vaguely remembered as going on in his own boyhood and which some of his older workmen had practised.' His own experience however was in aniline dyeing although he was anxious to learn of any other techniques which he could apply to his own particular interest, the production and dyeing of silk.[18] Wardle had spent a number of years experimenting in sericulture[19] and the successful dyeing of tusser silk (a type of silk yarn which had previously resisted colour) which he perfected by adopting a preliminary bleaching process. He imported a great deal of silk from India often already woven, much of which was dyed and overprinted in Leek. The Hencroft Works afforded the luxury of two dyehouses; one which Wardle used for the aniline dyeing of his own commercial products and the other was, for a period of two years, almost solely engaged on Morris's work. Although Morris inspired Wardle's first experiments with natural dyestuffs,[20] Wardle was pleased to undertake this work both as a profitable commercial venture[21] and for the experience which he was to use for his own textile manufacture some years later. Wardle, who seems to have been a modest and generous man, wrote later of the experiments 'I should have known little of printing but for him [Morris] I undertook the task, being led on by the charm of his personality and the wide range of his artistic ability.'

In July 1875 Morris travelled to Leek and started experiments with Wardle and three of his dyers, 'About this time his hands were habitually and unwashably blue, and in no condition to do fine work,' Mackail wrote.[22] Morris was exhilarated by the work and wrote to a friend, 'I daresay you will notice how bad my writing is, my hand is so shaky with doing journey-man's work the last few days; delightful work; hard for the body and easy to the mind.' In August, on his return to London, Morris began a long correspondence with Wardle which lasted the full period of their experimental dyeing period. 'My bundle of fents were very much admired by my artist friends and myself, all of them seem good in colour when they come among other things here.' The dyes that had been used for these samples were a mixture of artificial and natural dyestuffs set by steam. After the disaster of *Tulip and Willow* Morris became anxious to use indigo or woad for blue dyeing and although he was satisfied generally with the initial results at Leek, the Prussian blues used disappointed him. The results were 'worse than Clarkson blues, in fact worse than any I have ever seen.' The problem, as Morris saw it, lay in the inexperience of Wardle's staff. Of the two dyers employed on his work Hayworth was a steam-colour printer and therefore knew nothing about the natural red dye madder, and Kay was a madder printer who knew nothing about steam. Morris's hope that Kay would use his experience of traditional techniques combined with modern dye fixing methods was a complete disaster and the dyer became the bane of Morris's life. He wrote to Wardle about the dyer in despairing mood 'If only you could get an intelligent man, even if he were only moderately experienced, it seems all would be gained.' Kay left Wardle's employ in 1876.

Accepting that Wardle's success lay in the production of steam colours, Morris wrote to Wardle listing those colours he would need to print his own patterns 'leaving indigo blue and madder apart.' This vital list is rather modest in content.

1 outline blue
1 outline green which would be of an olive character
1 blotch [by this he meant solid colour] yellow – green to be diluted
1 blotch blue
1 yellow greenish in character as above for shades
1 brown always dark and sometimes very dark
To these one might add a black (if such a thing is to be fast in steam colours).

All the new printed textile designd by Morris from this time were sent to Wardle to print with instructions for different colour schemes. Samples (fents) would be returned to Morris by post who would write in reply quoting dye pattern numbers with his comments,[23] and Wardle's own pattern books, with samples of Morris's prints, are now in the Whitworth Art Gallery, Manchester (illus p. 50). Early complaints concerned the use of the Prussian blue and samples of the *African Marigold* pattern show the brightness of this dye. Wardle attempted a number of different systems to introduce woad and indigo dyeing but, again, his staff were the problem. The ancient profession of 'wadman' (as the woad dyer was called) was a most important and highly skilled job involving a seven day week of care and constant attention of the woad vat. Without the experience and commitment required, Wardle's dyers could not undertake this work, however enthusiastic Wardle and Morris were themselves.

Both read a great deal (and recommended books to each other) on the subject and in 1876 they visited probably one of the few surviving woad dyers in Nottingham, but the use of this dye for block-printing was never successfully achieved at Leek although hanks of wool and silks were dyed adequately. Obtaining an unstreaky solid blue was the main problem with this time consuming and complicated process. As it involves the submersion of yarn or cloth in a deep vat (sunk into the floor), it is essential that the dye solution is of a uniform strength. After the prescribed time according to the depth of blue required, the yarn or cloth is then exposed to the air and the dye swiftly oxidizes and becomes insoluble. Because of the properties of the dye and the method by which it is used it is not possible in its normal state to print cloth with it, as it will oxidize on the block. A system of resist or discharge printing is therefore necessary.

Morris chose the latter as the only successful means of printing *Tulip and Willow* but he had to wait a number of years before it was successfully manufactured. In November 1875 Morris sent to Wardle a sample of pencilled cloth, achieved by dipping a chewed willow twig into a solution of 'pencil-blue' dye, an early nineteenth-century system of printing indigo in lines. Morris also saw the use of this technique as being a solution to Wardle's staffing problems, 'Of course you would have children for the pencilling, our boys at 5/6d a week would be up to it. I should have thought (with deference) that we scarcely wanted more printers.' In reply Wardle explains that there was a great difference between what could be achieved by a twig and what Morris expected for his own designs and the proposal was abandoned as impractical.

Morris's attitude to all textile techniques was as up-to-date and labour saving as could be managed without sacrifice of finish and appearance. He used modern chemicals mixed with alum in mordants (dye-setting agents) which proved not only quicker to use but more efficient, although the processes involved in natural dyeing and the preparation and finishing of the printed textiles often including a number of soapings, washing and drying of the cloth could never be curtailed without some loss of brightness or fastness to the dyes themselves.

On 9 May 1876 Morris wrote to Wardle asking him to undertake the dyeing of the firm's piece-goods — serges and Utrecht velvets, which were supplied to Morris and Company from the Manchester firm of J. Aldam Heaton & Co. There are no examples of colour fents of these fabrics in the Wardle's pattern books although it is likely that the firm undertook the work. Wardle was already dyeing Morris's embroidery silks by this time, carpet wools for the firm's manufacture of Kidderminster and Wilton carpeting, and silks and cotton yarns for woven fabrics being produced in Macclesfield and Halifax.

It is difficult to explain either Morris's determination to achieve the results he required or to describe the pressures that Wardle must have felt without quoting all Morris's letters to Wardle. Morris's criticisms escalated towards the end of 1876 and colours perfected previously (madder reds in particular) were now being dyed disastrously badly. Wardle continued to badger his dyers and even turned down a lucrative order from another retailer[24] in

Design for AFRICAN MARIGOLD, *1876. Originally printed by Thomas Wardle with Prussian blue dye.*

his loyalty to Morris and anxiety to concentrate on achieving the required results. Morris blamed Wardle's failures on 'a lack of constant supervision on the spot' and can not have been surprised to hear from Wardle in August 1876 that the mental, physical and financial pressures of the work were too great and that he might have to abandon the experimental dye-house. Whether this was an attempt by Wardle to moderate Morris and get him to accept more responsibility for the results achieved, is difficult to assess but if it was then it failed. Morris wrote in reply that although sympathetic to the pressures involved he was unwilling to accept the responsibility (and presumably the costs) of pieces wrongly dyed nor was he willing to let his own standards slip. 'I mean that I can never be content with getting anything short of the best, and that I should always go on trying to improve on goods in all ways, and should consider anything that was only tolerable as a ladder to mount up to the next stage – that is, in fact – my life!' Wardle turned down Morris's offer to take over the dye-house himself and continued production.

By February 1878 Wardle was printing fourteen designs for Morris & Co.; *Tulip, Marigold, Carnation, Indian Diaper, Acanthus* (velveteen), *Iris, Bluebell, Snakeshead, Little Chintz, African Marigold, Honeysuckle, Pomegranate, Peony* and the now unnamed sunflower and acanthus pattern.[25] At the same time Morris's correspondence tailed off; having controlled the dyeing and printing of patterns as far as he was able, and accepting particular colour schemes, he now left it to the staff of Morris & Co.'s newly opened shop at 264 (later 449) Oxford Street to order new stock when it was required.

The Merton Abbey Works

Disillusioned with the Wardle partnership and determined not to design any other printed fabrics until more satisfactory results, particularly indigo discharge, could be guaranteed, Morris made plans to open his own works. As early as March 1877 he had written to Wardle 'I have been thinking much since I saw you about beginning manufacturing in a small way as soon as I can: my trouble is that for the thing to be done satisfactorily it must be done in London (since I live there).' By 1881 the situation was becoming critical, with samples of bad dyeing being returned by clients to the shop. Morris was not only in danger of losing business but also a friend and business colleague; he wrote to Janey on February 23rd 'Tom Wardle is a heap of trouble to us; nothing will he do right and he does write the longest winded letters containing lies of various kinds ... we shall have to take the chintzes ourselves before long and are now really looking for premises'. For his factory Morris required purpose-built or easily adaptable premises with plenty of natural light and endless supplies of soft water for

Contemporary photograph of the Merton Abbey Works, taken from across the bridge. The works no longer exist.

washing and dyeing fabrics. He had a liking for 'some place on the Colne, say about West Drayton', but none of the few available empty factories were in this area. A silk yarn processing works in Blockley near Chipping Campden was viewed but turned down on the advice of George Wardle and similar premises in Crayford in Kent, an important textile printing centre, were pronounced as unsuitable by Morris himself. William de Morgan, who was at that time looking for a suitable area in which to produce his own pottery, came across the Merton Abbey factory and in March 1881 Morris went to see the buildings which he found entirely satisfactory. The factory which had been erected in the early eighteenth century by Huguenots for silk throwing was taken over as a printworks in the nineteenth century and had, until just before Morris & Co. took over, been run by Welch Brothers who were calico printers. Apart from the buildings, which already contained a dye-house and croft room (for clearing prints after dyeing) Morris was pleased to find the river so close to the premises, 'The River Wandle ... runs through them, turning a water wheel and supplying water of the special quality required for madder dyeing – we brought away bottles of water for analysis – to make sure that it was fit to dye with'. The works stood on a seven acre site including a large meadow, an orchard and a vegetable garden. There was a

43

manager's house, a caretaker's lodge and offices. The workshops, of two-storey red tiled and weatherboarded sheds were grouped irregularly around the site and were of the shape and size easily adapted later for glass-painting, carpet, tapestry and fabric weaving and block-printing.

The move to Merton Abbey in June 1881 gave Morris the impetus to start designing again and within a short time of moving equipment from Queen Square and adapting part of the buildings he was busy in the dyehouse directing experiments in indigo-dyeing. The atmosphere in the dye-house and the technique of the blue vat were described by an American visitor on a tour of the works in July 1886:

In the first out-house that we entered stood great vats of liquid dye into which some skeins of unbleached wool were dipped for our amusement;[26] as they were brought dripping forth, they appeared of a sea-green colour, but after a few minutes exposure to the air, they settled into a fast, dusky blue. Scrupulous neatness and order reigned everywhere in the establishment; pleasant smells of dried herbs exhaled from clean vegetable dyes, blent with the wholesome odors of grass and flowers and sunny summer warmth that freely circulated through open doors and windows.[27]

The dyehouse staff were trained by Morris and few had previous experience (Kenyon being an exception). Boys employed by Morris & Co. were not selected for suitability to the job, but put on to each job as a vacancy occurred. John Smith, who had helped Morris in the early years at Queen Square, was taken into the dye shop because at the time it was set up he was getting too old to remain an errand boy. By the late nineteenth century he had become chief dyer at the factory. Wages were above average and the dyers were paid on piece-work with the foreman dyer and colour-mixer, both highly rated in the hierarchy of staff, receiving weekly salaries.

Dyes used

In his 1889 Arts and Crafts lecture 'Of Dyeing as an Art' Morris described his own preferences for the colours and dyes he used in the successful production of his own textiles. He believed that all colours could be derived from four basic colours; the primaries red, blue and

A page from the Merton Abbey Dyebook which lists dyes and recipes for fabrics printed at the works 1882–91.

yellow, plus brown. For these colours he used the following dyes:

RED: Madder, lac-dye (derived from tree bark), cochineal and kermes (the last two are insect dyes). Morris's and Wardle's greatest success was the re-discovery of the technique using kermes, a dye Morris called 'the King'. Hardly known since the Middle Ages, a supply of the dye was brought for Morris from Athens by Aglaia Coronio.

BLUE: Indigo and woad. Woad, the Northern hemisphere's version of the Eastern indigo is best used on wool, indigo on cotton and silk. Both are 'substantive' dyes and do not need mordanting.

YELLOW: Weld (wild mignonette). quercitron bark (inner bark of the American black oak) and a wood dye called 'Old Fustic'. Yellow, Morris said 'is the commonest to be found in our fields and hedgerows ... saw wort, popular twigs, birch, heather and broom.' Yellow dyes are the least permanent and have to be treated with a solution of bran after dyeing to fix them.

BROWN: Roots of walnut tree and the husks of walnuts. Catechu, an Indian plant. Like Morris's choice of blues, neither of these dyes needed a mordant.

Secondary colours

BLACK: Dyed in indigo or woad until dark and then in walnut roots.

GREEN: Indigo and then weld or quercitron.

PURPLE: Indigo and then cochineal, kermes or madder. Shades of mulberry or claret were obtained by the 'saddening' (darkening) of purple with walnut.

ORANGE: Madder or cochineal with weld. By saddening with walnut all shades between yellow and red were obtained.[28]

Printed textiles

Before Morris's introduction to Thomas Wardle and the transfer of the firm's dyeing and printing to Leek, Morris & Co.'s textile range consisted of only a few items, but these suited most domestic needs. From Clarkson's manufacture there were three designs – *Small Stem*, *Large Stem* and *Coiling Trail*, all printed on to a fine wool and suitable for curtaining – and *Jasmine Trellis*, a glazed cotton, for use as summer curtains and loose covers on chairs and couches. Heavyweight curtains were made of plain woollen serge, available in a number of colours, and a woven mohair pile fabric stamped with a floral design called *Utrecht Velvet* (after original seventeenth-century Dutch fabrics) was used for chair upholstery. The Manchester firm of Heaton and Company supplied the firm with woollen serges,[29] and it is likely that the velvet was also one of their products. The design is not by Morris and when in 1914 the fabric was used for part of the decoration in the ill-fated liner Titanic it was chosen by Heaton's, who were employed by the White Star Line

as interior decorators (illus. p. 129). Utrecht velvet had been used for furnishing since the beginning of the nineteenth century and, because of its hard-wearing qualities, proved ideal for chair upholstery. The design adopted by Morris & Co. and sold through their own shop became very popular, and today can be seen not only on examples of Morris & Co. furniture but on chairs by other designers and manufacturers. One example, now in the Victoria and Albert Museum, shows the textile used on a chair designed by the architect and designer William Burges (1827–1881). *Utrecht Velvet* was available in a number of popular Victorian colours and a series of small samples at the William Morris Gallery, Walthamstow, show bright chemically dyed shades of yellow, rose, turquoise and red alongside the more usual sage green and olive.

Thomas Wardle's early experimental block-prints of Morris's designs have a number of different background fabrics and samples of woven spun and tusser silk, challis (a mixed fabric of silk and wool) and fine wools can be seen in the Wardle Pattern Books with plain and combed (fluffy) cottons. As Wardle was particularly interested in silk it is understandable that he was keen to use this in the initial trials and examples of the patterns *Marigold*, *Larkspur*, *African Marigold* and *Honeysuckle* all printed on to silk were exhibited under Wardle's name in the British India Section of the 1878 Paris Exhibition.[30] Morris would not have been greatly interested in the use of silk for his designs wishing to produce furnishings not dress fabrics and must have been doubly hampered by the narrow width of the silk (usually 19 inches) being imported by Wardle from India. Few of Morris's designs fitted into this restricted format and examples of the pattern *Honeysuckle* show only half the design. Silk backgrounds were, therefore, abandoned and there is no evidence to suggest that any silk lengths were sold commercially. Other aspects of Wardle's own trade were more successfully adopted by Morris and the influence of Indian patterns seen both in Wardle's own products and those imported by him is evident in a number of Morris's designs made between 1875 and 1877.

The first four of his patterns printed by Wardle, however, show a preoccupation with designing for other media: wallpaper and tiles in particular. *Larkspur* and *Marigold* were both designs first used for wallpaper and

Tulip was derived with the same feeling for all over flat pattern; the small alternating flower-heads providing the only relief of flat colour from the densely detailed ground. The fourth design *Carnation*,[31] registered on 15 October 1875 was probably designed by Kate Faulkner (d. 1898) sister of Charles Faulkner, a founder member of the firm and the first book-keeper. She is known to have produced a number of designs for wallpapers and tiles for the firm as well as free lance wallpaper patterns for Jeffrey & Co. and this textile design could also have been used on either technique. She was also an accomplished craftswoman contributing to the firm's production of embroideries, painted tiles, painted pottery and gesso decoration, and her china painting skills were employed by Doulton's. Little is known about the designer apart from her involvement with Morris & Co. and her close friendship with the Morris and Burne-Jones families. She lived in Queen Square close enough to his workshop for Morris to make frequent calls on her and her family. Her sister, Lucy, married in 1861 and Kate felt her own responsibilities lay in the care of her mother and her brother (whom she nursed for three years before his death in 1891). Georgiana Burne-Jones noted that she had a gentle nature and sympathetic understanding and keen sense of humour and it is clear that she was one of the few women that Morris felt close to. In 1878 he proposed that she should go to live with the Morris family in their newly found home, Kelmscott House in Hammersmith but being an independent yet responsible person she declined. It is interesting to conjecture that Kate Faulkner's own career would have developed much further and more of her attractive designs would be available today had she allowed herself more freedom. *Peony* printed on to cotton by Wardle in 1877 has already been tentatively attributed to her[32] and it is likely that the following two designs *Vine and Pomegranate* (for three-ply carpeting and woollen hangings) and a printed design of sunflowers and acanthus leaves, were also designed by her. Stylistically, these three designs are very similar and all were drawn at a time when Morris had been side-tracked from printed cottons and was preoccupied with setting up a jacquard loom for the hand-weaving of cloth at the firm's premises at Ormond's Yard (close to 26 Queen Square).

After *Larkspur* Morris's next printed textile design *Indian Diaper* has a strong eastern pattern and this together

A trial fent for IRIS *printed cotton designed in 1876. The Victorian date stamp denotes registration. The design is reversed.*

with *Snakeshead*, *Little Chintz* and *Pomegranate* all show Morris's awareness of contemporary imported Indian textiles. Although Morris must have seen many Indian designs at Leek these were widely available in all the most fashionable London shops. In 1876 £260,811 worth of Indian silks were exported from British India, an increase of £180,000 on exports quoted ten years previously. This colossal rise was mainly attributed to the continued use of natural dyestuffs in the printing and dyeing of the silks in India. This was because of the heavy (45 per cent) levies and, in parts of India, prohibition on the import of aniline dyestuffs, particularly magenta.[33] Many of Morris's early designs have small, square or diaper motifs, a characteristic of the contemporary designs being imported at that time and printed trials show 'hot' colour schemes of dark and even black grounds with the patterns printed in brown, terracotta and maroon. Even the more western-looking designs *Iris* and *Tulip* did not escape this attempted transformation but all settled down to more usual colour schemes for commercial use. Only the dark over-printed background of *Snakeshead* and a pre-

The indigo dye-vats at Merton Abbey. These were in use until the closure of the firm in 1940.

dominance of madder reds in other designs are evidence of this transient fascination.

Morris's interest in contemporary Indian patterns was soon forgotten and all his subsequent designs show his love of historic textiles from Italy, Persia and Turkey. His great dislike of contemporary British designs and a general abhorrence for the eighteenth century made him turn to more distant periods and his knowledge of the growing collections of the South Kensington Museum, first analysed by Peter Floud in 1959,[34] is now well known. The dates of many of the textiles most admired by Morris have been reassessed since Morris studied them (and in some cases since Peter Floud's article was published) and it is ironic that they are now generally thought to have been woven much later than had previously been supposed. Whether Morris would have chosen them for study had he been aware of this is questionable because it is not known if it was their supposed period or their pattern which first attracted him. In his article Peter Floud cited five historic textiles which influenced Morris in his designs. Only one printed textile

is included but, in 1876, this provided the repeating structure for two of Morris's printed textile designs, *Iris* and *Bluebell*, in which flowers duplicate the bird motifs of the original. Thought to be a Rhenish printed linen of the fifteenth century – and one of the earliest known examples of the craft – this has now been proved a fake, printed in the nineteenth century onto an earlier background fabric.[35] Ignorant of this, Morris adopted the twirling plant forms of this pattern for a number of designs of the period including woven textiles, a printed ceiling paper and for the re-painting of part of the Oxford Union in 1875. The use of willow leaves in the background of *Iris* and the earlier design *Tulip and Willow* shows a keen eye for commercial detail as this was a favourite design motif of the successful contemporary 'Aesthetic' designers B. J. Talbert (1838–1881) and E. W. Godwin (1833–1886). Because of their use in many designs Morris's own patterns must have looked far less unusual in their time than is now thought. The style of pattern and colouring used by Morris was quite different however.

Another characteristic Morris pattern style, first seen in designs printed at Leek, was that using a turn-over or 'mirror' repeat: *Acanthus*, *African Marigold* and *Honeysuckle* (illus. p. 51) all show this device. Because of the nature of this type of design patterns tend to be wider than those with straight or half-drop repeats and Morris took full advantage of this by using the whole width of the fabric (36 inches for linens and cottons and 24 inches for this velveteen) for the designs. Morris was already producing repeating patterns for woven textiles and machine-made carpets and had realized that this type of design was particularly suitable for the loom. It had also influenced his designs for other textiles and in the 1880s he used it in designs for large embroidered wall-hangings and bed-covers and hand-knotted carpets. Morris clearly preferred working on a large scale, 'Do not be afraid of large patterns', he advised, 'if properly designed they are more restful to the eye than small ones: on the whole, a pattern where the structure is large and the details much broken up is the most useful ... very small rooms, as well as very large ones, look better ornamented with large patterns'.[36]

Acanthus was to prove Morris's only design for printed velveteen although the firm later produced a range containing five other designs.[37] Morris was clearly put off by the complicated finishing processes the textile required involving the 'padding' of the front and back of the fabric before drying to retain the true tactile qualities of the cloth. *Acanthus*, registered in April 1876, is significantly early enough to have influenced the fashion for furnishing velveteens at their height in the 1880s when Thomas Wardle and the Lancashire firm of Turnbull and Stockdale (established in 1882) led a very competitive field. By the end of the century these fabrics were considered rather too heavy for general domestic use and although they remained in the firm's range they were printed only for special orders of 30 yards or more.

Morris loved the practical labour of drawing patterns and by the summer of 1876 he was so pre-occupied with designing that even his rest became affected. To Aglaia Coronio he wrote, 'I am drawing patterns so fast that last night I dreamed I had to draw a sausage, somehow I had to eat it first which made me anxious about my digestion'. His determination to succeed as a retailer of printed fabrics did not waver either by excess of hard work or by Wardle's expensive, time-consuming experiments. Work at Leek had contributed to a loss of £1,023 to this section of the firm and in a letter of 21 October 1875 a note of desperation showed, 'I don't suppose we shall get many people to buy them', Morris wrote of his printed cottons. It was not until 1877 that their commercial viability became evident and an increase in sales was related by Morris to Wardle with all the confident air that all was now saved.

Born into an age of art theorists and a contemporary of Christopher Dresser, Lewis F. Day and Walter Crane (who all wrote books on repeating design), Morris was never secretive in describing his own ideas on good design nor in declaring his own theories concerning the history of repeating pattern, and the role of designer and craftsman within society. He lectured to many different groups and those lectures concerning textiles – 'Hints on Pattern Designing' (to the Working Men's College, London, 10 December 1881), 'Textile Fabrics' (given at the Health Exhibition 1884) and 'Textiles' (Arts and Crafts Lecture, 1888) were given to audiences of quite a different social standing. His belief, that great fulfilment could be derived, irrespective of skill, class or status, from the honest toil involved in the design and production of decorative domestic goods, and that all men were capable of such artistic work, illustrated his naivety in attempting to re-establish an artistic social structure probably not successfully practised since the guilds of the Middle Ages. This utopian dream which was described more fully in his visionary work *News from Nowhere* (first published in book form in 1891) was formulated in the century of the Industrial Revolution and can only have been strengthened by Morris's own experience of the growing commercialization seen in the Victorian textile trade. He was aware of the deprivation and boredom inflicted on workers brought by the so-called improvements in technology.

Equally simplistic in approach, if not terminology, were Morris's lectures on the history of pattern making which were well received but it is questionable if they were understood by the inexperienced. However, at no time did he treat his audience with condescension. His theory that all pattern essentially has two basic elements – the diagonal line and the diaper in its various forms – is axiomatic. His own descriptions of how these could be used (illustrated with diagrams from Owen Jones's *Grammar of Ornament* (1856) and F. Fischbach's *Ornamente der Gewebe* (Hanau, 1874–78)[38] show true originality however and all his own designs can be classified between the 'branch' (diagonal line) and 'net' (diaper) patterns as described by him. Morris always recognized that within this framework intuitive inspiration was the element that differentiated between a good and an excellent design and he was totally committed to the idea that designs must be sympathetic to the recipient craft and that the designer should have experience of the technique he designed for. 'The special limitations of the material should be a pleasure to you, not a hindrance: a designer, therefore, should always thoroughly understand the processes of the special manufacture he is dealing with'. A sympathy for technique is shown in all Morris's designs and this, above all other factors singles him out from many of his contemporaries who sold designs to whatever manufacturer was interested, irrespective of purpose or finished product.

January 1878 saw the registration of the last new design to be printed at Leek during Morris's own lifetime. Frustrated with Wardle's inconsistent results and his inability to print with indigo dye, Morris became pre-occupied for the next three years with weaving and carpet production. With the anticipated move to Merton Abbey only months away and the hope that, at last the indigo vat would be successfully used for printing, Morris drew three designs, *Brother Rabbit*, *Bird and Anemone* and *Rose and Thistle*, to be printed by the indigo discharge method. Experiments with indigo started as early as April 1881 at Queen Square and Morris, and his new dyer Goodacre, an East Londoner with experience of 'dipping' (the term Morris used for indigo dyeing) were encouraged by the results. These three designs were not however registered until the printing process was perfected at Merton Abbey in 1882.

Morris & Company's registration of textile designs is rather haphazard although a lot more printed textile designs than woven appear in the Patent Office Register of Designs. All Morris's designs for indigo discharge printing are listed however, so covetous was he of the technique he had revived. Morris and Company was not the only firm to sell textiles printed by this process as Japanese cottons were being imported and registered by British companies as their own work. Japanese designs had so influenced the market by the mid 1870s that differentiation between western imitations and the original fabrics had become difficult.[39]

Of the nineteen patterns registered by Morris & Co. between May 1882 and September 1885, seventeen were designed to be printed by indigo discharge. These included two colour designs of the natural dark indigo blue and white (*Brother Rabbit*, *Rose and Thistle*, *Bird and Anemone* and *Borage*), those with additional half tones of indigo and weld providing two shades of blue, white, yellow and green (*Wreathnet*, *Wey*, *Kennet*, *Eyebright* and *Lea*) and those with half-blues, weld and madder producing blues, white, yellows, greens, reds, oranges, browns and purples (*Flowerpot*, *Wandle*, *Evenlode*, *Strawberry Thief* and *Medway*). *Windrush*, *Rose* and *Lodden* were all designed to be discharge printed leaving a white ground. The blocks for *Windrush* were cut for discharge printing (the blue blocks show a negative of the design) but only one sample, a trial in madder red, now at the William Morris Gallery, Walthamstow, shows this colour balance. All other prints of this design show a coloured ground indicating that the blocks were re-cut for surface printing.

Surface block-printing

Before moving to Merton Abbey it is likely that Morris sent his designs first to Clarkson's[40] and then to Thomas Wardle's block-cutter to be made into printing blocks. Although it was usual, in large textile printing works, to have a block-cutter on the staff this was not the case at Merton Abbey and all the firm's blocks for wallpaper and printed textiles were cut by Alfred and later James Barrett of 489 Bethnal Green Road, London. Morris was quite specific in his instructions to the block-cutter and many of his existing designs have notes to the block-cutter written on them. The pattern was transferred from drawing to block by means of tracing paper but this had

Indigo discharge wood-block for FLOWERPOT, *originally designed as a lining fabric.*

Double page from one of Wardle's dyebooks showing four colourways of BLUEBELL *with dates and sample numbers.*

to be matched to the pattern for accuracy and all tracings were submitted to Morris before rubbing onto the pearwood block to provide a guide for cutting.[41] This checking ensured that all the blocks, each cut for a different colour of the design, matched one another. The pattern on the blocks was originally carved but later nineteenth-century replacements (and the life of the block was limited) were more hard-wearing with metal insets taking the place of the raised sections of the wood. These were padded with felt to absorb the dye.

The cloth to be printed was prepared and stretched onto a blanket on one of the long printing tables which ran the length of the printing shop in front of the windows. The printer, equipped with a large dye-pad which was kept on a trolley near-by (mounted on rails for mobility) pressed his block on to the pad and then laid it in position onto the fabric. It was then rapped with the handle of a mall (a lead weighted mallet) which ensured an impression on the cloth. Morris advocated dusting the printing tables with powdered glass so that if the dye did impregnate the blanket it could be brushed off the surface of the table. The printer then lifted the block, applied more colour and repeated the impression until the whole length of the fabric was completed. The area first printed was now dry enough to receive the second colour and the process was repeated with the next set of blocks. To

The Printing Shop at Merton Abbey. The mobile trolley on tracks held the dye pads and other equipment.

A Morris & Co. dyer washing cotton lengths in the Wandle. This was necessary before and after dyeing.

Original watercolour design for HONEYSUCKLE *printed fabric, designed by Morris in 1876.*

ensure a perfect registration of colours each block was fitted with a series of small projecting pins which left tiny dots of colour, a guide for the subsequent printing.

May Morris wrote of family visits to Merton Abbey and how she climbed the stairs to the printers' shop on the first floor (over the carpet weaving section) to the thump-thump of the printers' blocks. This became one of the most characteristic noises of the works. The shops were kept warm and moist and of the most equable temperature possible 'some boil a kettle in the shop to keep the air moist; some hang up damp clothes; this last is best' Morris wrote in his 'Printers Notes'.

The system of finishing the prints, ensuring that the colours were fast and whites cleared, depended on the dyes used although this was always a time-consuming and exacting process especially when dealing with cloths printed by indigo discharge. 'We are not getting on as fast as we should with the printing: it is very tough work getting everything in due order, the cloths seem to want so much doing to them after' Morris wrote to Jenny on 28 February 1883. The soft waters of the River Wandle were utilized in the washing of the cloth and on at least one occasion Morris clogged the water-mill with madder dye. Drying was also completed out of doors whenever possible and in fine weather lengths of brightly coloured cottons lay drying in the meadow at the back of the workshops where poplar trees had been planted to act as windbreaks. Morris recommended soaping as a good finishing technique for the clearing of whites and fixing of madder reds. The usual clearing process was lengthy, consisting of washing the cloth and passing it through two soap and bran baths (the second of which it was boiled and turned in for 30–40 minutes); it was then washed and 'crofted' (dried naturally) for 5–8 days. It was then soaped again, bran washed and crofted for 7 days and this was followed by a further soaping and a 3, 4 or 6 day drying period. If the colours had not cleared by this time, a fifth soaping was recommended.[42] It is not surprising that Morris & Co.'s textiles were generally more expensive than that of their competitors but, bearing in mind the time and labour involved in printing and finishing the cloth, the firm would have been justified in raising their prices even higher. Obviously, this would not have been a prudent move commercially and Morris was more content to keep the workshops running than to make a large profit.

Indigo discharge method

After washing, the undyed cotton was submerged into the indigo dye vat for the required time. On lifting it out the dye on the cloth, which appeared dark green quickly oxidized with the air, producing the characteristic blue colour. A bleaching agent was then block-printed onto the areas of cloth not intended to be blue (for light blue, or half-blue as they were known, a weakened solution was used). The cloth was then washed and the blue cleared from the bleached areas producing a print of dark blue, pale blue (if the pattern dictated it) and white (illus. p. 54). The cloth was then half dried, warmed and prepared for the next colour, yellow, by block-printing with a mordant in those areas of the pattern requiring this colour. The cloth was then submerged in the weld vat, cleared and prepared for dyeing in the same manner in the madder vat. Both weld and madder are adjective dyes and need a mordant so any areas of the submerged cloth not mordanted did not take up the dye. There is evidence that later printing methods adopted more labour-saving techniques, first to cut out madder and weld vat dyeing by using colour instead of mordant on the blocks,[43] and, secondly, as a substitute for discharge altogether to use

Design for FLOWERPOT *printed cotton, 1883, with instructions to the block-cutter in Morris's handwriting.*

surface block-printing on lighter dyed grounds. These later colours did not require a mordant.

The move to Merton Abbey began in June 1881 with the erecting of fabric and carpet looms, the equipping of the glass painters' shop and setting up of dye vats and printing tables and it was not until 1882 that indigo discharge dyeing was put into production.

Indigo discharged cottons are easy to recognize as the blue dye can always be seen on the back of the cloth. In the case of patterns with light grounds, where most of the blue has been bleached out (*Rose* and *Lodden*) blue selvedges are noticeable. Some production delays were caused in the dyeshop by Kenyon, the colour mixer who, although much liked by Morris, needed standing over to get the work done. By December the firm's blocker William Hillier had successfully printed *Brother Rabbit* and was working on *Bird and Anemone*. The development of fabric printing and dye recipes used at Merton Abbey from c. 1882 to 1891 can be traced today through a dye-book now in the collection of Sanford and Helen Berger[44] (illus. p. 44). The advantage of ready-built premises, soft water and attractive surroundings made the Merton Abbey Works particularly pleasant to work in. Morris continued to produce numerous designs at his easel at the works where inspiration was provided by the surrounding gardens (a small kitchen garden was divided between some of the men for them to plant and care for). In April 1882 a visitor wrote, 'white hawthorn was out in the garden; we had tea with Mr. Morris in his room in the house and left laden with marsh-marigolds, wallflowers, lilac and hawthorn'.[45] George Wardle summed up the atmosphere admirably when he wrote, 'there seems nothing to say except that it was altogether delightful'.[46]

With the exception of three designs for woven textiles[47] and a few special commissions for Hammersmith carpets for 1883–4, Morris concentrated on designing for printed textiles and took on a new printer called Hill to cope with the extra work.[48] Later designs show a significant change in style and subject matter from those printed at Leek. Although still concentrating on floral patterns these show a more sophisticated stylization than the botanical cross-sections seen in earlier works. Merton Abbey designs show animals, birds and flowerheads arranged in vertical and horizontal rows with the main emphasis of movement, and repeating motif, made by the stem of the flower. This scheme, which achieves a perfect visual balance, was derived from a study of traditional patterns, especially animal and bird patterns in the South Kensington Museum; and was inspired by those of the fourteenth and early fifteenth century, thought in Morris's day to have been woven in Lucca in Italy. It has been suggested by Peter Floud that this close study of the past was a waste of Morris's inherent talents but Morris was experienced enough to select details from those patterns which he most admired (usually technical repeats) and use these in his own original designs. At a time when historic patterns were copied verbatim by commercial designers from the pages of books such as *The Grammar of Ornament* it is no discredit that Morris sought inspiration in this way. It was, after all, this practice of study and selection which has been advocated in art schools throughout the twentieth century; just as a study of the human form improves draughtsmanship, a designer's ability to control colour and line is improved by a study of successful patterns.

Morris employed Philip Webb to draw birds and animals for his wallpaper and tapestry designs, and

Seventeenth-century Italian cut velvet, seen by Morris in 1883 when it was acquired by the South Kensington Museum.

Webb is credited with providing these for the textile design *Brother Rabbit*.[49] Morris's own letters and sketchbooks do, however, show evidence of his own attempts at bird drawing and it is possible that he alone drew the designs *Bird and Anemone*, *Strawberry Thief* and *Rose*.

Between 1883 and 1885 Morris's designs show two distinctive pattern types not seen before, large-scale meandering 'branch' designs and small 'net' patterns for lining fabrics. *Wreathnet*, *Borage*, *Eyebright* and *Flowerpot* were all initially printed on cotton twenty-seven inches wide and were intended to be used as linings for Morris & Co.'s heavy woollen curtains (two widths of cotton matching the width of most woven wools). The provision of dress fabrics was of no interest to Morris although he saw in these small-scale designs, (and in a number of plain dyed fabrics) a good opportunity for commercial expansion. On 6 January 1883 he wrote to May, 'There is a new block come in for the printed dresses [presumably *Borage*] and we can dye piece cotton goods for such like things so give your orders ladies as even the humble can indulge in these simple articles'.

Morris's last designs for both wallpapers and printed cottons show a strong diagonal slant, and *Evenlode*, *Wey*, *Kennet*, *Windrush*, *Wandle*, *Cray*, *Medway*[50] follow the design of a seventeenth-century velvet (illus. p. 53) (then thought to be fifteenth century) which had recently been acquired by the South Kensington Museum.[51] Morris utilized this diagonal bias in a unique way and the meandering flower stems of the original take on an inanimate appearance in *Windrush* and *Cray*: in *Wandle* they become striped poles, echoing medieval motifs.

By 1885 Morris's visits to Merton Abbey were cut to three or even two days a week and although he had a bed there he seldom stayed overnight. The journey to Merton from Hammersmith was arduous and took two hours involving travelling by tube into London and then crossing the city to Farringdon Street in order to catch a train.[52] On arrival at the works Morris immediately discussed any new business with George Wardle. He would tour the workshops with Henry Dearle who was now supervising most areas of the textile workshops, and finish the day designing at his easel.[53]

John Henry Dearle (1860–1932)

Born and brought up in South London (he lived in Upper Tooting for a number of years before his death) Henry Dearle was taken on by Morris and Company in 1878 to assist in the newly opened shop in Oxford Street. He was transferred to the glass-painters' shop but showed such promise that Morris, 'influenced by the evident intelligence and brightness of the boy',[54] chose him to assist in setting up a tapestry loom at Queen Square. As the first apprentice tapestry weaver he was trained by Morris himself and two years later, when two other boys were employed for this side of the business, Dearle was responsible for their training.

It is difficult to determine when Dearle first supplied

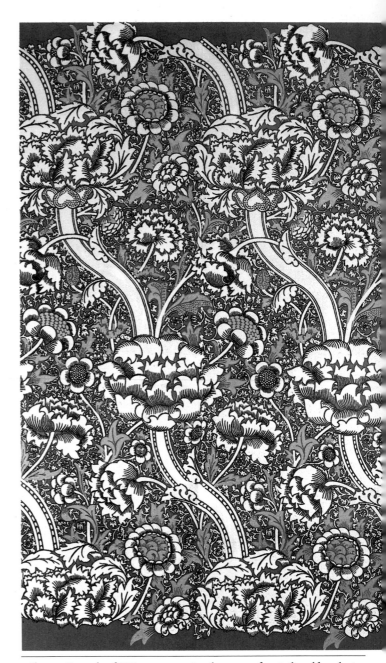

Above: Length of WANDLE *printed cotton after indigo blue dyeing and discharging and before other colours were printed.*
Right: Watercolour design for EVENLODE *printed cotton, 1883. Printed at Merton Abbey by indigo discharge.*

designs for Morris & Co., although in 1887 a tapestry of his design *Fox and Pheasant* was woven by the firm. It is likely, therefore, that he started to design repeating textiles soon after this date. Morris is often credited with drawing the designs of all the textiles produced up to the year of his death, 1896, despite historic and stylistic evidence to the contrary and even J. W. Mackail and May Morris in their biographies of William Morris uphold this myth. Far

more confusing, however, are the Arts and Crafts Exhibition catalogues which are often grossly inaccurate in their description and dates of patterns and it is likely that some entries attributing exhibits to William Morris do, in fact, simply mean Morris and Company. Even his own memorial exhibition at the Arts and Crafts show for 1899 appear to concentrate on the achievements of the firm he founded rather than on his own designs.

With the foundation of the Socialist League by Morris in December 1884 he became far more deeply involved in political action than previously and his attendance at meetings kept him very busy. At the same time he continued to write and produce a few designs for tapestries and hand-knotted carpets. It is unlikely that any more of his designs for repeating printed textiles were produced by the firm. He was now content to leave his daughter May in charge of the embroidery and Henry Dearle, who had already proved himself as a craftsman and draughtsman, to supervise woven and printed textile manufacture and most designs made for these sections of the firm were provided by these two. Dearle continued to produce designs until his death in 1932 and although he provided fewer printed textile designs than Morris (25 to 36) recognition of the importance of his contribution to the firm is long overdue. He was not the hack imitator of Morris's work that many now claim and his later work compares favourably with many of his more famous contemporaries.

Avon is likely to have been Dearle's first printed design. The style is uncontrolled, naively drawn and, in parts, badly constructed. Adopting Morris's preference for small subsidiary patterns there is an imbalance of dark and light tones which gives the design an unfortunate patchiness. While accepting that this could have been drawn by an inexperienced designer only Morris in the midst of a brainstorm would have produced such a result. The following two Morris & Co. fabrics *Cherwell* (used on velveteen) and *Trent* show better control but the busy background details have little form. In these three designs Dearle copied the drawings of a number of flowers (carnations, thistles, chrysanthemums and roses) from earlier Morris designs but also his own characteristic motifs, of pointed-headed tulips and dark veining on flowers and leaves, appear for the first time.

From 1889 Dearle represented the textiles section of

Design for DAFFODIL *printed cotton by Dearle, 1891. One of Morris & Co.'s most popular fabrics.*

the firm in schemes for interior decoration and all new textiles used in commissions from this time, including Bullerswood in Kent, Stanmore Hall in Middlesex and Wightwick Manor and Compton Hall near Wolverhampton in West Midlands, were all provided by him. *Compton* designed as a wallpaper and printed on to fabrics using the same blocks, has for many years been mistakenly considered to be Morris's last repeating design (if not his finest) which shows the considerable development of Dearle's talents. His designs for the 1890s are considerably tighter in format than those seen before and in four particularly successful designs, *Trail*, *Daffodil*, *Florence* and *Graveney*, a development of the diagonal bias

DAFFODIL *printed cotton, available with both light and dark grounds. Ten blocks were needed to print this design.*

in Morris's later work can be seen, with controlled floral patterns appearing between vertical stripes.

Dearle's historical preferences lay in the designs of Middle Eastern textiles and *Persian*, *Rosebud* and *Eden* in particular, show this. *Rosebud* is a copy of a Turkish textile and a watercolour of the original fabric in the South Kensington Museum, is now in the Victoria and Albert Museum. His increasing interest in historic designs unfortunately produced less original patterns. Lacking Morris's ability to select, his designs become imitative and, in some cases, especially woven textiles, it is often difficult to differentiate between patterns based on old designs and straight reproductions.

Morris's own designs continued to be printed and sold by the firm and two originally used for wallpaper, *Willow Bough* and *Powdered*, were adopted for textiles, their blocks re-cut to fit a 36 inch wide cotton. *Colne* and *Ribble* on the other hand were printed with the original wallpaper blocks. Both of these patterns were probably designed by Kathleen Kersey however, who, in the early twentieth century supplied Morris & Co. with a number of similar art nouveau patterns for wallpaper.

In 1905 a change of management at Morris & Co. took place. F. and R. Smith, who had become partners of Morris during his lifetime both retired from active management and a Board of Directors was set up. A great change in the style of goods sold by the firm followed this in an effort to modernize its now fading image and improve trade. The emphasis on textiles now lay with the production of high-quality reproduction fabrics popular in fashionable homes, and two or three printers worked continually. A stamped plush called *Acorn* and a second Utrecht velvet, *Musgrove*, joined the range of upholstery fabrics and a range of glazed cottons, named after country houses became popular. With the exception of *Haddon*, which shows an Indian floral sprig design, the remaining three designs in the range *Holkam*, *Tangley* and *Hadfield* are all based on English cottons of the early nineteenth century. Not all the firm's twentieth-century printed textiles were reproductions and Dearle introduced six original designs of attractive lightly coloured open floral patterns (*Briar*, *Sweet Briar*, *Brent*, *Rambling Rose*, *Merton* and *Indian Pink*).

On Henry Dearle's death in 1932 management of the works fell to his son Duncan who, although not greatly interested in the production of textiles, is known to have produced some designs.[55] Standards at the works declined and the company found the competition from manufacturers with more modern designs and production too great to stand, but a few established patterns continued to be printed and sold from the shop which in 1917 had moved to 17 George Street, Hanover Square. Morris and Dearle were now out of fashion but attempts to follow fashion were equally unsuccessful. Only one design from this period has been traced; showing a sub-Jacobean design in red and white, it shows neither the originality of design nor the technical excellence associated with Morris & Co.'s name.

Woven Textiles

Textile weaving is a much lengthier and more complex process than printing and it is, therefore, not surprising that although sixty-three woven fabrics[1] were eventually sold under the firm's name the earliest did not appear until 1876, eight years later than the earliest printed samples. By this time Wardle had established acceptable colour samples of the first original printed designs at Leek and Morris was able to concentrate first on learning the technique of weaving and, secondly, on deciding how he wished to use it in the manufacture of his own furnishing fabrics. Without facilities at Queen Square he was, once again, obliged to look outside the firm and his first five designs were woven by contractors.

Out of the vast field of available manufacturers Morris did not approach a newly established factory as he had done for his dyeing and printing of textiles, but instead chose leaders in the fields of silk, wool, cotton, and gauze weaving. No documentary evidence is available concerning Morris's direct dealings with these firms and it is likely that negotiations were made either through an agent or through the individual firm's local offices in London. Morris did, however, refer to this work in his letters to his family and to Thomas Wardle at Leek (who provided the dyed yarns for most of the work) for the two years before successfully setting up the first loom at Queen Square in November 1877. This information is scanty and at times ambiguous so no clear picture of which early designs were used or the type of cloth woven can be formed. The facts, such as they are, derive from design registration and existing samples. Morris's own technical terminology is also very confusing and usually described the visual effect of the cloth rather than its technical make-up. Most of his fabrics were called either 'tapestries', meaning heavy woollen fabrics or 'damasks' which were lightweight silk fabrics. These erroneous titles which covered a number of types of cloth continued to be used throughout the nineteenth and the twentieth centuries by the firm in their catalogues[2] and were further expanded to include 'tapestries' not only of two and three-ply weaves and woollen compound twills but also silk and wool double cloths and any other cloths containing wool. The term 'damask' referred to any smooth-surfaced lightweight fabric containing silk.

It has been claimed that Morris's first interest in weaving was sparked off by the use of a toy loom[3] although his ambitions to produce textiles of richly woven patterns and textures were always more important to him than the technique itself. A rudimentary loom would have been of little use to him, beyond learning the basic principles of plain weaving as he was never interested in developing the geometric patterns such a loom would be restricted to producing. Ironically it was this type of simple work, where the loom and the yarn control the patterns, that emerged from the crafts movement of the twentieth century, founded on a number of Morris's own principles. Morris's aim was to produce the luxury of texture and colour and complexity of pattern that his paper designs dictated and for these ends there would be no compromise. Having learned how the loom worked he set out to make it weave a variety of patterns and techniques not seen since the seventeenth century. Furthermore, within his own workshop, he was able to achieve this variety with only four looms.

Six manufacturers are known to have woven textiles under contract to Morris & Co. and most of the patterns they wove continued to be produced outside throughout the firm's history. Large orders for designs later woven at

THE POND AT MERTON ABBEY. *Watercolour drawing showing the Morris Works by Lexden Lewis Pocock (1850–1919).*

Queen Square and Merton Abbey were also contracted out, leaving the firm's limited facilities for the production of new designs and small orders, including stock for the shop. Of the six firms employed, Warner & Sons of Braintree produced only one woven silk, *Flower Garden*, from 1911 and the East Anglia Weaving Company of Macclesfield wove late versions of *Tulip and Rose* and *Acanthus* with a cotton warp and spun-silk wefts.[4] Founded in 1919 this firm was not established in Macclesfield until 1923 so its importance in terms of the early history of Morris & Co. is negligible. More significant work was provided by J.O. Nicholson of Macclesfield who wove silk fabrics and those containing a mixture of silk and cotton; H.C. McCrea wove silk and wool mixed fabrics and Dixon's of Bradford were the manufacturers of lightweight woollens such as *Mohair Damask*. Cotton fabrics were woven by an, as yet, unknown manufacturer identified in the firm's large sample book (now in the Victoria and Albert Museum) as 'B and A'[5] and woven muslins and wool and silk

double cloths were woven by Alexander Morton & Co. of Darvel in Scotland. The weaving of three-ply Kidderminster carpeting had already been established in 1875 at the Heckmondwike Manufacturing Company in Yorkshire and these were later sold as 'triple cloths' for wall-hangings and curtaining.

Morris's first five designs – *Tulip and Rose*, *Anemone*, *Honeycomb* (illus. p. 61), *Crown Imperial* (*Mohair Damask*), *Swivel* were woven by contractors each as a number of different fabrics, some of these much later in the nineteenth century. Apart from the triple weaves being produced at Heckmondwike it is probable that McCrea was the first weaving manufacturer to be approached by the firm and *Anemone* and *Honeycomb* were subsequently woven as silk and wool fabrics. The yarns for these were either provided by the manufacturer or were specially dyed for Morris & Co. in France and for this reason there is no mention of the project in Morris's letters to Thomas Wardle. However, as early as November 1875 Morris refers to another manufacturer in

Design for ANEMONE *woven wool and silk, 1874. One of Morris's early so-called 'tapestries'.*

ANEMONE *woven wool and silk fabric, woven on a jacquard loom by H. C. McCrea of Halifax. Also used for damask.*

his letters concerning the production of silks in the Macclesfield factory of J.O. Nicholson.

Nicholson's rise to fame in Macclesfield was quite meteoric. He started his manufacturing career in 1872 at the Prestbury Road Mill with a small office in Cheapside in London and it is likely to have been through this that Morris first negotiated a contract. In 1887 he opened the much larger Hope Mill, then one of the largest in the town and soon gained a good reputation in the manufacturing and retail trades. In 1891 the *Art Journal* printed the following eulogy, 'that the richest furniture silks in brocade and damask can be woven in Macclesfield is proved in the production of Mr J.O. Nicholson.'[6] A local pillar of society, Nicholson founded a local embroidery school and published two books on the history of Macclesfield. Morris's visits to the factory led to a friendship between the two men and Morris, whom Nicholson greatly admired, took some part in the town's local affairs; on one occasion acting as guest of honour, with Nicholson in the chair, at the prize-giving ceremony of Macclesfield Technical School, part of which was developed later as the School of Art. The Yorkshire factories of McCrea and Dixon's were equally well known and respected although Morris's dislike of contemporary living and working conditions in towns and factories of the industrial north, towns which had developed around the nineteenth century cotton and woollen trades, did not encourage social visits.

All Morris & Co.'s contractors used the most technologically advanced power-driven jacquard looms in their factories. Morris was not against modern weaving methods and said, 'since the manner of doing it has with some few exceptions varied little for many hundred years: such trivial alterations as the lifting of the warp threads by means of the jacquard machine, or throwing the shuttle by steam power, ought not to make much difference in the art of it'.[7] In fact, he would have adopted these himself in his own manufacture some years later had he enough capital[8] but instead made do with jacquard looms in which the weft thread was directed through the warp by hand. Fortunately, Morris was not as interested in historical accuracy in his weaving as he had been in the production of print textiles. The drawloom, predecessor of the jacquard, would have been cheap and easy to build had Morris been able to find a carpenter in late

Design for HONEYCOMB, *1876. Registered as a carpet, the design was also used for woven fabric.*

and a draw-boy, who lifted the group of lashes tied to the cords controlling the warp threads for the pattern. The jacquard did away with this, and by a system of punched cards mounted on top of the loom the warp threads were lifted automatically. The introduction of power meant that one weaver could look after a number of looms.

Although Morris's use of hand-activated jacquard looms was forced on him by economic stringencies he soon realized that this system gave the weaver a greater control of the process and resulted in far less mechanical looking fabrics. The 'hand-woven' textiles boasted of by the firm were, however, a far cry from the fabrics associated with the term today.

Morris's letters to Thomas Wardle first mention the dyeing of yarns for contractors' use in November 1875 and the same subject was periodically referred to over the next two years. On 7 April 1876 he wrote of a visit to Macclesfield where he saw 'a good piece of silk in the loom and I am happy to say that it seemed quite satisfactory'. By 27 April he had received the first piece of this 'blue damask' which must have been the pattern *Larkspur*, the only design established before this date that is known to have been woven as a silk damask. The design was woven in a number of colours, the silks being dyed at Leek (Morris refers to blues), as well as in Lyons (greens) and Tours (reds) in France. None of this early dyeing was satisfactory, however, as the colour rubbed off. 'For curtains this will not matter', Morris wrote to Wardle, 'but it makes the damask impossible for seats'. It is important to note here that Morris designed woven textiles only as furnishing fabrics and although a few of what May Morris described as 'some broché silks for dresses'[9] were available, these would have been lightweight furnishing silks of small-scale design adapted for the purpose. May goes on to describe dresses made for herself and her mother of black 'anemone' damask worn, probably, for mourning. Most of the other fabrics were totally unsuitable for the costume of the period, however, and one existing example, a dress of *Flower Garden*[10] silk displays the kind of sumptuous effect desirable for being presented in at court but quite inappropiate for more general use.

The bad dyeing of weaving yarns was not the only difficulty holding up production and Morris's letters continually asked Wardle for long overdue lots of silk,

nineteenth-century industrial Britain who had known what it was. While the drawloom had certain technical advantages over the jacquard, weaving upon it was much slower. The jacquard attachment was introduced into Britain in the 1820s and was widely accepted by industry in the 1830s. Previously, weaving had been carried out in the homes of weavers but, because the adaptation of the drawlooms to the jacquard was expensive (and manufacturer's realized that if driven by steam, much more could be produced) there was a strong incentive to set up and work the looms together. Thus the jacquard indirectly contributed to one of the most socially evil products of the age – the textile factory. The drawloom had required the employment of two people; a weaver

and then cotton for Nicholson whose 'moans are shortening my life!'[11] By 1877 Morris had already decided that the time had come for him to start manufacturing woven textiles himself and a letter to Wardle written in March of that year asks for his help and advice in this undertaking. 'I want very much to set up a loom for brocade weaving, would it be possible to get a Frenchman over from Lyons under the present circumstances of the trade there? I would give a year's engagement certain to a real clever fellow who would do what I wanted him to do: I am dazzled at the prospect of the splendid work we might turn out in that line'. Wardle made enquiries, and, through a French correspondent, found a weaver willing to undertake the work. 'We are willing to agree to his terms of 3,000 francs for the year,' Morris wrote in reply to Wardle, 'and think it would be prudent not to guarantee for longer, but if he suits us, no doubt the situation will be a permanent one

PEACOCK AND DRAGON *woven compound twill, 1878. The nearest woven fabric to Morris's ideal of a medieval hanging.*

Above: GRANADA *woven silk velvet, brocaded in gold thread with blue block-printing. The most expensive Morris fabric.*

Opposite: Original design for BIRD *double cloth, 1878, in watercolour and pencil.*

for him ... but I think before we strike a bargain we should see his specimens of work: meantime we send a parcel of examples of cloth such as we are likely to want as far as the weaving is concerned'.[12] It was arranged that the Frenchman should bring a loom with him and measurements of this were relayed to Morris who arranged for space to be made in the Queen Square annexe in Ormond's Yard, where furniture was being made. The size restriction of patterns woven at Macclesfield (Nicholson could only weave a nine inch pattern) made Morris insist that the new loom should give more variety, 'we should certainly want to weave damasks', he wrote, and expressed a hope that it would weave the widest cloth possible without steam; at least a twenty-seven inch pattern. Morris looked to future production with some excitement and arranged to receive instruction in the painting of point-papers, and for jacquard-cards to be cut ready for use. The first design used was the *Willow* adapted from an earlier wallpaper, which was prepared as a damask and cards were cut in Lyons, France.

The long awaited M. Bazin arrived in London in June 1877 and was immediately put to work erecting the loom which had been transported in pieces. Delays ensued, caused by Bazin spending time in St Thomas's Hospital with an undisclosed illness, and no proper weaving was started until October. It was then found that the *Willow* design was not weaving correctly and it was clear that the cards had been mounted on the jacquard attachment in the wrong order. 'I have been having an afternoon with Froggy (M. Bazin) the loom and our Coventry "designer" so-called; the loom was the wisest of the four of us and understood much more of what the other said than anybody else did – at least I think so', Morris wrote to Jenny, but the problem was eventually solved by an elderly Spitalfields weaver employed to assist Bazin. From this time Morris designed exclusively for his own looms and initially only two fabrics, *St James* and *Oak*, went to Nicholson to weave because of the large quantities needed in the decorations of St James's Palace for which they were designed.

Morris is now more widely known for his printed textiles than for those designed for the loom and, in many respects, the speed of technique involved in block-printing was better suited to his intuitive style. His earliest woven textiles do, however, show him at his most characteristic and best; fully conversant with the medium and confident of his own handling of it. The bold patterns of these designs show a mixture of the pseudo-medieval with the modern and, in *Anemone* (illus. p. 60), reach a sophistication in form not seen in printed textiles until much later in his career. The use of non-naturalistic, gently waving branches preceded the 'tributaries' series of printed designs by seven years. It also predated the acquisition by the South Kensington Museum of the seventeenth-century Italian velvet said to be Morris's main design source for these designs.[13]

In a letter to Wardle of March 1877, Morris mentioned that he was studying birds and hoped to include them in his next designs.[14] Subsequently, four of Morris's following six designs contain birds in their patterns. The first, *Bird* (illus. p. 63), was designed to hang on the walls of the drawing room at Kelmscott House to which the family had recently moved. The structure of the design is very similar to the earlier *Swivel* pattern, which shows formal, interlocking ogee compartments, and particularly to *Flower Garden* designed some months later. In this later design much of the *Bird* background pattern is repeated with the central motif of a flower-head with fanned-out leaves copied directly from the earlier pattern.

The pattern of these bird designs – *Bird*, *Peacock and Dragon* (illus. p. 62), *Bird and Vine* and *Dove and Rose* – is particularly interesting. The background foliage is designed in a formation of net or ogee repeats with the birds placed on top of this in pairs facing each other; although providing the main interest to the viewer they have no structural importance to the pattern. *Bird and Vine* and *Dove and Rose* both repeat one pair of birds throughout, whereas *Bird* and the more complex design of *Peacock and Dragon*, show two different sets of birds which repeat alternately through the width of the fabric. This makes the pattern much larger in size and in *Peacock and Dragon*, which has a repeat of 43 inches × 35 inches (109 × 90cm), a great deal of the fabric is needed to see the design at its best. Of all Morris's textile designs this is the closest he ever came to his early ideal of English medieval hangings. The inspiration for the design actually comes from the Middle and the Far East and it has been suggested that the 'dragons' do, in fact, represent phoenixes which had been seen by Morris on Chinese

BIRD *woollen double cloth. Designed by Morris in 1878 for the drawing room at Kelmscott House, Hammersmith.*

textiles.[15] The pattern inspiration for the earlier bird fabrics came from more classical sources, especially from silks, thought in Morris's day to have come from Sicily and Lucca in Northern Italy.

In 1873, on his second visit to Iceland, Morris met the 'scholar and archaeologist'[16] John Henry Middleton whose interest in, and knowledge of, oriental textiles was to have a great influence on him. Morris already had a fine eye for quality in period and style and was well acquainted with the collections at the South Kensington Museum but this friendship further heightened his own awareness of pattern and colour as seen in Middle Eastern textiles and carpets. Morris's four most orientally inspired

designs; *Peacock and Dragon Granada, Brocatel* and *Ispahan,* move away from his usual colour schemes and are instead an attempt to imitate the terracottas, lapis blues, ruby reds, and emerald greens generally seen in Islamic art of all kinds. This type of colour and pattern was also favoured by Henry Dearle, when in 1885 he began to design repeating textiles for the firm.

Morris & Co.'s designs for silk and wool double cloth were woven by the firm of Alexander Morton & Co. of Darvel in Scotland and it is likely that early samples of *Dove and Rose,* the first design produced by Morton's for Morris & Co., were woven by out-workers.[17] Two warps were used in the weaving of this design and the

later fabric *Helena* designed by Dearle in 1890. By varying the lifting patterns of threads of either wool or silk warp, a number of textures and effects were obtained showing areas of silk, wool, or a mixture of the two. This fabric was not recommended for upholstery because of the strain that would be put upon the silk areas, but for curtaining it was more successful. Morris was particularly pleased with the subtlety of the colours gained by Morton, although these were not always fast, and, on recommending them to George Howard for curtains at 1 Palace Green, he wrote, 'It will last as long as need be, since the cloth is really very strong: I can't answer so decidely as to the colour; but the colours in it when looked at by themselves you will find rather full than not, 'tis the mixture that makes them look delicate'. This subtlety of shade made up of pastel pinks, greens and blues was to be developed further in Morton's own textiles of the same technique and experiments in the improvement of

Section of point-paper for DOVE AND ROSE. *Painted in the Morris & Co. workshops from Morris's original design of 1879.*

Detail of DOVE AND ROSE *woven silk and wool. This clearly shows the double weave structure of the fabric.*

chemical dyestuffs by Morton were to prove of great value later to the industry as a whole. It is probable that *Dove and Rose* was the first silk and wool double cloth woven at Darvel but this became one of the Morton firm's most popular products and a number of later examples were woven from designs by such notable designers as C.F.A.Voysey, Lindsay P.Butterfield, Arthur Silver and Lewis F.Day. It is not known now if the *Helena* range of silk and wool double cloths was called after the Dearle design of the same name or vice versa. Alexander Morton, himself a hand-weaver, had established his firm in 1862 by reorganizing the sagging local hand-weaving industry which had developed an expertise for woven gauzes following the late eighteenth- early nineteenth-century fashion for hand-embroidered 'Ayrshire white-work'. Although Morton was anxious to develop lace

weaving at the time, in 1881 Morris commissioned him to weave a patterned gauze (leno) for him from his design *Madras Muslin*, which was influenced in design and technique by the fine contemporary Indian imports of similar cloth. Morris's design made a strong impression on Morton, as did the designer himself, and later lenos, *Cherwell* and *Cray* are not, as thought by some, original Morris designs but adaptations of these by Morton himself.[18]

The St James's Palace commission of 1881, already described in a previous chapter, gave Morris the opportunity to design two new silk damasks which he called *St James* and *Oak*. At first sight both of these appear conventional in their patterns and the arching oak leaves of *Oak* make it comparable to French Napoleonic silks. Both designs rely on leaf forms for their patterns but

MADRAS MUSLIN, *a cotton and silk gauze woven by Alexander Morton, from 1881. Used as curtaining.*

the framework of these is more openly drawn than in previous designs, especially in the *Acanthus* damask of 1879. They therefore lack the small subsidiary background detail which is now associated with Morris's most famous designs. This may also account for the designs proving the most universally acceptable of all Morris's textiles for curtaining and particularly for upholstery. The self-destructive nineteenth-century habit of weighting[19] silks to improve their hanging qualities was fortunately not adopted by Morris & Co. and many samples of these silk damasks, in particular, can be found in public collections and are still in use in private houses. This is a little surprising because the silk was so expensive. Estimates for 1 Holland Park quote £245 for a set of green *St James* curtains, 'lined and finished with tufted fringes for the Bay Window opening into the Drawing Room. Poles and Fixing'.[20] Samples of this silk in the Victoria and Albert Museum include a small piece of the drawing room curtains at Old Swan House Chelsea.

The popularity of these designs did not only flourish in circles preferring traditional forms of furnishings in their homes. *Oak* was used in 1898 on the upholstered seat of an embossed leather chair made by the Guild of Handicrafts and designed by M.H.Baillie Scott for the Palace of the Grand Duke of Hesse in Darmstadt, one of the most modern and influential interiors of the late nineteenth century. Both designs were revived in the 1950s after the closure of Morris & Co., *St James* by Warner & Sons of Braintree and *Oak* (re-named *Whittingaeme*) woven by Courtaulds for Sanderson, but neither remained in production for very long.[21]

Similar open designs of scrolling leaves are seen in *Campion* and *Violet and Columbine* both woven in wool. These designs lack the type of interest that would have earlier been provided either with the additional decoration of birds or by the texture of the silk and linen fabrics and silk damasks but both have proved successful when used as wall-coverings and for upholstery where the design is either broken up or acts as a background for other patterns. A Morris & Co. adjustable-backed chair from The Grove, Harborne, Birmingham (now in the Victoria and Albert Museum) is covered with *Violet and Columbine*, and the buttoned back gives greater interest to this spaced out rather droopy design. *Campion* was used

very successfully as flat wall-covering at 28 Bruton Street where the design provides a rich background to the otherwise conventional yet richly furnished drawing room.[22]

Morris's last woven designs show his increasing interest in technique and in both *Granada* and *Brocatel* he attempted to reproduce complex woven structures in the weaving shed at Merton Abbey. A special loom was built in 1884 for *Granada* (illus. p. 62), a silk brocaded in small areas with gold thread[23] and with other areas of blue block-printing, but the cloth proved far more expensive to weave than was commercially viable. It is said that only 20 yards (1829 cm) of the fabric was woven and it was sold at the prohibitive price of £10 a yard. Not all of that woven was sold, however, and a six foot length (548 cm) was found at Merton Abbey in 1919. This was sold to the Victoria and Albert Museum for £35.[24] A small sample of the same material, showing three-quarters of the lengthwise repeat had previously been given by the firm to the museum in 1912. In *Brocatel*, Morris attempted to recapture the quality of historic silk brocatelles with their prominent, raised patterns and textured, ribbed surfaces. To some extent he was successful in reproducing the weight and stiffness of the original and with the use of bright yellow silk came close to suggesting a rich gold effect. Because of its tightly woven structure the fabric proved hard-wearing and ideally suited to upholstery. Its large-scale design was seen to best advantage in bigger areas however, especially as curtains or wall-coverings.

The last three designs attributed to Morris, *Ispahan*, *Brocatel* and *Golden Bough* were all designed for the Arts and Crafts Exhibition of 1888[25] and these must be 'the stuffs' that one of the Smith brothers was pressing Morris to finish earlier the same year. The patterns *Brocatel* and *Golden Bough* both lack the originality of early work and, at first sight could be mistaken for the work of Henry Dearle. It is possible, as has been suggested in the designing of the *Bullerswood* carpet, that both men were involved. It is as difficult to believe that Morris would have produced these weak designs as it is to believe Dearle was capable of such sophisticated repeating structures so early in his design career. The original design for *Golden Bough* now at the City Museum and Art Gallery, Birmingham does, however, have the

The weaving sheds, Merton Abbey. Three hand jacquards are in use. An apprentice winds hanks of wool on to bobbins.

slickness of hand associated with a great deal of Dearle's later work.

Throughout the nineteenth century Morris & Co. were kept very busy producing large quantities of woven textiles for the interior decorators' market in particular; a service provided by themselves as well as by other companies. Whereas the avant-garde were always quick to use printed cottons in their homes (and, after all, Morris had made this respectable once more) the more conventional London decorator preferred the richness of effect gained from woven fabrics and silk in particular. Nevertheless it is unlikely that there were ever more than four looms set up at Merton Abbey and four weavers, listed in the Arts and Crafts catalogues of the 1880s and

1890s, are known by name – Frederick Chadwick, T. Bailey, J. Taplin and Arthur Dudson. The Chadwick family seem to have provided a number of workmen for the firm and existing photographs[26] from the 1920s show another member of the family and his young nephew attending to the indigo dye vats. There seems to have been no specialization amongst the staff of the weaving sheds and the men set up their looms with whatever type of warp was needed for the next order relayed from the shop.

The first weavers employed by Morris at the Merton Abbey establishment were all experienced weavers from the dying silk industry at Spitalfields. May Morris wrote that it 'was always somewhat pathetic to watch the weavers at work ... on their handlooms – old men from Spitalfields who had been prosperous once and had been through bad times saddened by the changes in industrial life that with its scurry and thrusting aside had passed them by'.[27] Her sympathies were somewhat misguided however as their employment at higher than average wages, in pleasant working conditions, must have been envied by many other redundant craftsmen. The skills of these weavers were gradually handed down to younger men recruited by Morris from the surrounding areas of Merton and Wimbledon and one such apprentice can be seen winding spools from hanks of weaving yarns in the only known existing photograph of the weavers' shop. The conditions found in this room were better than most but the technique of jacquard weaving can never provide the weaver with a totally pleasant and peaceful occupation.

In her account of a visit to the Works in 1886 Emma Lazarus described Morris's own reservations:

There was plenty of air and light even in the busiest room, filled with the ceaseless din of whirring looms where the artisans sat bending over their threads, while the lovely play of colours and beauty of texture of the fabrics issuing from under their fingers relieved their work of that character of purely mechanical drudgery which is one of the dreariest features of ordinary factory toil. This was evidently the department that entailed the most arduous and sedentary labour, for as we went out again into the peaceful stillness of the July landscape, Mr Morris reverted with a sigh to the great problem, and asked why men should be imprisoned thus for a lifetime in the midst of such deaffening clatter in order to earn a bare subsistence, which the average professional man pockets in comfortable ease.[28]

J.H. Dearle: *Designs for woven textiles*

Henry Dearle's first attributed design for the loom was woven in 1888 and over the next thirty-four years he was responsible for thirty original designs and eight reproduction patterns sold by Morris & Co.; more than double that supplied by Morris. His style was well suited to this technique and some of the firm's most attractive woven textiles were made from his designs under his direction. Many of these, woven at the turn of the century, are little known today and it is hoped that their

Pencil portrait of Henry Dearle drawn at the Merton Abbey Works. The artist, Edward Payne, was an employee.

illustration in the catalogue of this book will give them the publicity they deserve. Dearle's finest period as a designer were the years 1888–1905 when he interspersed the output of derivative designs based closely on historical textiles from Persia and Turkey, with groups of bold highly original patterns. It is true to say that the initial driving force (and in some cases the repeating system) came from Morris's own work but Dearle's mature style was quite different. He was not as imaginative or ingenious but made up for this in many ways with his own skills as a draughtsman. Whereas his flowers look more suited to the vase than to the garden this was a popular nineteenth-century approach and within the conventional commercial market his work is likely to have been more saleable. But Morris & Co. was not founded to be a conventional company and by manufacturing goods from Morris's designs it had evolved a characteristic style of its own. Unfortunately

Detail of design for PERSIAN BROCATEL *woven silk and wool fabric, designed by Dearle especially for Stanmore Hall* c. *1890.*

Dearle's critics tend to judge his work purely within these criteria rather than as part of the industry as a whole.

A strong Persian influence can be seen in Dearle's first woven designs – *Small Figure, Tulip and Net* and *Persian Brocatel* and these show his own preoccupation at the time with designing for hand-knotted carpets. Dearle was far less able to differentiate successfully when designing for different techniques at the same time than Morris and *Persian Brocatel*, in particular, echoes the style and copies many of the motifs seen in his own contemporary 'directional' carpet patterns. This silk, which was designed specifically for wall-covering at Stanmore Hall, Middlesex, was woven in two qualities; the original heavy 'brocatelle' (the same structure as Morris's earlier design) and a lightweight silk. An indication of Dearle's inexperience in designing for the loom is shown in the fact that slight modifications had to be made in the pattern before the lightweight fabric could

be made. This pattern appears to have been particularly popular on the continent and examples can be found in museums in Copenhagen, Zurich and Trondheim.[29]

The following three textiles woven from Dearle's designs, *Vine, Golden Stem* and *Sunflower*, show him at his most powerful and successful as a designer. All are strongly coloured, with an emphasis on green and the designs show a final severance from the strong influence of Morris. The patterns still show Morris's device of diagonally waving lines but Dearle's use of these in his own very characteristically tightly drawn and disciplined way is quite unlike the inherent naturalism of Morris's own work. Dearle's great interest in historic textiles continued to show in his designs especially *Helena, Rose and Lily* and *Squirrel*. For *Rose and Lily*, he used an Italian seventeenth-century brocaded silk as his source, simplifying the design and substituting the crowns of the original with roses. The original textile is an exquisite example of its period, with a gold ground and pattern brocaded in polychrome silks. Not even Dearle's careful use of colour could recapture the beauty of the original and the most successful example of the design was woven with a woollen ground providing a strong contrast to the silk pattern. So popular was this silk design with the

Henry Dearle's design for HELENA *woven wool and silk double cloth, 1891.*

ROSE AND LILY *woven wool and silk compound twill, designed by Dearle, 1893. This example has a red ground.*

Early seventeenth-century Italian silk brocaded with gold. Used by Dearle as the source for ROSE AND LILY.

public that in the twentieth century the firm sold one of Thomas Wardle's early printed cottons, *Crown*, which shows a direct reproduction of the Italian brocade. *Squirrel* is a far less successful design than either *Helena* or *Rose and Lily* and the animals are so strangely drawn that it is not surprising that the original title, *Fox and Grape* (from *Aesop's Fables*), is now no longer used. The design for this textile is copied from Morris's earlier woven designs showing birds but Dearle's greatest failing, his inability to control small subsidiary background patterns, shows in this piece. Having made this aesthetic criticism, it is important to note that not only was this design commercially popular but it has often been mistaken for Morris's own work.

More variety in colour was introduced into the Morris & Co. woven range with Dearle's designs made between 1895 and 1900 and a series of patterns called after fruit and flowers, *Apple*, *Bluebell*, *Poppy*, *Tulip* and *Pomegranate* all show the designer's interest in and experimentation with surface texture. Silk and linen mixtures (*Apple*, *Poppy* and *Cross Twigs*) reproduce the mixture of glossy and matt surfaces first seen in silk and wool double cloths woven by Morton's at Darvel. By clever manipulation of

the two yarns (worked out initially on the point-papers) a three-dimensional quality is given to some of the subjects depicted. From 1915 an extra texture was obtained in the form of artificial silk[30] which could be substituted for silk for further effect and, of more importance to some buyers, thus providing a cheaper fabric. *Tulip* and *Pomegranate* continued the bold approach of the silk and linen fabrics in heavyweight woollen hangings and Dearle's characteristic bunches of flowers spring from all parts of the two designs.

The development of these designs provided disappointing results and Dearle's attempts to historicize and refine his own natural style as seen in *New Persian*, *Carnation* and the later *Millefleurs* does not succeed, especially in the two later designs which simply copy the style of Flemish medieval *millefleurs* tapestries. This change in style coincided with Morris & Co.'s change in management and commercial direction and frequent changes in the board of directors are evident in an unsettled period of both design and production. With a few isolated exceptions all the later woven textiles were produced by power-loom and Dearle's later designs show both a consideration of the mechanical aspects of such production and the firm's desire to compete in the market for reproduction textiles. Eight woven reproductions were sold by the firm and it is likely that some of these, the two Genoa Velvets in particular, were manufactured abroad in France or Italy. Morris & Co.'s catalogues also hint that a number of other fabrics were also available in individual pieces or single lengths:

Morris & Company have made a collection from France, Italy, Portugal etc., of some of the best reproductions of rich antique materials, suitable for the decoration of great houses, and for the covering of handsome furniture. These include Cut Velvets, Brocades, Silk Damasks, Tapestries and Oriental Embroideries of which the colouring and period are both good. Special mention may be made of the inexpensive silk Brocades woven on the old Portuguese looms in traditional designs and colours. The firm are also willing to undertake the reproduction, in sufficient quantities, of any special fabric that a customer may wish copied.[31]

For this reason alone, the catalogue at the end of this book cannot hope to include all designs sold by Morris & Co. However, the eight reproduction designs that are included – *Alva, Venetian, Pineapple, Musgrove,* two *Genoa velvets, Sistine* and *Trinitas* – were all textiles kept in stock which could be ordered in any quantity and so must be considered the firm's products. Two of these, *Pineapple* and *Musgrove* were hand-loom jacquard woven at Merton Abbey and all the others are either individually advertised by the firm's printed catalogues or found as samples in the Morris & Co. pattern book at the Victoria and Albert Museum.

Many of these reproduction designs were used for ecclesiastical furnishings and it is probable that this side of the firm's retail output expanded in the first quarter of the twentieth century against heavy competition from other companies. *Pineapple*, a design adapted from a sixteenth-century specimen in the South Kensington Museum, was seen in a number of advertisements for vestments and altar cloths and was also used by a competitor, A.R.Mowbrays & Co. Ltd of St Margaret St, London in whose catalogue it is shown used for copes and chasubles. In Morris & Co.'s catalogue *Church Decoration and Furniture etc (c. 1910)* a number of earlier designs were also recommended for church use including *Utrecht Velvet* at 9s per yard, *Elmcote* and *Pomegranate* at 18s 6d, *Vine* and *Tulip and Net* at 22s 6d and 'Golden Bough soft hanging' at 27s 6d. Power-loom fabrics were cheaper and *Alva* cost 16s a yard and *Sistine* 13s 6d.

Henry Dearle was a conscientious, efficient and well respected organizer of the weaving sheds at Merton Abbey and, although it is known that May Morris had both experience and an interest in the technique of weaving, she took no part in the firm's activities either before her father's death or afterwards. Dearle's hard work was not enough to retain the popularity and commercial success the firm had once known. Although the scale of reproduction fabrics brought a short lived revival of interest, by the mid 1920s this section of the firm was suffering both from the general economic problems of the country and from the changes in fashion which it had not been capable of reflecting. The high quality of the firm's goods was maintained but they were expensive and, at a time when one of the most fashionable London firms, Gordon Russell, were selling original hand-woven woollen fabrics by their leading designers at 11s 3d a yard,[32] it is clear that Morris & Co. had begun to outprice themselves. By 1929, Merton Abbey employed just two weavers and a boilerman-cum-colourmixer to produce fabric dyes both for printing and dyeing yarns.[33] The weavers, who were now housed at Merton Abbey in a wooden shed erected outside the original buildings spent the last few years of the firm's existence by weaving textiles, mostly silk damasks, of classical design, especially *St James* and *Oak* tweeds,[34] and high quality plain materials including a wool ribbed cloth *Merton Plain Arras* (which sold for 14s a yard) and light-weight shot-silks in attractive blue/purple, red/orange and green/blue combinations.

Many of Morris & Co.'s printed textiles have been reproduced since the firm went into liquidation and surviving printing blocks have helped to make this an easy process. Woven reproductions have been far more difficult to arrange as all the company's sets of jacquard cards were destroyed in 1940. A few manufacturers have attempted to re-weave designs but this has proved too complex and costly an operation to be viable.

Carpets

MORRIS AND COMPANY sold two different types of carpets, hand-knotted and machine woven, and the design and manufacture of these were treated quite differently. Morris was not obstinately historical in his approach when designing for carpets and although clearly preferring hand-knotting as a technique, because of the traditions of the art, he realized the need for well designed, good quality cheaper floor coverings and produced one design for linoleum and a number of others for machine woven carpets, restricting the line and colour of his patterns to the limitations of the technique whether flat, looped or pile surface. Morris's machine carpets were particularly popular and were used in many types of house; on the stairs and in the bedrooms and billiard rooms of the rich, to the drawing rooms of the less wealthy and, from 1886, they were even used on the cabin floors of the ocean-going liners of the Orient Line.[1]

Machine woven carpets were initiated in the 1870s, when Morris was already involved in the mass-production of printed and woven textiles and this formed an important part of the original 'Morris' interior, where different designs met, crossed and complimented one another. Hand-knotted or 'Hammersmith' carpets as they were known are, in contrast, individual works of art like the firm's embroidered hangings and tapestries, and were meant to be considered quite separately whether used in the home or in a gallery. Today these carpets can often be seen shown to advantage hung on a wall, a habit Morris adopted with historical examples from his own fine collection.

In the past, writers have often dismissed Morris machine carpets as secondary in importance to hand-knotted examples but this view misunderstands their purpose and design. Because of the great contrast between these two types of design and manufacture they should be considered as quite different techniques.

Machine made floor-coverings

LINOLEUM   William Morris's first design for any type of floor-covering was registered on 7 June 1875 for printed linoleum called 'Corticine floor cloth'. Manufactured while the firm was still at 26 Queen Square without suitable manufacturing facilities this design must have been produced by an outside contractor. Although no records exist today to identify the factory, the likely manufacturers were Nairns of Kirkaldy, Scotland, the most prolific linoleum firm in the mid 1870s who included in their range a number of 'modern' designs in total sympathy with Morris's own work, and quite unlike other popular manufacturers' products which show dense floral and imitation oriental designs of brash, strident colouring. Linoleum was very popular in the third quarter of the nineteenth century and the search for new, original designs for it competed with carpet manufacture.[2] It is thus surprising that Morris did not produce more than this one design, which was available in two colourways. The pattern, of African marigolds arranged in arched trellises, is very similar in subject and repeat to Morris designs for painted tiles, wallpapers and printed textiles, especially the *Marigold*, which was registered as a textile twenty-one days previously. Few examples of this linoleum exist today, although much was sold at the time. It was available in 72 inch widths and cost 3s 10d per square yard at the beginning of the twentieth century. In 1915 the fashion for inlaid linoleum took over from printed linoleum and from this time the

Linoleum designed by Morris in 1875. Sold by the firm as 'corticine floor cloth' in two different colourways.

firm sold very little and by the 1920s it is doubtful if this was still in the Morris & Co. range. Although their late catalogue, advertising items at George Street, Hanover Square,[3] shows a piece of the linoleum under the 'Kelmscott' sectional bookcase, it is without identification or advertisement.

CARPETS The idea of improving the standards of design of mass-produced carpeting came to Morris early on in his career as a manufacturer and although he expended much energy and time on their production he always considered machine carpet 'make-shifts for cheapness' sake'.[4] Whatever he believed, his designs for machine-woven carpets are extremely successful and show no lack of commitment. He succeeded in his aim 'to produce pure and shapely forms with simple colouring' doing the best he could with the material,

'without straining its capacity for decoration'[5] and lifted the standards of the technique from the imitative, dull and inferior craft of the mid-nineteenth century to one accepted in the most fashionable households.

Machine carpets were not fitted skirting to skirting as they are today and the convention of a square or rectangular carpet with matching borders was as important in machine woven as in hand-knotted carpets. Morris's borders, therefore became as important a part of the design as the centre – 'filling' or 'field' – as it is variously known. Available in three widths: nine inches, thirteen and a half inches or eighteen inches, even stair carpets were sold with a border, which could take the form of a complicated floral design or, if preferred, a stripe, zig-zag, chevron or barber's pole stripe. Morris was in favour of more than one design being used on the edge of his carpets, 'All borders should be made up of

75

Drawing of a Wilton carpet design submitted by Morris & Co. for registration on 24 December 1875.

several members, even where they are narrow, or they will look bald and poor, and ruin the whole cloth'[6] and his hand-knotted Hammersmith carpets in particular show this multifarious, yet toning effect. He believed that there were two types of carpet borders. One of wide proportions was to be added merely to finish the cloth and keep it from looking frayed, 'Such a border will not vary much from the colour of the cloth it bounds, and will have in its construction many of the elements of the construction of the filling pattern; though it must be strongly marked enough to fix that filling in its place.' The other kind he described as 'meant to draw the eye to it more or less, and is sometimes of more importance than the filling: so that it will be markedly different in colour and as to pattern will help out at the filling by opposing its lines than by running with them'.[7] This type of pattern border should be narrow in width.

Some border designs were used by Morris and Company for both machine and hand-knotted techniques and also repeated with different filling designs for the same technique. Hammersmith carpets are particularly identifiable in this respect; the palmette border of the *Little Flower* rug can also be seen on the smaller *Swan House* carpet and the *Little Tree* and *McCulloch* borders were used on hand-knotted and Axminster carpets of plain and patterned centres.

Of the two types of carpet techniques, Morris turned to the machine first and it is unlikely that any of his carpet designs were woven before 1875 although designs were drawn before this date. On 27 May 1875 he wrote to Charles Fairfax Murray (at that time an assistant in Edward Burne-Jones's studio), 'I am up to the neck in trying out designs for papers, chintzes and carpets and trying to get the manufacturers to do them. I think we are doing some good things in that way'.[8]

Morris's first designs for carpets were registered on Christmas Eve 1875 and comprised two patterns: one was for a border of intertwining poppy-type flower heads and foliage which is now known on only one carpet (that illustrated in the sitting room at Great Tangley Manor) but which was also used as an embroidery design.[9] The other has a repeating motif of acanthus leaves and peonies. The latter was woven as a Wilton pile carpet and was used by Morris and Co. in the furnishing of Great Tangley Manor, Surrey (on the same carpet mentioned above) and Torrens Park, Adelaide in Australia. The furnishers Howard and Sons purchased a quantity of it to use as part of a bedroom scheme at 15 Hyde Park Gardens, London.

During the following year five further designs were registered by Morris & Co. from 26 Queen Square including the *Honeycomb* (11 February 1876), and four registered 31 March 1876, one a very fine design of peonies, foxgloves and lilies (illus. p. 83);[10] *Rose*, and two border designs, one of curling leaves the other of alternating squares of leaves and flowers, both obviously designed to use with the earlier pile carpet designs. Also registered this year was a square design in which naïvely drawn leaves and flowers radiate from the centre. Alternating corner flowers denote that this design was intended for a repeating machine technique although no examples have been found. The flowers in the design are a mixture of medieval and naturalistic in influence and show Morris's transitory style from the gothic forms of the 1860s to the free-flowing originality of the 1870s. This is the full extent of Morris & Co.'s registration of its carpet designs. Other firms were to take advantage of this lack of protection by plagiarizing some of the firm's patterns and the Heckmondwike Manufacturing Company, in particular, registered a number of designs based on Morris's own including *Tulip and Lily* and *Daisy*. A Morris & Co. brochure warns customers of the 'dishonest' copying of their Kidderminster carpets 'of inferior make and colouring'.

Morris employed five different techniques of machine carpeting in the weaving of his designs – Kidderminster three-ply; Wilton pile; Brussels loop and Patent and 'Hand-knotted' Axminsters – and at least two outside manufacturing firms produced these for Morris and Co. under contract and all the firm's dealings with these went through an agent, Whitwell & Co. Ltd. of 69 Carter Lane, London. Unfortunately, all this company's records were destroyed in the 1939–45 war, so specific details are no longer available.

KIDDERMINSTER CARPETS Also known as 'Scotch' or 'inlaid' carpets these are made by hand weaving two or three fabric layers together on a loom to form a single structure. They were woven for Morris & Co. by the Heckmondwike Manufacturing Company Ltd. of Yorkshire which was incorporated in 1873. It had previously taken over the carpet and blanket weaving firm Michael Swallow and used the latter's experience of weaving flat structures in their production of Kidderminster two- and three-plys. Although comparatively new to the trade in 1875, it was already competing against the leading manufacturers of the day – John Brinton & Co.; John Crossley and Sons; T.F.Firth and Benjamin Woodward & Co. — and by 1880 was registering more carpet designs than any other firm.

Early attempts to transfer one of William Morris's designs on to point-paper[11] at Heckmondwike as a preparation for weaving, had produced an unrecognizable result and the manufacturers insisted that the design was too simple. In Morris's opinion the Heckmondwike draughtsman, whose job it was to transfer the designs into a working graph, could not draw and from this time all Morris & Co.'s point-papers were filled in at the firm's premises. At first this was done by Morris himself, then when he had trained them satisfactorily, by other workmen.

Kidderminster carpets were woven in two qualities for Morris & Co. in two- and three-ply at an initial cost of 4s 6d and 5s 6d per square yard. Originally available in plain colours at 27 inch widths and patterned at 36 inches, the plain carpets were no longer available by 1914. Stair carpets with integral borders were sold in three different widths: 22 inches at 4s 5d; 27 inches at 5s 3d and 36 inches at 7s per yard, and fringe could be bought at 9d per yard to decorate unbordered floor carpets. In 1884 Morris & Co. charged Alexander Ionides £4 18s 2d for a Kidderminster carpet of 13 yards with fringing. The cost of 'making up' was 5s 6d.

For the first year of production Morris accepted the factory's own yarns and colours.[12] He was soon dissatisfied with the chemical dyes used and wrote to Thomas Wardle at Leek asking him to dye '200 lbs a week of low quality wool for the 3-ply carpets made in Yorkshire.' By April 1876 he was detailing the dyes needed to produce the colours he desired: 'Indigo for blues, combined with fast yellow weld for greens, madder for scarlet, brick-red and salmon; cochineal for crimson and cochineal or madder for pinks. For bright, clear yellow, weld is to be used, mixed with madder for ochre or orange shades'. Black was to be made by toning down deep indigo. Satisfied with the results when woven he wrote to Wardle on 10 April 1877, 'nothing could be better both to tone and relief of colour — so that is settled'.[13] Constant recall to Morris was made whenever new colour schemes were tried in established patterns and a sample of three-ply *Tulip and Rose* in the collection of the Victoria and Albert Museum is labelled 'Whitwells make, approved Sept 4/80.' Morris & Co.'s catalogues mention seven designs[14] available in 36 inch width Kidderminster carpeting although ten patterns[15] can be recognized today. Of these, four are known primarily as textiles – *Tulip and Rose*, *Campion*, *Vine and Pomegranate* and *Honeycomb* and samples of *Bluebell* also survive in curtain form. Only the *Tulip and Rose* and *Campion* were registered specifically as textiles however and *Honeycomb*, always considered as a woven fabric, was registered only as a carpet.

Believing that Kidderminster carpets called for 'a small design in which the different planes ... are well interlocked,'[16] Morris's earliest design, the *Daisy* (or *Grass* as it was also known) is reminiscent of his early tile and embroidery designs based on medieval manuscripts and was clearly evolved many years before any carpets were woven. This was woven in the three carpet techniques – Kidderminster, Brussels and Wilton pile – and a very early example, a stair-carpet in three-ply with an integral chevron border, can be seen at Kelmscott Manor. The popularity of this design was noted by the Heckmondwike Manufacturing Co. and their own range departed from the conventional floral and geometric designs to include light, colourful patterns reminiscent of Morris's own. A design very similar to the *Daisy* was registered by the company at the end of 1876[17] and from then onwards the same motif was used many times in their field and border designs. Another design plagiarized by them was the *Lily and Tulip*[18] registered on 27 December 1878 eighteen months after the first weaving trial of Morris. The delivery of this sample on 25 June 1877 was meticulously noted at Queen Square by Morris's temporary secretary, the Rev. Guy's son, 'The Heckmondwike Company sent up a woven pattern of 3-ply green tulip carpet. M. called it dove-like – and so it is, the colours are very nice and well toned down'.[19]

It is likely that all William Morris's designs for Kidderminster carpeting were made before 1880 and even *Artichoke*, which is probably the last to have been woven, shows very strong stylistic similarities to Morris's designs for other techniques used in 1876–8, weaving and embroidery in particular. Two designs can be identified as being by Henry Dearle, namely *Bluebell* and an unidentified pattern of loosely-petalled flowers encircled in leaves, the only known existing sample of which is in the collection of the William Morris Gallery, Walthamstow. *Bluebell* is a very successful design in which Dearle has not attempted a large-scale traditional pattern as in his designs for Wilton pile carpeting. In this small neat repeating pattern, rows of flowers are seen in bright colours against a dark ground. A watercolour design for this carpet is now in the Sanford and Helen Berger Collection.

Morris and Company's Kidderminster carpets were very popular in the United States and the collection of the Cooper-Hewitt Museum in New York contains a range of small samples donated by Cowtan and Tout, Morris & Co.'s New York agents. The collection comprises *Tulip and Rose*, *Daisy*, *Honeycomb*, *Tulip and Lily*, *Artichoke*, *Bluebell* and *Campion*. This is, almost certainly, the range of seven designs advertised in the firm's catalogues for 1910–15. Samples of *Bluebell* show a matching border labelled '5/- per yd smaller width made in designs and colours to go with each body carpeting'. The prices of 12s 6d per yard for *Campion* and 14s for *Daisy* show that these carpets were available well into the twentieth century and these prices point to post-First World War inflation.

The excellent hard-wearing and dirt resistant qualities of the Heckmondwike carpeting must have made it a popular choice for the furnishing of many halls, landings, passages and stairs. Fashions do dictate supply, however, and eventually the technique lost much of its popularity. By 1928 Morris & Co. had ceased to deal with the Heckmondwike factory.[20] They, like Morris & Co., had started to look at other carpet techniques and had, by this time, already established themselves as manufacturers of Brussels and Wilton carpeting in wool and worsted and had invested in looms for the production of machine-tufted Axminsters. To weave their designs in these techniques Morris & Co. relied on other manufacturers.

WILTON PILE AND BRUSSELS CORD CARPETS

'Wiltons must be classed as the best kind of machine-woven carpets. The patterns they bear are somewhat controlled as to size and color by the capability of the machine ... If well made the material is very durable, and by skilful treatment in the designing, the restrictions as to color are not noticeable'.[21]

William Morris's designs for Wilton and Brussels carpeting are very similar in many respects to his work for Kidderminster three-ply, with their small regular repeating designs with cross-sections of lilies, tulips, daisies, roses and other distinctive floral forms. The finished effects are quite different however.

Brussels carpeting was the first to be woven with a jacquard attachment on the loom enabling designs of two to six colours to be made. The pattern is formed on the surface of the carpet by different coloured looped warp threads of worsted yarns on a strong woven foundation of linen, jute or cotton. The forerunner of present day cord carpeting, it is the most durable machine-made carpet structure. Wilton carpet is practically the same structure and a similar loom is used. The loops are cut, however, and three weft threads are used in each row of pile instead of two as in Brussels. Wiltons have a soft velvety texture (50–150 tufts to the inch) and Saxony-Wiltons, often called 'Velvet carpets' have an even closer and more resilient pile. Subsequently they were more expensive; Morris & Co. charged 10s 6d for Wilton carpet and 12s 6d for Saxony-Wilton.

Morris & Co.'s Wilton and Brussels carpeting was woven for the firm by the Wilton Royal Carpet Factory Ltd., of Wilton near Salisbury in Wiltshire, the oldest carpet factory in existence in Britain, established in 1701. Brussels was developed as a result of an influx of French weavers in the mid-eighteenth century and was the first carpeting to be loom-woven at the factory. It was closely followed by the Wilton pile evolved from this technique and named after the town of its birth. The carpeting was originally woven on hand looms by outworkers but with the adoption of the jacquard attachment in the nineteenth century, factory production was developed. Morris & Co.'s Brussels carpets were all 27 inches wide, while the plain Wiltons and Saxony-Wiltons were in four widths varying from 18 to 36 inches. Patterned borders became very popular and when sewn around two or three attached widths of plain or mottled Wilton, they provided an economic and attractive carpet which, because of its plain centre, could be used in most interiors. Although the Wilton factory was capable of producing much larger seamless carpets, up to nine feet in width, there is no evidence that Morris & Co. used these.

It is not known at what date Wiltons and Brussels carpets were first woven for Morris & Co. although it was probably soon after the initial trials at Heckmondwike. Unfortunately, the first design used exclusively for pile carpeting, *Lily*, was not registered with the Patent Office, although this design was in production together with a number of others in October 1877 when Morris sailed to Ireland to advise the Countess of Charleville of Tullamore, King's County, on the decoration of her house. According to Guy's diary Morris took with him,

The Wilton carpet factory, showing (to the left) the type of jacquard loom used to weave Morris carpets.

in the form of packages made up at Queen Square, 'patterns of carpets, silks, chintzes etc'.[22]

Wilton was the most popular type of machine-made carpeting sold by Morris & Co. and was available in twenty-four different designs, all available in different colour schemes. Because the same jacquard cards could be used for both, these were also available in Brussels carpeting although very few examples of Morris's designs in this technique have survived. Of the twenty-four designs by Morris and Dearle only seventeen are identifiable today although recognition is further confused by existing patterns no longer having specific titles and, in the Arts and Crafts Exhibition catalogues, by names listed without illustration. It is known that the Kidderminster designs *Daisy*,[23] *Wreath* and *Artichoke* were also used for Wilton carpets and others may also have been adapted.

Of William Morris's many fine designs for Wilton carpeting made in the 1870s three deserve particular mention – *Lily*, *Rose* and *Bellflowers*. They are the quintessence of Morris's design style showing his love of and use of nature and its simplification to its purest form. The pale pastel colours of the *Rose* carpet contrast sharply with the *Lily* and *Bellflowers* where the floral designs are worked in white and pastel colours on a dark indigo

A bedroom at 37 Augustus Road, Edgbaston, Birmingham. A distinctive Morris Wilton carpet was used.

ground. In these there is no attempt to disguise the repeating devices used and each motif is designed as a single square unit. It is almost as if Morris was trying to reproduce a tiled floor surface with the warmth and comfort of woollen pile. This simplicity of form however was not obtained by copying tile designs but was due to the restrictions of the woven carpet technique itself and many of his designs when painted onto point paper look much the same as in the original design. This ability to provide an instantly transferable image can be seen in L.F.Day's illustrations for the *Rose* carpet,[24] in which he shows the preliminary design next to the point-paper. Another attractive design, worked in soft greens and beiges is the *Wreath*, a design of willow leaves and periwinkles arranged in eddying circles. Only a small strip of this carpet is now available in a public collection[25] although a point-paper of part of the design is in the collection of the William Morris Gallery, Walthamstow.

Other Morris & Co. Wilton carpets are known only from nineteenth-century photographs of house interiors and two designs in particular show how well these could be used in rooms already full of other patterns. The bedroom carpet at 37 Augustus Road, Edgbaston, Birmingham was of a repeating shield-shape design of floral in-fills now difficult to recognize clearly, but this

The sitting room, Great Tangley Manor. Morris & Co. furnishings included a bordered Wilton carpet.

contrasts well with the rest of the fairly cluttered room in which Morris & Co.'s *Daffodil* printed cottons (shown on the couch, window curtains and bed-hangings) are the only other products of the firm. A very good example of Wilton used successfully in a Webb/Morris interior is shown in the contemporary photograph of the sitting room at Great Tangley Manor, Surrey, where one of William Morris's earliest designs is seen combined with later Morris & Co. furniture and furnishings.

It is difficult to determine which carpets were designed by Morris and which by Dearle for the period 1885–96. As with other textile techniques, it is probable that Morris produced few designs in the 1880s although

because production did not start till late, his interest in hand-knotted carpets lasted longer than his involvement in designing for the machine. Very few designs for machine-made carpets can be traced to the 1880s and most of those already mentioned belong to the period 1875–83, which was his most prolific as a designer.

Henry Dearle first entered employment with Morris in 1878 as an assistant in his Oxford Street showroom and can barely have been equipped with the technical knowledge or artistic maturity required to produce designs before 1887 when his first printed textile designs were produced by the firm. Yet by the end of the decade he had successfully produced all the new repeating designs used in the furnishings of Stanmore Hall, Middlesex, a sizeable commission. Unlike Morris, who chose to design his machine-woven carpets with simple naturalistic images, Dearle's work shows a strong influence of traditional Persian carpets; his repeats are much larger and more formal, stylized and complex in design. Two unnamed designs which both have matching borders, made by him in the early 1890s[26] show this classical style very clearly. Examples still exist[27] showing that these were very popular with the general public and carpets of these two designs have been found in houses and church interiors not normally associated with Morris or the Arts and Crafts Movement. One carpet used on the stairs and hall of 18 Stafford Terrace, London, the home of Linley Sambourne the *Punch* cartoonist (illus. p. 139), plays an important part in a cluttered, yet exciting, Victorian interior, one in which a simplified William Morris design would not have worked so well. Dearle's interest in the technique of machine-woven carpets was not in its ability to produce a different type of all-over patterned floor covering, but as an economic means of reproducing large scale designs for bordered carpets. Many of his designs for machine and for hand-knotting are very similar. Designs in the Sanford and Helen Berger Collection show formal shield and jewel shaped motifs linked in ogee patterns made by Dearle for body carpets with small additional patterns for decorating borders. Far more imaginative in design, these borders are all brightly coloured on a cream ground with guard stripes in dark colours. One drawing in the Berger Collection is for a rug designed by Dearle and closely copied from a seventeenth-century Indian carpet now in the Victoria and Albert Museum. Because of its repeating motifs this may well have been intended for Wilton machine carpeting. Even at a preliminary stage Dearle's designs were envisaged as large bordered carpets, one monochrome design for example is labelled 'for 27″ carpet, to have 13″ border'.

A number of Wilton carpets and designs were exhibited at the 1899 Arts and Crafts Exhibition, including *Stanmore*, designed specifically for the house in Middlesex, the *Artichoke* and the *Vine*; of these only *Artichoke* is recognizable today and then only as a Kidderminster carpet. Later Wilton products were also advertised in the firm's catalogue *Church Decoration and*

A carpet made from two widths of machine-made Wilton carpeting. Designed by Dearle c. 1890.

Furniture (c. 1910)[28] and include a copy of a bokhara rug, 'specially suitable for the covering of sanctuaries and chancels', at 8s 6d per yard. Wilton and Brussels carpets were particularly popular for church furnishings and accounts dated 1901 for the now disbanded Forest Gate Unitarian Church in London, show the purchase of a Dearle designed Wilton carpet 13 ft 3 inches × 6 ft 9 inches (three widths) at the competitive price of £10 2s 6d.

AXMINSTER CARPETS The Wilton Royal Carpet Co. Ltd. wove two types of Axminster carpeting for Morris & Co.; the 'Rough' or 'Patent Axminster', which is power-loom woven and the so-called 'Fine Seamless Real Axminster Hand-made Carpet', in which the weft and pile threads are laid in the warp by hand. Patent Axminsters are woven with a ready-patterned chenille weft (itself woven in a preliminary technique). This chenille, which forms the pattern and pile, appears only on the surface of the carpet and is loosely woven onto a coarse woven backing which, in the case of Morris & Co. carpets, shows as a plain black cloth on the reverse. Because of the blurred effects of the chenille only the most positive designs could be used for this type of carpet. Morris & Co. advertised two patterns (available in five colourways) and stated that the bolder Wilton designs could also be supplied to order in Axminster. Patent Axminster was available in 27 inch widths for body carpet and $22\frac{1}{2}$ inches, 27 inches and 36 inches widths for stairs, the same as for Kidderminster, Wilton and Brussels.

The difference between the two Axminster techniques and the Wilton firm's use of these is first recorded in Morris & Co.'s text for the 1883 Boston Foreign Fair. Patent Axminster, it says 'can be easily distinguished from real Axminster if the backs of the two are compared. Patent has a foundation of hemp; the real Axminster wool. As the Patent is also a coarse fabric, the designs are much bolder than for Wiltons or Real Axminster. When a large pattern is wanted, therefore, and Hammersmith carpet cannot be had, this patent cloth should be chosen'.

PATENT AXMINSTER The first of Morris's two designs for Patent Axminster is said to have been drawn in 1873,[29] this was not registered until March 1876, unfortunately no examples of carpet of this design have been found. A second design was used for the stairs in 1 Holland Park, London, and a bill, dated 1880 includes $54\frac{1}{2}$ yards bought at 12s 6d per yard. £2 was charged for 'making and laying same'. A second bill for October 1888 mentions a further supply of the same carpet for a total cost of £44 with additional services – 'making up and laying and supplying the brass rods and eyes' – a further £7 0s 6d.[30] Supplied in light blue, cinnamon and dark red the design of this stair carpet is particularly attractive although, because of the technique, it shows a larger scale design of a less positive pattern than one is

Point-paper of Axminster carpeting – each square represents a thread. This design was registered in March 1876.

The staircase, 1 Holland Park, showing a Morris Axminster machine-made carpet of blue and cinnamon, laid in 1880.

used to in Morris's work. The large centrally placed motif is successfully adapted for this use and hits the rise and fall of the staircase in a pleasing pattern. The pattern also looks good as a flat carpet and as well as being used in the billiard room of 1 Holland Park (designed incidentally by Thomas Jeckyll as a pilot scheme for his later 'Peacock Room') is known to have been used in at least two other houses; Torrens Park, Melbourne where, in its widest form with a nine inch striped border, it provided slip matting for the polished floor and as a vast floor-covering in the dining room at Clouds near Salisbury in Wiltshire. Dearle designed at least two pieces of Patent Axminster, but as with other carpet techniques, these are of large scale design and follow in style his designs for Hammersmith rugs. Originally designed for Hammersmith carpets, borders were also woven in Patent-Axminster carpeting and in 1906 the Beale family of Standen in Sussex ordered staircarpets, wider hall

runners, and small square rugs with the same plain apricot mottled centre and patterned borders. Copied from the *Little Tree* and *American Spray* Hammersmith rugs, the border was used at a $13\frac{1}{2}$ inch width.

FINE SEAMLESS REAL AXMINSTER HANDMADE CARPETS Handmade carpets were made in Axminster in Wiltshire from 1755 until 1835 when the looms were transferred to the carpet works in Wilton and from this date Wilton Royal Carpet Co., as it later became known, produced hand-knotted carpets of various qualities. It is these carpets produced by Wilton's for Morris & Co. in four grades, at 28s, 38s 6d, 50s and 60s that have been responsible for more confusion (because of the distinctive difference between the two-knotted techniques of Wilton and Morris & Co.'s own) than any of the firm's other carpets. The 'Real Axminster' carpets are of much poorer quality when compared with Morris's 'Hammersmith' weavings; the pile is not as dense nor as deep and the finished result is far more like machine-woven carpets than hand-knotted ones. A number of previously attributed hand-knotted Hammersmith carpets can be traced to this manufacture, especially those with plain centres of extended width, where the central body of the carpet exceeds 36 inches without seams. The weaving of plain centres would have been a waste of time for the Hammersmith weavers and exorbitantly expensive to clients, so it is likely that all those with borders of repeating designs were manu-factured by the Axminster technique. As with Patent Axminsters, many Hammersmith border designs were used, and the most popular of all, the *McCulloch*, taken from Dearle's design of 1898 was used a number of times, usually with a red/maroon mottled centre. A selection of 'Seamless' borders also copied from earlier hand-knotted Morris rugs can be seen advertised in the catalogue *Church Decoration and Furniture*, issued by Morris & Co. in about 1910. Four patterns, which could 'be made in any colouring, plain or patterned from 27/- to £4/5/6d per square yard according to quality and fineness'. There was no restriction on size in the manufacture of Real Axminsters at Wilton Royal Carpet Co. Ltd. and C.E.C.Tattersall[31] quotes one of 62 feet by 35 feet made in one piece by the firm for a London club.

Morris & Co. contracted Wiltons to weave all their

Wilton pile, Brussels and Axminster carpets during Morris's own lifetime and, from 1912 they were employed to hand-knot Hammersmith quality rugs for the firm. In 1896, the year of Morris's death the firm approached another manufacturer, Brintons Ltd. of Kidderminster with the idea of further production. Brintons have reference to 'a private pattern' produced for Morris and Company in 'Beacon' gripper Tufted Axminster[32] quality but neither design nor further details of the commission are known today.

Hand-knotted carpets

Britain has never proved a successful long term manufacturer of hand-knotted carpets. Nevertheless, from the seventeenth century various attempts have been made to establish manufacturing centres and for short periods of time since then, a number of carpets of great individualism and skill have been made in Britain. When Morris first decided to try hand-knotting in 1877 there were no other contemporary manufacturers working on the scale he envisaged, which gives some insight into the confidence, determination and tenacity of the man, intent to succeed where others had failed before.

A great admirer of the designs and techniques used for Eastern carpets, Morris began buying historical rugs before his marriage and used these for the furnishing of the Red House in 1859. He continued to collect with great enthusiasm, so much so, that in March 1876 he wrote to May of his latest purchases of Persian carpets: 'It will make you feel as if you were in the Arabian Nights'. This collection was of the finest quality and at least one piece, a seventeenth-century Persian garden carpet is now in the Victoria and Albert Museum.[33] His knowledge of the history of Eastern carpets was used extensively by the Victoria and Albert Museum (then known as the South Kensington Museum) during the last quarter of the nineteenth century when he was acting as an Art Referee and it is due to his enthusiasm and good advice that the collection developed at this period when it was possibly to buy at moderate prices. Two of the museum's finest Persian pieces – the *Ardabil* and *Chelsea* carpets – were acquired at this time following Morris's recommendation and, in the case of the former, financial assistance.[34] The *Ardabil* carpet, bought by the museum

for £2,000, was woven in Persia, and is now considered one of the most famous carpets in the world. Morris described it in his report as 'the finest Eastern carpet which I have seen.'[35] The *Chelsea* carpet, called after the location of the dealer from which it was bought, is a superb seventeenth century 'medallion Ushak' with centre and corner medallion devices, a composition Morris was to adopt in a number of his own carpet designs.

It is interesting to note that Morris used only oriental carpets in his own home and his finest pieces often hung on the walls in defiance of western fashion, 'its use as a floor-cloth degrades it especially in northern and western countries where people come out of the muddy street into rooms without taking off their shoes'.[36]

There is no evidence that Morris & Co.'s hand-knotted 'Hammersmith' carpets were ever used by the Morris family either at Kelmscott House or Kelmscott Manor. However, economic reasons may well have contributed to this decision, since the carpets were expensive to weave, and loom and weavers' time could not be wasted on unprofitable business.

William Morris had very strong views on the subject of hand-knotted carpet design and, with the exception of dyeing, his lectures mention this more than any other textile technique. Formulating his ideas from his knowledge of ancient Persian, Turkish and Chinese carpets his advice on how to design successfully covers all aspects of the art from colour to motif and general composition. He insisted, as did his contemporary Christopher Dresser,[37] that the fashion for developing a three-dimensional effect by adding shading to the design should be discontinued. These carpets should represent rather more than just pretty, colourful flat patterns: 'I, as a Western man and picture lover, must still insist in plenty of meaning in your patterns. I must have unmistakable suggestions of gardens and fields and strange trees, boughs and tendrils or I can't do with your patterns'.[38] But what type of design did he favour and how did he suggest that this be achieved? His own designs complement the old as they do not attempt to copy the historical rugs he admired so much. His debt was more selective as he tried to emulate the symbolic tradition behind the designs rather than specific motifs from the old. 'In their own way they meant to tell us how the

Wall rug, 1878–80, one of Morris's earliest Hammersmith weavings. The rug has a worsted warp.

flowers grew in the gardens of Damascus, or how the tulips shone among the grass in the mid-Persian valley, and how their eyes delighted in it all and what joy they had in life'. This eloquent prose tells little of his own designs and even less of the reasons for his first attempts at carpet hand-knotting in 1878.

He deplored the decline in standards in imported contemporary eastern rugs at this time, due primarily to the use of artificial dyestuffs and the mass-production of indifferent westernized designs to satisfy a large and enthusiastic export market, but he did not underestimate the task he set himself to remedy this situation and

proceeded with his usual vigour and determination.

We people of the West must make our own hand-made Carpets, if we are to have any worth the labour and money such things cost; and that these, while they should equal the Eastern ones as nearly as may be in material and durability, should by no means imitate them in design, but show themselves obviously to be the outcome of modern and Western ideas; guided by those principles that underlie all architectural art in common.'[39]

In April 1877 Morris wrote to Thomas Wardle at Leek that he was not prepared to weave tapestry 'till I get my carpets going'.[40] It seems likely that at this time he had already finished designs for the technique and within the next twelve months experimental carpet knotting was attempted on small looms or basic carpet frames in the attic at 26 Queen Square. In 1879 the coach house and adjoining stable of Kelmscott House, Morris's home overlooking the Thames at Hammersmith were converted into weaving sheds, and twelve feet wide looms were set up by Morris with the technical assistance of a Glasgow carpet-weaver.[41] From this time until Morris & Co. ceased the manufacture of hand-knotted carpets at least six women were involved in knotting at any one time. Two pairs of sisters are mentioned as carpet weavers in the Arts and Crafts Exhibition catalogues[42] suggesting that, like the embroidery section of the firm, it became a family affair. All rugs made at this time bear the 'Hammersmith' mark; that of a letter 'M' with a hammer and waves to represent the Thames. Usually the hammer dissects the other motifs but other variations have been noted. Whether the omission of water signifies a later date (when the looms moved to Merton away from the Thames) is doubtful, as the pattern and format is of the early period. There are few existing examples which show this early marking in what today is the only true test of the earliest samples woven at Kelmscott House, and all these rugs are small in size so there is no evidence that the full twelve feet width of loom was ever used at this time.

On 7 June 1881 Morris signed the lease on his new factory at Merton Abbey. Within the month alterations were made to the building including the raising of the roofs, and carpet looms were built into the ground floor area, running the length of the windows. Mackail's description of trout leaping in the River Wandle outside the windows of the 'long cheerful room where the carpet looms are built', depicts an idyllic setting. The extra height and roominess of the sheds enabled the construction of much larger looms, one of which was twenty-five feet in width. An article in the *Spectator* magazine for 24 November 1883[43] describes a visitor's view of the Merton Abbey factory and, in detail, the scene in the carpet weaving shed:

In the middle sits a woman finishing off some completed rugs; in a corner is a large pile of worsted of a magnificent red ... On the windowsill are pots of musk ... The strong, level afternoon light shines round the figures of the young girls

Girls hand-knotting Hammersmith carpets at the Merton Abbey Works in the late nineteenth century.

seated in rows on low benches along the frames, and brightens to gold some of the fair heads. Above and behind them rows of bobbins of many-coloured worsteds, stuck on pegs, shower down threads of beautiful colours, which are caught by the deft fingers, passed through strong threads (fixed uprightly in frames, to serve as a foundation), tied in a knot, slipped down in their place, snipped even with the rest of the carpet, all in a second of time.

TECHNIQUE USED   The warp threads were wound onto two horizontal wooden beams between which they were stretched horizontally. The beams were carried by upright posts on which they could revolve, the space between the posts determining the width. The weavers sat side by side in front, and as the carpet was woven this section was gradually wound onto the lower beam and the warp correspondingly unwound from the upper beam. The yarn for the pile was cut into two inch long tufts and was knotted around two warp threads tuft by

CLOUDS *carpet, first woven in 1887 for the Wyndham family. This shows three-quarters of the 39ft length.*

tuft according to the paper design (point-paper) which was attached in front of the weavers. As each row or part of a row was finished two weft threads were put in alternate sheds of the warp, the first one loosely, the weft was then beaten down. The weavers followed the pattern on ready prepared point-paper which hung in front of them on the loom above the area they were working. Morris & Co. used Turkish knots to weave their carpets in which the two tuft ends of the knot appear together

between two warp threads. Early warps of worsted wools were soon changed in 1880 to cotton and the pile-making wefts were of wool. At least one carpet, the *Redcar*, shows evidence of mohair mixed with the wool and a few other carpets were woven with a silk pile and jute binding wefts.

With approximately ten warp threads to the inch and subsequently five knots to each two warp threads, Morris carpets were usually of a thickness of twenty-five knots to the square inch although with heavy beating down the 'count' was more like twenty-eight to the inch. This is by no means a fine carpet and even within the limited output of the firm, the count varied greatly in their own carpets. The difference between the quality of weaving of the original *Clouds* carpet in 1887 and that of a large double-sized copy of the design made for Stanmore Hall in the early 1890s is dramatic, the latter is much thinner and has not been able to stand the usual amount of wear expected of it. Earlier carpets and rugs, those made in the early 1880s especially, are astonishingly resilient to time and many are still used in homes and look in much the same condition as they did when first woven. Of the two types of knot available, it is surprising that Morris did not select the Persian (or Senna type) used in the manufacture of the rugs he admired the most. Instead he chose the coarser Turkish (or Ghiordes) knot having no illusions of the capabilities of his weavers. He did not expect them to produce fine lines and small details and he designed accordingly, his patterns showing a broad treatment of both colour and composition. Dearle treated the technique quite differently and his designs often show stilted details brought about by expecting the firm's weavers to produce fine and graceful minutiae on a coarsely woven fabric.

Although May Morris is likely to have produced at least one rug design,[44] William Morris and Henry Dearle were responsible for all the others produced by the company. Preliminary designs were approximately an eighth full size and usually showed a quarter or a half of the carpet itself depending on the method of design repeat. These were then presented to the firm's draughtsmen to enlarge onto point-paper, each painted square representing one knot. The designs were often painted up into scaled miniatures to represent the whole carpet and these very finely worked paintings were used for publicity and for showing to prospective clients. Some were sent with other samples on approval to the Victoria and Albert Museum in December 1918 when the museum expressed an interest in acquiring a Morris & Co. carpet. It is unlikely that Morris himself was responsible for any of these paintings as his own style of drawing as seen in preliminary designs was much freer. Henry Dearle and George Wardle, on the other hand, were both accurate draughtsmen and had enough

technical knowledge to enable them to translate a partial design into a full plan.

It is very difficult to determine just how many rugs were woven before the move to Merton Abbey and any study has to depend on existing makers' marks and Morris's own correspondence. Unfortunately, his earliest most exciting sounding carpet, the *Orchard*, is now unidentifiable although the design may have been repeated at a later date and can not now be differentiated from his other carpet designs. Its completion in August 1880 gave him a great deal of pleasure although he worried about the results. 'I have just been busy over my carpeteers; all going pretty well the 'Orchard' being finished is a fair success as manufacture – lies flat on the whole – and as a work of art has points about it, but I can better it next time'.[45] The same month he wrote to Jane with reserved pride, 'The Orchard, spread out on the drawing-room floor, though not perfect as a piece of manufacture is not amiss as a work of art. I am a little disappointed with it: if I do it again it shall have a wide border I think; otherwise I will somewhat alter the colour'. He goes on to write of other carpet work, 'The 4 × 4 is out and much improved by the alterations; the 3 yellow bordered pots are not flat as they should be: I fear the worsted warp is to blame for this: I should use cotton in future and perhaps dye it blue roughly'. This almost certainly refers to a series of small square rugs depicting pots of flowers and floral designs in which the pattern develops from the centre of the lower border (illus. p. 86); very similar in design to his contemporary embroidered cushion covers. Although the rugs are square the pattern forms a horizontal section across the warp in a 'door-mat' arrangement. These were intended for wall-hanging, not for use on a floor. Three of these rugs, of pastel coloured patterns on blue and cream grounds with dark blue and camel outer borders still exist. Each has a worsted warp and an early 'Hammersmith' mark.

Morris's first large carpets were commissioned by two of his most enthusiastic clients, George Howard (to whom he also sold the three small pieces mentioned above) and Sir Isaac Lowthian Bell, for their houses Naworth Castle and Rounton Grange. The Bell carpet, which was woven at Kelmscott House is known today only from a photograph (illus. p. 137). Three alternative designs[46] were prepared in February 1881 for the

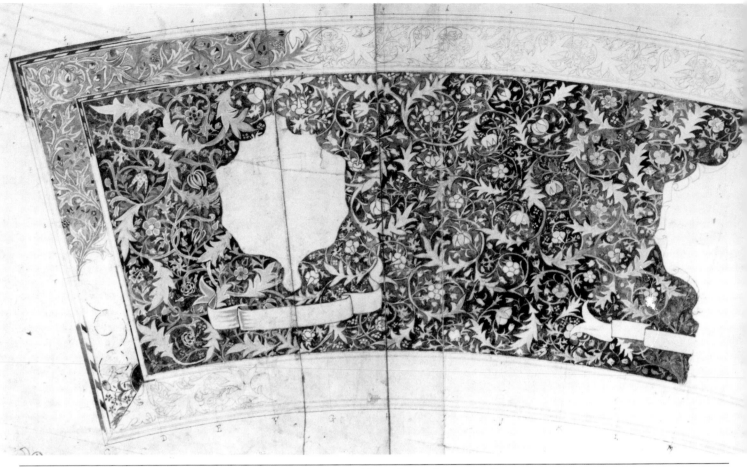

Design for the HURSTBOURNE *Hammersmith carpet. Woven in 1881–2 for Lord Portsmouth.*

Naworth Library carpet and the chosen design had an heraldic motto around its edge. A month was taken painting the point-paper in preparation for weaving and, because of its massive size (31 feet 3 inches × 15 feet 2 inches) the carpet must have been woven on the large loom at Merton Abbey. It was completed in October 1881 and on 3 November Morris wrote to Howard, 'Your carpet has been finished for a week or two: I have been keeping it back to try for a fine day to spread it on the lawn, so that I might see it all at once: at present I have only been able to see it piecemeal ... What are your orders about it? as I shall have to send some-one down to Naworth to get it into place: it weighs about a ton I fancy'.[47] This carpet has altered ownership a number of times in the twentieth century and was last heard of in a Bournemouth hotel in the 1950s, unfortunately it is no longer there.

Another large carpet of the same period of similar foliage design to those described above was that made for Lord Portsmouth for his seat Hurstbourne Prior near Andover. An immense piece, it formed a wide arc spanning some 60 degrees. Its greatest length was 49 feet 6 inches and its radial width 13 feet 6 inches. Emblazoned with the arms of Pease and Wallop and mottoes, the carpet was woven with a dark indigo ground and bright red border, a mix Morris was to use on many carpets.

In 1882 Morris announced his first exhibition[48] and offered to give 'estimates and execute Carpets of any reasonable size, in design, colouring, and quality, similar to the goods exhibited'. One can only hazard a guess at the possible 'Hand-wrought' pieces displayed in London and, one year later at the Boston Foreign Fair.

Stylistic Developments

It is difficult to identify a definite development in the patterns of Morris & Co. carpets, as many examples are

The BULLERSWOOD *carpet, first woven in 1889. Despite its size and subsequent cost three versions were made.*

Hammersmith rug with Chinese-inspired design c. 1880. This version was a wedding gift to Margaret Burne-Jones.

difficult to date. Without the benefit of a catalogue from the firm, other evidence has to be relied on especially the dates of construction and decoration for houses for which specific carpets were woven. This can be confusing as designs were often repeated much later than their original weaving and sometimes it is only the later samples that have survived. For example, the design *Carbrook* was used in a number of later decorative schemes and is now thought by some to have been designed by Henry Dearle[49] because of this. In fact, the design pre-dates the designer's work. Although woven in 1883 for the Antiquity Room at 1 Holland Park, its likely origin is even earlier as Morris was involved in the decoration of Carbrook between 1879 and 1881.[50] Neither the design nor the original carpet are known today although the Ionides example is now in the Victoria and Albert Museum. Despite this confusion, a series of types or styles of carpet can be discerned when studying the firm's output, commencing with the small, squarish shaped

wall carpets already described. Two other contemporary rugs, both with 'Hammersmith' marks are worth noting. These rugs were approximately twice the width of the wall carpets and were made to be used on the floor as their designs read equally well from all sides. Using Chinese inspired motifs and pastel colours the designs show Morris in experimental mood and although repeating one of the designs a number of times,[51] he was never again to look to the Far East for sources of design.

The direction of the design on a carpet was a factor that greatly interested Morris. He later developed a two-way pattern for many of his rugs and carpets intending them to be looked at from all sides, but earlier floral designs of fruit trees and shrubs in dispersed *millefleurs* patterns show quite different variations with the motifs placed vertically or horizontally to the warp. Both types of pattern can be looked at only from one side of the rug. Whereas horizontal patterns were used in many later carpets, few examples of vertically placed designs are

Hammersmith wall rug with vertical design. A late weaving of an earlier style.

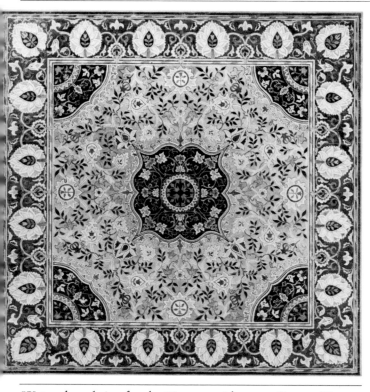

Watercolour design for the Hammersmith carpet SWAN HOUSE *designed for Wickham Flowers.*

known. Illustrations of *Flowery Field* and *Cherry Tree* designs, both exhibited in the Arts and Crafts Exhibition of 1889 show earlier adaptations of this type of composition developed from the earlier wall carpets and an example in the William Morris Gallery, Walthamstow bought from 449 Oxford Street in 1898 is almost

certainly woven from an earlier design.

To follow Morris's developing style further it is necessary to turn to large carpets, as the rug patterns follow the general lay-out of these. Morris's first large carpets – those made for Hurstbourne, Naworth Castle, and Rounton Grange – all show complex patterns of random curving acanthus and willow leaves with small flower-heads and buds wreathed inside; the leaves providing a dense all-over floorcover of similar effect to Morris's earlier designs for wallpapers, fabrics and painted wall decoration. These carpets were woven with a dark blue ground often with a contrasting red border on which a more regular leaf design can be seen. By 1883 Morris had already adopted a more classical format for his carpet designs, one which he continued to use until 1889. These designs have symmetrical proportions, and are 'quartered' (each quarter of the design being the same but reversed as in a mirror) often with a central medallion or other device in the case of large carpets as in the *Swan House* and *Large Swan House* and *Holland Park* or with looping branches or leaf designs in the case of rugs, like the *American Spray*.[52] The two *Swan House* carpets were designed for Wickham Flower's house on Chelsea Embankment and date from 1881 when, according to Morris's diary, he is known to have first produced work for this patron. These carpets are Morris's most traditional designs and resemble Persian 'medallion' carpets. The magnificent borders of repeating palmettes are the most

93

Watercolour designs for CARBROOK *(above) and* LITTLE FLOWER *carpets. Drawings like these were sent to clients.*

arresting parts of the designs, however, their inspiration owing much to the patterns seen in Turkish cut velvets of the sixteenth and seventeenth centuries. A version of the *Swan House* carpet with a red field and indigo border (possibly the original scheme) is now in the Art Institute of Chicago. This had been commissioned by Mr Glessner, an enthusiastic American client for his own home. The *Large Swan House* design was copied for Stanmore Hall. The borders of both carpets were repeated on later pieces with different field designs including the *Little Flower* and a large cream carpet now in a private collection in which the field design shows curving acanthus leaves, peony flower-heads and distinctive sprays of olive branches.

Original watercolour design for REDCAR carpet, designed by Morris c. 1881–5. This colouring was used in weaving.

The *Holland Park* carpet (illus. p. 96), made for Alexander Ionides in 1883 for £113, is probably Morris's most original carpet design and shows traces of all his greatest influences: medievalism, floral realism and eastern precision. Many of the motifs and separate elements used in the design can be traced to other techniques – wall-paintings, wallpapers and textiles in particular – and although the design is complex with a strong border design, field and subsidiary background patterns, Morris succeeded in controlling these to make a balanced composition. The design was repeated for Clouds, the Hon. Percy Wyndham's Salisbury house, with an indigo field and red border. A third weaving exists today made in an exquisite combination of cream coloured ground with the pattern picked out in pale blue, duck egg, beige, pale pink, strawberry pink, grey, turquoise and red.

The increasing size of the medallion and stylized flower motifs in the patterns of Morris carpets developed to such an extent that by 1885 these gradually took over in importance from the previously dominant all-over ground cover of leaves, flowers and background sprigging. A new repeating composition was evolved consisting of large motifs often cut off at the borders in similar vein to Turkish velvets and, more importantly, to oriental carpets. This is probably Morris's most imitative carpet style, but his designs are quite easy to differentiate from the original and look very Victorian in comparison, and decidedly English in their floral detail. This type of composition was used throughout the decade and

The HOLLAND PARK *carpet, designed by Morris in 1883. At least three versions of this design were woven.*

elements can be seen in the earlier designs *Carbrook*, *Redcar* and *Little Flower*. It was, however, manifested in the designs for *Black Tree* rug (exhibited in the 1889 Arts and Crafts Exhibition) and the enormous *Montreal* a carpet woven with a length of twenty-eight feet.

From 1887 a number of carpets woven by Morris & Co. show a one-way directional sweep through their design, the most fundamental change seen until this time. This change can be attributed to two factors, firstly Morris's interest in Persian 'vase' carpets which have this pattern bias and secondly to Henry Dearle's increasing involvement, both in the running of the firm and in the designing of carpets. This is not to suggest that the first datable design of 1887, *Clouds* made for the Wyndham family, is not a Morris design although this is likely to be the last designed by William Morris alone. It is the longest carpet woven by Morris & Co., measuring 39 feet

with a width of 12 feet 3 inches. It is only on this immense scale that Morris's large motifs can be fully appreciated as they tend to overcrowd the pattern surface on a smaller scale. The pattern shows the earlier device of using a design branching from centre to sides and back again but in this instance all the pointed artichoke motifs are facing in one direction. The border design of curving leaves appears in a much earlier paper design, dated 17 October 1878, in the Victoria and Albert Museum. Fortunately, the carpet survived the fire which destroyed most of the original Clouds house; it was sold in 1936 to the University of Cambridge and is currently on the floor of the Combination Room in the Old Schools.[53] Although this type of pattern was never used in rug designs it became the stock in trade of a number of large carpets from 1887–89, and variations on the *Clouds* design, substituting flower-heads and medallions for rosettes and artichokes, are known today.

The *Bullerswood* carpet (illus. p. 91) made in about 1889 for the Sanderson family shows a return to the bird motifs which first appeared in Morris's early designs for small wall rugs and in the Naworth Library carpet. It is probably Morris & Co.'s most famous carpet design and it displays elements characteristic of the work of Henry Dearle. The central theme of two meandering branches forming intersecting ogee compartments, is too positive and obvious in its repeating motif to be by Morris, whose designs are more subtle, but it compares favourably with Dearle's contemporary textile designs, *Florence*, *Vine* and *Golden Stem*, which are arranged around very strongly drawn design repeats. The design of the carpet, as a whole, is far too competent however to be entirely the work of Dearle, (who had only designed a few textiles by this date) and it is probable that both men had a hand in it with Morris possibly correcting, softening, and to some extent, trivializing Dearle's monumental style. Although the carpet is extremely large (24 feet 3 inches × 12 feet 10 inches) and would have been expensive, at least three versions were woven. The original was presented to the Victoria and Albert Museum in 1923, another was given to Bath City Council in 1954 as part of the Henderson bequest and is now on indefinite loan to Kelmscott Manor, and the third is thought to be somewhere in Australia.

The *Bullerswood* is the last carpet that Morris had any

part in designing and although he is mentioned in the 1889 Arts and Crafts Exhibition catalogue as 'superintending' the rugs exhibited, his involvement at this time was directorial rather than directional; his interests straying to tapestry weaving and book production.

Many of Morris's earlier designs continued to be copied often with changes in size, colour and border designs and there seems little evidence of a shortage of orders at this time. Late commissions for Stanmore Hall and for the Barr-Smith's home Auchendarroch near Adelaide in Australia show a plethora of carpets copied from earlier pieces, but often used in unison with more modern designs for other furnishings. Whilst clients were responsive to new patterns for textiles and furniture they were less willing to commission new designs for Hammersmith carpets, possibly preferring Morris's already established patterns.

Dearle was responsible for the design of all new carpets made after 1890, and the change in style seen from this time is quite dramatic. Dearle's attitude to designing for hand-knotted carpets differed little from that for machine-made and often the designs are very similar, showing a more traditional style than Morris's with complex crowded compositions of many small colourful designs. His greatest design, the *McCulloch* (illus. p. 98) is a masterpiece of its type and comes very close to Morris in its masterly use of form and colour.

Designed for George McCulloch, a fellow Australian and friend of A.K.D'Arcy (for whom Morris & Co. had decorated Stanmore Hall) the carpet was designed to be used in the same room as a set of *Holy Grail* tapestries. Much of the design – the mottled ground and border in particular – is modelled on Morris's style although the ground design, with its clumps of flowers pointing haphazardly in all directions, has the characteristic ambiguities of direction seen in many of Dearle's other designs. The carpet attained international fame when exhibited in 1902 as part of the English Arts and Crafts Exhibition in Turin[54] and became a very popular design. The border in particular was used a number of times with plain and mottled centres for machine-made and hand-knotted carpets.

The *McCulloch* was the last original carpet design in what can now be called the 'Morris' style. By the twentieth century, in keeping with the firm's embroidery section, the design and production of carpets tended to follow the mode of the day. In 1912 the manufacture of Hammersmith carpets was transferred to the Wilton Royal Carpet Co. for economic reasons as it was simply not worth Morris & Co. continuing to employ a permanent weaving staff and maintaining looms, when orders were beginning to decline. All later carpets show a change not only in style but also quality. It is easy to criticize the firm for changing the style of its products, but the prevailing difficulties experienced by all manufacturing firms at this time in attempting to maintain profits must also be recognized. Morris's designs were no longer fashionable and whilst accepting that they were no longer leaders of style, Morris & Co. maintained much of their quality market by accepting those styles most acceptable to it. Point-papers from Wiltons[55] show small-scale designs for rugs of undistinguished repetitive patterns and although it is probable that old designs were used and adapted, new uncharacteristic ones also appeared. One design, dated 1917, for a library carpet for Australia House, is in a typical eighteenth-century style based on the ceiling designs and plaster decoration of Robert Adam architecture. It is likely that this carpet was designed not by Henry Dearle but by another, probably free lance, designer.

Twentieth-century rugs, on the other hand, are more characteristic of the Morris tradition of the firm and the maintenance of high standards of design, colour and technique is evident in a few surviving examples. These later rugs usually show a design emphasis on the border which, in many examples, is as wide or wider than the field. Often of 'hearth-rug' shape and size, these follow the fashion set by the Arts and Crafts Movement in its search for cosy interiors. A few small rugs were woven at Merton Abbey some time between 1934 and 1939 as an attempt to revive the flagging company in its last years but neither the technique nor the patterns used are known.[56]

Hooked rugs were another form of carpet manufacture adopted by the firm in the twentieth century and kits comprising printed canvas with dyed woollen thrums could be bought in London, from 449 Oxford Street, and later from George Street. Two examples are known today; one was bought at the Kelmscott sale of 1939, and may have been worked by May or Jenny Morris,[57] the second, showing a typical 'Morris' design in bright

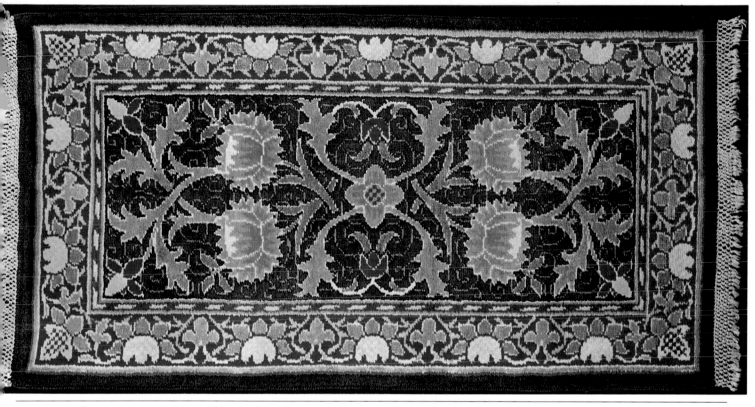

Hammersmith rug, woven at Merton Abbey in the early twentieth century. The rug has a cotton warp.

colours, was made over a period of time by the present owner's mother as her morning 'chore' whilst still a young girl.

Other services supplied by Morris & Co.

CARPET WEAVING FOR OTHER ORGANIZATIONS   Although this was their own most busy manufacturing period, Morris & Co. wove a collection of small wall rugs for the Century Guild from designs by A.H. Mackmurdo between 1884, the year of the Guild's foundation, and 1888. Of identical format to Morris's own early wall rugs at least three examples have survived two of which were bequeathed to the William Morris Gallery, Walthamstow by Mackmurdo himself. Morris and Mackmurdo were friends, and there were close links between both organizations. It is clear that the Guild's rugs were sold through Morris & Co.'s shops and that Morris & Co. advertised through the Guild's magazine the *Hobby Horse*.

Left: the McCulloch carpet designed by Dearle c. 1900–02. Woven for the furnishings of 184 Queens Gate, London.

CARPET WASHING   Morris & Co. provided this service both for their own and for historical carpets. Initial trials used the river Wandle outside the Merton Abbey factory. In February 1883 Morris wrote to Jenny about the washing of a Persian carpet: 'I was frightened at first: for after we first put it into the river it cockled up … the cotton warp shrinking with the wet; I thought my £80 had gone down the Wandle: but all came right when it was dry.'

Whether Morris succeeded in his aspirations for carpet manufacture remains a matter of personal opinion. His designs for machine-made carpets certainly lifted the technique from the doldrums into which it had sunk, and can be said to have contributed to its acceptance today as rather more than a minor art form. The influence of Morris's hand-knotted carpets is more debatable. Morris's designs are often seen today as a Victorian's vision of oriental design. While this does describe Dearle's work to some extent, it underestimates the abilities of both men in their selection of elements from the old in the construction of new designs. Their carpets never simply mimic, they are original in design and often surpass many earlier British examples.

Tapestries

The noblest of the weaving arts is tapestry: in which there is nothing mechanical: it may be looked upon as a mosaic of pieces of colour made up of dyed threads, and is capable of producing wall ornament of any degree of elaboration within the proper limits of duly considered decorative work. As in all wall-decoration, the first thing to be considered in the designing of tapestry is the force, purity and elegance of the silhouette of the object represented, and nothing vague or indeterminate is admissible. But special excellencies can be expected from it. Depth of tone, richness of colour, and exquisite gradation of tints are easily to be obtained in tapestry; and it also demands that crispness and abundance of beautiful detail which was the especial characteristic of fully developed Medieval Art.

This extract from William Morris's 1888 Arts and Crafts lecture, 'Textiles', proved to be his most pertinent statement on the art of tapestry. The lecture was given only eight years before his death but he was still to produce some of his finest examples. Despite being a fine botanical draughtsman, Morris never succeeded in drawing the human form with the same intuitive flair and he saw the production of tapestries as his one opportunity of aspiring to the higher aesthetic realms of fine art. In his own words, the technique of tapestry was 'so deep, rich and varied, as to be unattainable by anything else other than the hand of a good painter in a finished picture'.[1] At last he was able to break away from the confines of the domestic interior with its need for practicalities and conformity of purpose and instead relive the fantasies of his own boyhood and student dreams; scenes of Arthurian legend, mythology, and medieval romance, first inspired by Chaucer, Malory, and Sir Walter Scott.

Morris's first known reference to the technique was to 'a room hung with faded greenery', seen on a boyhood visit to Queen Elizabeth's Lodge, Epping Forest. The use of tapestries in a domestic setting was unusual in the mid-nineteenth century. Tapestry was fashionable as chair upholstery in the eighteenth century but from the 1730s, the practice of using tapestry hangings as furnishings declined in popularity and was revived only in the second half of the nineteenth century, along with an awakened interest in other forms of Gothic art. Morris's own precocious awareness of tapestry went beyond a liking of the scenes depicted however (the Queen Elizabeth's Lodge verdure panels would have shown scenes of natural greenery with animals) and he was clearly attracted by the tactile qualities and texture of the cloth itself; qualities he tried to reproduce in his earliest embroidered hangings.

Long vacation college trips to France first in 1854 and then with Edward Burne-Jones in 1855 gave Morris the opportunity to see medieval figurative tapestries for the first time hanging in the cathedrals of Amiens, Beauvais, Chartres, and Rouen as well as in the Hôtel (later Musée) de Cluny. The cathedral at Rouen particularly impressed him, and he spoke of the experience almost forty years later in *The Aims of Art*, 'No word can tell you how its mingled beauty, history, and romance took hold of me: I can only say that looking back on my past life, I find it was the greatest pleasure I have ever had'.

Since tapestry was the first textile technique to attract Morris's attention, why did it take so long for him to achieve his 'bright dream'?[2] Possibly, simply because he held the technique in such high esteem, he did not feel capable or confident enough to succeed early in his career but preferred to wait until he had the necessary technical

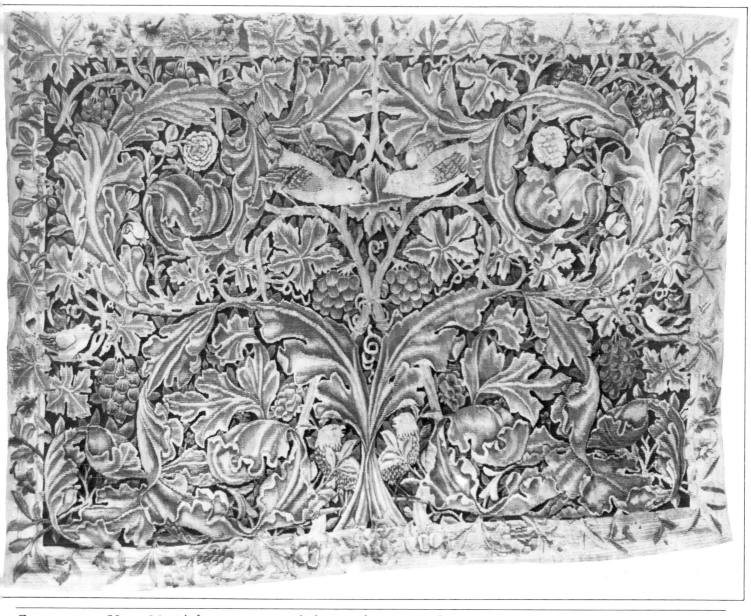

CABBAGE AND VINE, *Morris's first tapestry, woven by him at Kelmscott House between May and September 1879.*

and artistic experience to satisfy his own high expectations of the art.

Morris's first tapestry loom was set up in 1877 and many of his first thoughts on production and the components required were included in a letter to Thomas Wardle in November 1877. Wardle had previously written suggesting a joint venture in manufacturing tapestries and whilst Morris clearly hoped to put Wardle off the idea – having set up his own loom a month before – his views provide a valuable insight into his own aspirations at the onset of manufacture. Upset by Wardle's commercial approach to the subject Morris emphasized the importance of good design and

draughtsmanship. As a non-mechanical technique, Morris felt it was pointless to use anything but the finest pictorial subject matter for tapestry. To use any other type of design was a waste of the technique, as he said, 'the shuttle and loom beat it on one side, the needle on the other'. For practical purposes he recommended the use of 'greeneries, des verdures' (panels of woodland scenes, often showing animals, birds and insects) to help the making of series of figurative panels more economical, as less skill was required for these and the work would be completed more quickly. He was to act on this advice himself some years later when planning the *Holy Grail* series of tapestries for the dining room of Stanmore Hall,

Middlesex. Morris believed that to obtain good designs there could be no compromise: the artist employed should possess the following qualities:

1 A general feeling for art, especially for its decorative side.
2 He must be a good colourist.
3 He must he able to draw well; he must he able to draw the human figure, especially hands and feet.
4 Of course he must know how to use the stitch of the work.[3]

These were exacting standards and even Edward Burne-Jones, Morris's own first choice as designer, was not able to qualify on all points, being quite inexperienced in the technique itself although, having seen the loom in use, he was aware of the limitations imposed.

Morris's first loom was built in his bedroom at Kelmscott House and after initial experimentation to familiarize himself with the technique, he began on 10 May 1879 to weave his first panel. The tapestry was called *Acanthus and Vine* and nicknamed *Cabbage and Vine*, (illus. p. 101) because of the leaves' unruliness. It took 516 hours to weave, and was finished on 17 September. A design for the panel and a notebook listing the hours worked at it each day are both in the Victoria and Albert Museum. The design of this tapestry, which owes a great deal to the verdures seen in boyhood, uses the mirror repeating device of contemporary carpets and embroideries and depicts facing birds and swirling acanthus leaves, all motifs to be seen in Morris's woven textile designs produced at the same time.

Morris claims to have taught himself tapestry weaving with the assistance of one of a series of books concerning the applied arts called *Arts et Métiers*, published by the Paris Académie des Sciences. These manuals, written by various experts between the 1760s and 1780s cover a wide range of techniques from candle-making to tailoring and embroidery. No volume on tapestry weaving has yet been traced and, as Morris said that he found the volume on carpet weaving very useful,[4] it is possible he used that.

Of the two tapestry weaving techniques available and in use in the nineteenth century, Morris chose the *haute lisse* or upright loom in preference to the *basse lisse* which is horizontal. Working on the *haute lisse*, the weaver weaves with the back of the tapestry facing him and is guided by looking through the warp threads at a mirror which hangs in front of the work. This is the technique used in the production of Flemish medieval tapestries and was adopted by the state-run Gobelins Works in Paris. Morris visited the factory during his holiday in 1854 but he did not like what he saw. The work being carried out at that time was mostly the copying of oil paintings and small domestic panels of floral design. 'It would be mild to say what they do is worthless, it is more than that, it has a corrupting and deadening influence upon all the lesser Arts of France . . . a more idiotic waste of human labour and skill it is impossible to conceive', Morris wrote, believing that it had helped to lower the status of the art to no more than an 'Upholsterer's toy'.[5] *Haute lisse* weaving was used at Beauvais in France and the contemporary British factory, The Royal Windsor Tapestry Works, opened in 1876. The weaving at Windsor emulated the French work, producing popular Victorian designs, and Morris was equally critical: 'I am sorry to say that an attempt to set the art going, which has been made doubtless with the best intentions, under Royal Patronage at Windsor, within the last few years, has most unluckily gone on the lines of the work at the Gobelins, and if it does not change its system utterly, is doomed to artistic failure whatever its commercial success may be'.

One of Morris & Co.'s greatest assets, a fact Morris was quick to acknowledge himself,[6] was his chief tapestry designer, Edward Burne-Jones, whose designs of figures established Morris & Co. tapestries as the most artistic pieces woven in the nineteenth century. Burne-Jones was not felt to be the ideal choice by all contemporaries however. W. Graham Robertson in his autobiography *Time Was* (published in 1932) felt he was 'the least fitted to depict the full-blooded folk of Morris's romances, men and women full of joy of life and love of woods and waters and open skies'. Robertson clearly misunderstood Morris's own romanticism in seeing him merely as the purveyor of unsubtle Icelandic mythology and not the melancholic dreamer of dreams represented by Burne-Jones's dream-like figures which were far closer to Morris's vision. Although Burne-Jones's contribution to each tapestry was vital, in terms of effort it is often overestimated, as his drawings consisted only of figures within a general compositional scheme. It was the manner in which these drawings were adapted to cartoons, and then decorated and bordered, that make them such successful works of art and these sections were designed by Morris and later by Henry Dearle.

Just how original was Morris in the style he set for his firm's production of woven tapestries? It has already been noted that Morris studied tapestries as a student and from his own writings and lectures it is clear that his preference was for medieval Flemish hangings of the fifteenth and early sixteenth centuries. As Art Referee to the South Kensington Museum, Morris advised on the acquisition of a number of such tapestries, notably *The War of Troy* woven in Tournai in 1475–90 (bought by the museum in 1887) and *Pity Restraining Justice*, a Brussels tapestry of the first quarter of the sixteenth century and acquired by the museum in 1890.[7] He knew the collections well and the influence of such panels as *The Three Fates*, an early sixteenth-century Flemish tapestry depicting standing female figures surrounded by a dense floral (*millefleurs*) ground, are obvious in his firm's work.[8] The sheer enjoyment he experienced when studying these historical pieces was noted in Morris's diary for 1887, '(Wednesday) 26 Jan: Went to S.K.M. yesterday with Jenny to look at Troy tapestry again since they have bought it for £1250: I chuckled to think that properly speaking it was bought for me, since scarcely anybody will care a damn for it'. The advice of both Morris and Burne-Jones was highly valued by the museum and Thomas Armstrong wrote, 'There are no men in England so well entitled to be heard on the artistic value of work of this Jubial tapestry [Troy] and both, besides, have great archeological knowledge in the subject'.

Morris had a small collection of tapestries of his own, acquired with Kelmscott Manor in 1871. The room in which they hung was Rossetti's study from 1871–4 and then became known as the 'tapestry room'. Morris described the panels himself:

The walls ... are hung with tapestry of about 1600 representing the story of Sampson – they were never great works of art, and now when all the bright colours are faded out, and nothing is left but the indigo blues, and greys and the warm yellow browns, they look better, I think, than they were meant to look; at any rate they make the walls a very pleasant background for the living people who haunt the room and in spite of the designer they give an air of romance which nothing else would quite do.[9]

Morris was always more interested in faded colours than he was in those in their original state and it is these that he tried to represent in his own work.

There was a strong dichotomy between Morris and Burne-Jones in their pursuance of specific historic styles and this adds interest to the tapestries they made together. Whereas Burne-Jones's earliest drawings show a strong intuitive decorative sense,[10] his later drawings, at a time when he was designing for tapestry, are strongly influenced by classical and High Renaissance art, and are often devoid of surface pattern. This absence was more than made up for by the addition of patterned clothing and floral grounds and borders drawn by Morris and Dearle, which help to alleviate the Mannerist gestures of Burne-Jones's figures and draperies. Morris had no time for classical form and described it as 'bald ugliness'.[11] He much preferred the richly coloured and ornately patterned art of the Middle Ages. The composition of the figures in these early works was also noted by him, 'I have always noticed in good medieval design a peculiar kind of interest and ornamental quality which is quite lacking in most of those of the Renaissance and Modern times. And it seems to me to be caused by the planes of the figures being very near to each other'.[12] Burne-Jones's study of historical tapestry was no less thorough than Morris's, as his sketch books testify. One particular example in the Victoria and Albert Museum[13] shows figures from two German medieval tapestries, *The Search after Truth* and *The Buzzard* and others show details of dress taken from other medieval panels. His main source for historical costume for his paintings and tapestry designs, however, were from two books widely used at this period for reference, Thomas Hope's *Costume of the Ancients* (published in 1809) for classical dress and Henry Shaw's *Dresses and Decorations of the Middle Ages* (1843).

Having mastered the technique of tapestry weaving with *Cabbage and Vine*, Morris next set up a loom at Queen Square with the assistance of his first tapestry apprentice, Henry Dearle, who had previously been transferred from the glass-painters' shop. The first items to be woven were trial verdure panels, cushion covers, and furniture coverings. One panel described as a frieze of greenery with birds was sold to George Howard to hang in Naworth Castle.

Dearle proved a gifted pupil and was soon joined by

Tapestry panel depicting a bishop saint. Woven by an apprentice from a Dearle stained-glass design c. 1905–10. The figure probably represents St Thomas of Canterbury (Thomas Becket).

two other apprentices, William Knight and William Sleath. Dearle became responsible for their training and all of those who followed. The practice at Morris & Co. was that the most experienced weavers always worked those areas of the tapestry requiring the greatest skill; the tonal changes of colour required when representing flesh for instance, or the weaving of hands and feet. The apprentices graduated from being 'bobbin boys' (winding yarn on to bobbins for the weavers) to weaving repetitive areas of background and border, although they undertook a number of trial weavings before they were allowed to assist on commissioned work. One such test was the weaving of a small square of tapestry, the design taken from an English Sheldon tapestry bible cover of the seventeenth century. A set of these (now used as table mats) were collected by the aunt of the present owner on visits to Merton Abbey, when she took them from the weaver's waste baskets where they had been thrown on satisfactory completion. Apprentices then progressed to weaving larger tapestries depicting figures. Often copied from medieval tapestries, the figures were also taken from Morris & Co. stained glass cartoons and often depict religious characters. Others are of floral design copying the background details from larger narrative tapestries.[14]

Morris & Co. techniques

Burne-Jones's original drawings were never more than fifteen inches high. These showed figures 'grouped and drawn from carefully prepared studies; for the rest there is but little minuteness of detail and they are only slightly tinted.'[15] From these designs reduced drawings with colour were made (first by Morris and from 1887 by Henry Dearle). These drawings were then submitted to Burne-Jones for his approval, and if necessary, for alteration which usually took the form of suggestions.

The original drawing was then photographed (in the London studio of Messrs Walker and Boutall) to the full life size, mounted on stretchers and returned to Burne-Jones. Some slight details were added at this stage but most were left for Morris and Dearle, who next drew in the foreground and background details copied from their own studies made specifically for the purpose. The flowers and accessories throughout were added at this stage by means of a tracing; the weaver then took the tracing and the original and made a complete tracing of both. This was placed against the warp and retraced onto it from the paper.[16] Morris declared that 'a considerable latitude in the choice and arrangement of tints in shading etc. is allowed to the executants themselves who are, in fact, both by nature and training artists, not animated machines' and it is known that certain details, flowers in particular, were copied from nature at the loom.[17]

Morris preferred to employ young boys for tapestry weaving. They were easier to train and unlike two experienced weavers he employed from the Royal Windsor Tapestry Works (William Haines and George Eleman) they had no difficulties in adapting to the technique.[18] The boys were lodged in the house on the site and looked after by a housekeeper. They were given 'board and lodgings and a weekly stipend'. It is difficult to estimate at what age the boys joined Morris & Co. but one existing photograph shows youths of no more than thirteen years of age. This was better technically, Morris

Below: The tapestry looms at the Merton Abbey Tapestry Works. Weavers worked from the back of the warp.

Right: Two young Morris & Co. apprentices, aged about thirteen, weaving trial samples in the early twentieth century.

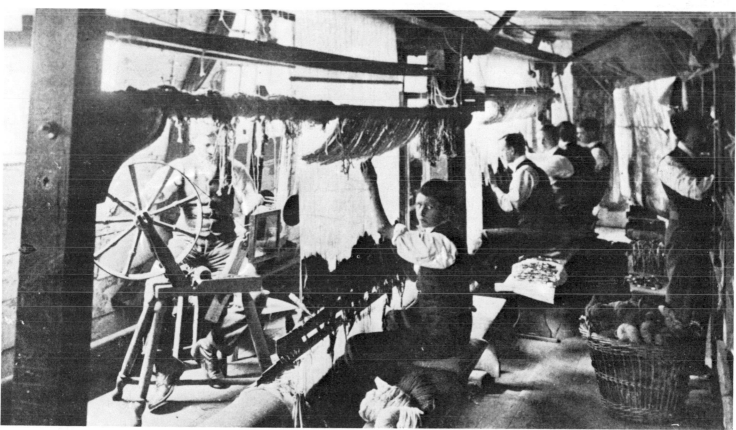

believed: 'The work of weaving is a kind which experience proves to be best done by boys. It involves little muscular efforts and is best carried on by small flexible fingers'.

Conditions of service and rules within the weaving sheds were strictly enforced and informal dress was not encouraged even in the hot summer months, when starched collars had to be worn at all times in case prospective clients were likely to visit. The weavers dressed as if for the office, with black striped trousers and black coats but were allowed to change their coats for a suitable smock or overall before sitting at the loom, although these were removed if visitors or a photographer appeared.[19] On moving to Merton Abbey in 1881 three tapestry looms were set up and up to three people worked at each at any one time. The looms ran the length of the ground floor windows and the weavers sat behind their looms looking into the light. Weavers did not prepare their own warps, this was usually done by a semi-retired weaver, but they were responsible for tying the warp on to the loom and for inking the design on to the warp. They were not paid for these initial preparations, only for the tapestry they wove, and could spend up to two days working on their knees without remuneration. Weavers earned an average of £2 5s per square foot woven and clients were charged from 12 to 16 guineas for the same area, depending on the design and weavers employed. The pattern was transferred on to the warp by means of a small piece of ivory with a sharp edge. This was dipped into the ink and each warp thread was marked by holding the inked marker in one hand and twisting the thread with the thumb and index finger of the other. Trial colours were woven on the edge of the warp until approved by Morris or Dearle and the weaver was then ready to start weaving.

The technique of tapestry weaving at Merton Abbey involved the plain weaving (alternate warp threads being picked up on each shoot of weft) of wool, silk and, for softer highlights, mohair on to a cotton warp. The weft threads when woven were then packed down on the warp with a comb so that no warp threads were visible. Morris & Co. tapestries were woven in a number of different thicknesses from twelve to sixteen warp threads per inch and although early experiments were made to add warp threads to some areas thus giving a finer finish

this was not successful. During Morris's lifetime all tapestries woven by Morris & Co. were in the medieval 'slit' method leaving holes at the junction of colours which were sewn together by hand afterwards. In the twentieth century, Morris & Co. adopted the contemporary French technique, whereby the horizontal joints were secured by intertwining the weft bobbins at the back of the work. Because the width of tapestry looms, for practical reasons, has to be limited in size, all tapestries are woven sideways as few need to be higher than the width of the loom whereas the width, because the warp is wound around rollers, has infinite dimensions. Morris & Co. followed tradition and wove even their smallest panels in this fashion although there was one exception to this rule; a panel depicting a map of South Africa, woven for Sir Abe Bailey in 1934, which was woven upright. Before 1935 the longest panel worked at Merton Abbey was *The Attainment* from the *Holy Grail* series at 8 feet × 22 feet 9¾ inches (244 × 695cm) but for the panels worked for Lancing College in 1935 a special loom was made to enable the weavers to cope with the vast required height of 35 feet (1066 cm).

The action of weaving was tiring and the weavers sat on a low form. One of the apprentices made a painted wooden stool for Morris to sit on.[20] A number of the weavers developed stomach complaints from the crouched position they were required to sit in and one weaver, Richard Carter, died of a gastric ulcer whilst working on one tapestry in 1929.

Morris & Co. weavers

The training given by Morris & Co. was a good one and, of the twenty-nine known weavers who worked for the firm between 1879 and 1939, a number distinguished themselves when leaving the firm by using their skills either on a free lance basis or in other establishments. The most notable was Walter Taylor who joined the firm in the 1890s at the age of fourteen. He left some years later to qualify as a teacher and, eventually, became Head of the Weaving Department at the Central School of Arts and Crafts in London when the subject was first introduced into the school in 1920. A contemporary of Luther Hooper, now considered the father of modern weaving methods, Taylor was equally important – instrumental in

Painted wooden chair made by an apprentice for Morris to sit in while tapestry weaving.

the training of many leading twentieth-century weavers. Initially, he taught in the attic at the Central School sharing this very limited space with the embroidery class under the direction of Miss Ellen Wright, who had also been trained by Morris & Company.[21]

William Sleath, whom Morris had employed at Queen Square, did a great deal of tapestry conservation work, both at Merton Abbey under Mr Marillier and, on a private basis, when he left the firm in the 1920s. He also wove a number of panels from private designs and two were exhibited in the War Memorials Exhibition of 1920 from designs by John D. Batten. John Martin became the first tapestry restorer to be employed by the Victoria and Albert Museum, and William Haines, who had previously been trained at Windsor before spending a few years at Merton Abbey, left to start his own restoration business run from his own home very close to the works. After his untimely death in November 1916 the business was continued by his wife until her own death in 1949.[22] George Fitzhenry and John Glassbrook were both

persuaded to leave Morris & Co.'s employ and join the staff of a new tapestry studio started in Edinburgh by Lord Bute in 1912. It was called the Dovecot studios and was to benefit greatly from the demise of Morris & Co. in 1940, when they obtained much of the tapestry weaving equipment. Both Fitzhenry and Glassbrook lost their lives in the 1914–18 war.[23]

Percy Sheldrick, after leaving the army disabled at the end of the 1914–18 war, went to the Central School of Arts and Crafts in London and trained for three years under Walter Taylor. He joined the staff at Merton Abbey in 1921 and worked there for nineteen years being one of the last to leave, as the firm's master weaver, in 1939. After a few years working on tapestry restoration for antique dealers, Mr Sheldrick started to teach embroidery, his first love, and combined teaching and lecturing with a number of professional commissions worked for clients all over the world. This prodigious work was only curtailed in later life by failing eyesight.

The development of tapestry design at Merton Abbey

The move to Merton Abbey in 1881 enabled Morris to envisage tapestry production on a much larger scale than before. There was little delay in setting up the looms, although the first panel woven at the works, *The Goose Girl*, taken from a book illustration by Walter Crane, was not finished until March 1883. Morris had mixed feelings about the results and wrote to Jenny on 14 April 1883, 'I thought the Goose Girl was not bad, my dear, on the whole: but when all is said it was not a design quite fit for tapestry, except for the landscape background, which looked very well indeed'. The suitability of designs for the technique was soon to be satisfied in Morris's own mind by using Burne-Jones's designs and he had already at the time this letter was written received two drawings, depicting the goddesses *Flora* and *Pomona*, for this purpose from the artist. Despite his close friendship with Morris, Burne-Jones designed for Morris & Co. on a strict commercial basis. His fees, however, were smaller than those paid to other designers. Walter Crane received £150 for the complete cartoon of the *Goose Girl*, which had previously been drawn to illustrate a story from *Grimm's Fairy Tales*,[24] whereas Burne-Jones was paid only £25 each for his original figure designs.

Flora and *Pomona* were woven between 1884 and 1885 by William Knight, William Sleath and John Martin, the latest recruit to the tapestry shed and the first weaver employed since moving to Merton Abbey. Using Burne-Jones's figures, Morris supplied all the decorative details of the tapestries, including background designs of swirling acanthus leaves very similar to those used in the earlier *Cabbage and Vine* panel. This type of tapestry pattern derives from the so-called *Large Leaf Verdure* tapestries of the sixteenth century, commonly thought to have been produced in Enghien but now known to have been manufactured throughout France and Flanders.[25] In these panels Morris's used the leaf motifs in a similar composition to the originals, with animals, birds, and flowers, peeping through the curves of the leaves. The backgrounds are really separate designs however, which overcrowd Burne-Jones's graceful delicate figures. The overall effect is rather too obviously that of two different ideas superimposed. The two original tapestries which were bought from the firm by the Whitworth Art Gallery, Manchester are both large – 9 ft 10½ in × 6 ft 10½ in (301 × 209.5 cm) – and have elaborate borders of fruit and flowers with inscriptions arranged on scrolls at the top and bottom edges of the panels. The verses, by Morris, were later published in 1891 in *Poems by the Way*. A number of later versions of these tapestries, woven from 1895 onwards, are smaller in size (5 ft 6 in × 3 ft 3 in or 167.5 × 99 cm). They lack inscriptions and have quite different backgrounds. Designed by Henry Dearle, these show *millefleurs* arrangements and although not as successful artistically as the Morris originals, they do complement more successfully the central figures, which now dominate the designs.[26] By the end of the nineteenth century, these small figure tapestries had become a significant new art form in their own right, small and cheap enough to be seen in many homes. At least eleven versions of *Flora* were woven and six of *Pomona*.[27]

A number of cushion covers and upholstery panels for chairs and couches were woven at Merton Abbey throughout the firm's existence, although few of these are listed by Marillier. It is clear, however, that they provided an important and lucrative outlet between commissions. Most of the first few tapestries woven by the firm were not commissioned, however, and the weaving of these small pieces helped to subsidize this side of the firm's business.

Four Morris & Co. panels. Above: One of six small versions of POMONA. *This example was woven in 1900.*

Morris designed only three tapestries himself although he provided the decorative details for a number of panels depicting Burne-Jones figures. The first of his own designs, The *Woodpecker*, is a most pleasing design of a bird sitting in a tree garlanded with flowers and swirling leaves and, in what was becoming a characteristic of the company, incorporating an embroidered inscription of

ST CECILIA *and* ST AGNES, *two panels woven in 1887 for Sir Thomas Wardle and exhibited in Manchester the same year. Both panels were re-woven 1888–9. Right:* FLORA, *a pair with* POMONA *tapestry. This panel is a later, smaller version showing one of the two backgrounds designed by Dearle. Both date from the end of the nineteenth century.*

his own poetry.[28] The borders again followed the successful format of the earlier panels depicting, in this example, trailing honeysuckle. A trial weaving of a similar border is now in the Victoria and Albert Museum.[29] The *Woodpecker* was bought by Sir Bryan Peters. It hung for a number of years in the billiard room at 24 Bedford Square, Bloomsbury, the home of George Prothero, President of the Royal Historical Society and[30] is now in the collections of the William Morris Gallery, Walthamstow (illus. p. 110).

Morris's two other tapestry designs depict female figures and were both woven in 1890. His own statement that all Morris & Co. figurative designs but one were supplied by Burne-Jones[31] is misleading, as he included only original designs in this assessment. For example, he omits *The Orchard*, a tapestry of his own design adapted from a cartoon drawn in 1866 for a ceiling painting in Jesus College Chapel, Cambridge. The original design, depicting angels carrying a scroll inscribed with the medieval hymn *Vexilla regis prodeunt* (both altered for the tapestry) was not personally painted by Morris onto the nave roof of Jesus College[32] nor is it likely that he redrew the design for tapestry. The background was supplied by Henry Dearle and the cartoon, now in the Victoria and Albert Museum, shows the figures attached separately and in a different hand, most probably the work of George Wardle. Morris did take some part in the production of the tapestry, in which the angels became female figures[33] and the inscription was taken from one of Morris's own poems. When the tapestry was acquired by the Victoria and Albert Museum in 1898 Dearle wrote, 'The colouring as well as the general design are by Mr Morris and parts of the figures have been woven by his own hand'. The rest of the tapestry was woven by Sleath, Knight and Martin (illus. p. 114).

Morris's only original figurative tapestry design is *Minstrel figure*,[34] (illus. p. 127) which was originally woven in lunette form, made to hang over a mantel-shelf. The figure was influenced by the small *St Cecilia* panel, woven in 1887 from a stained glass design by Burne-Jones, but it is not as competently drawn nor is it as emotionally charged. It is, however, a most attractive panel and Henry Dearle's background of fruit trees and architectural balustrade gives a visual balance to the arched top.

Background designs

Apart from the *Holy Grail* series of tapestries, it is unlikely that Morris produced any designs for tapestry after 1890. The number of panels he designed wholly or partially are comparatively few with Henry Dearle taking an active part in designing from as early as 1887. Whereas with repeating textiles it has proved difficult to tell Morris's and Dearle's work apart, this is not the case with tapestry.

Morris's background designs are strongly drawn and flamboyant in style. They work extremely well as verdures in their own right but, when added to a figurative design they tend to create an imbalance between

Above: THE WOODPECKER *tapestry, designed by Morris, 1885. The inscription was embroidered by May Morris and assistants.*

Right: *Design for* THE ORCHARD *tapestry, adapted from Morris's 1866 design for Jesus College Chapel, Cambridge.*

Above right: *Philip Webb pencil drawing for the fox in the tapestry* THE FOREST, *woven in 1887.*

subject and ground. Dearle's work, on the other hand, shows none of the confidence or style of Morris's designs but his own subordinate backgrounds allow the figures to predominate. Morris's backgrounds are always of curving leaves but Dearle's work shows random clumps of flowers in traditional *millefleurs* arrangements. It is this latter scheme which is now identified as Morris & Co's most characteristic form, although few realize that it was the pupil not the master who initiated it.

Probably Morris's most successful tapestry is *The Forest* (illus. p,. 115), a unique panel using animal and bird drawings supplied by Philip Webb. Many of the foreground floral details can also be seen in Webb's drawings and Dearle is thought also to have made some contribution to the foreground decoration. The general composition, the poetic inscription, and magnificent acanthus-decorated ground, was supplied by Morris. Morris arranged Philip Webb's animal designs in a most charming manner, peeping from behind tendrils and leaves, and, although caught momentarily motionless, they are still full of vitality and movement. The cartoon was transferred to tapestry in a most competent way and, although never identified by Marillier, the weaver is likely to have been William Knight, at this time Morris & Co.'s most gifted weaver. Bought by Alex Ionides for Holland Park, the tapestry hung with a small subsidiary panel of similar design created by Henry Dearle. The tapestry was sold to the Victoria and Albert Museum in

1926 and Webb's original drawings were bought by Lawrence Hodson of Compton Hall, Wolverhampton.

Burne-Jones's tapestry designs

Following the success of the *Flora* and *Pomona* panels, Morris & Co. produced a number of other single figure tapestries. Two panels woven in 1887 for Thomas Wardle, *St Cecilia* and *St Agnes* (illus. p. 109), were exhibited at the Manchester Centenary Exhibition of the same year. These were the first of seven tapestries adapted from existing Burne-Jones stained glass cartoons.[35] Both panels were re-woven in 1888-9. Other designs adapted from stained glass repeat the successful formula of Burne-Jones figures and Dearle background designs; a figure of *St George* was also woven in 1887 and repeated in 1895 and 1900, although no examples of this tapestry have been found[36] and in 1889 a slightly different format was used for the tapestry *Peace*. *Peace* portrays a seated female figure, the background area has been increased[37] and the border is wider than usual with putti in each corner, holding an inscribed scroll along the top edge. The design was first used for stained glass in the English Church in Berlin in 1886. The tapestry was sold for £160 at the Arts and Crafts Exhibition of 1889 to a Mr Whitehead of California.

The armoured figure depicted in the *St George* panel shows strong similarities to figures in another tapestry, *David Instructing Solomon in the Building of the Temple*, designed by Burne-Jones in 1883 for Trinity Church, Boston, USA. The tapestry was not woven until 1902-3 after the deaths of both Morris and Burne-Jones. The design is faithfully rendered and, of all Burne-Jones's tapestry designs, this is the closest to the original stained glass design. Little has been added to the original drawing, which must be classed as one of the most significant drawings in the development of Burne-Jones's career; its highly decorative composition included strange amorphous motifs anticipating *fin-de-siècle* styles. The tapestry was woven for the Hon. George Brookman, an Australian client, who already owned a small version of the *Flora* design and a *Star of Bethlehem* tapestry (now in the Art Gallery of South Australia, Adelaide). It was sold through Morris & Co. in 1922 and was bought by George Booth, a newspaper magnate from Detroit. It

Edward Burne-Jones's stained glass cartoon for DAVID INSTRUCTING SOLOMON, *1883. Re-used for tapestry 1902-3.*

now hangs in Christ Church, Cranbrook, Michigan, part of the foundation he established.

The revival of interest in church furnishings in the nineteenth century provided the Merton Abbey Tapestry Works, which this side of the business had now been named, with a number of commissions and this technique in particular was recommended in Morris & Co. catalogues, 'Tapestry is by far the most appropriate and beautiful form of decoration for a reredos or a blank wall space, and is less costly for its size than a printing by a good artist would be'. Three of Burne-Jones's designs became particularly popular for church decoration: *Angeli Laudantes* (illus. p. 123) and *Angeli Ministrantes*, both first designed in 1878 for stained glass windows in Salisbury Cathedral, can be seen in a number of different formats. Each of the original tapestries, woven in 1894, show two angels, although later versions show smaller panels with individual angels and larger panels with additional decoration.[38] The stained glass cartoons for this design, showing stunning bold figure drawings, coloured mostly in blue and green, are in the collection of the Fitzwilliam Museum, Cambridge. They are a little smaller than the finished tapestry measuring 6 ft 11½ in

(212.8 cm), against the tapestry height of 7 ft 9 in (236.2 cm).

Morris & Co.'s most popular ecclesiastical tapestry by far was *The Adoration of the Magi*, designed specifically for tapestry by Burne-Jones, with background decoration by Henry Dearle. It was woven originally for Exeter College, Oxford, where it is displayed to this day in the chapel. It was finished in February 1890 and Morris states that 'nothing better of the kind . . . has ever been done, old or new'.[39] The religious scene depicted was fashionably sentimentalized by Burne-Jones's figures and Dearle's foreground was scattered with a profusion of British garden flowers. This tapestry, in contrast to others woven at Merton Abbey, appealed to a more conventional market than had hitherto been interested in Morris & Co.'s work. A correspondent for *The Queen* magazine mentioned a visit to see the tapestry displayed at 449 Oxford Street on 26 April 1890. The tapestry was described as 'so perfect, indeed, in every detail, that there is nothing left to desire, and one feels inclined to linger over it until its perfections have been fully grasped'. The tapestry was not given to Exeter College as an outright gift but, because of Morris and Burne-Jones's connections with the college, it changed hands at much less than its market value. At least ten versions of this tapestry were woven between 1890 and 1907.[40] Other panels were woven for Wilfrid Blunt, Eton College, Manchester Town Hall, Museum für Kunst und Gewerbe, Hamburg, M. Stschoukine (now in the Hermitage Museum, Leningrad), M. Edward Mallet, George Brookman, the Colman family at Carrow Abbey (this now hangs in the keep of Norwich Castle), and for St Andrew's Church, Roker, near Newcastle. Each tapestry was woven by three weavers and cost, when sold

THE ADORATION *panel with figures designed by Burne-Jones. Each of the ten versions woven have different borders.*

to Wilfrid Blunt in April 1894, £545.[41] A large watercolour called *The Star of Bethlehem*, worked by Burne-Jones after the tapestry, is now in the Museum and Art Gallery, Birmingham and a study made by Henry Dearle of the dress decoration of one of the Kings is now in the Victoria and Albert Museum.

The Holy Grail series

Because of recent market developments, with panels being sold at record prices, this series of tapestries

Right: THE FOREST *tapestry. Designed by Morris in 1887 with animals by Philip Webb and foreground details by Dearle.*

Below: THE ORCHARD *tapestry woven in 1890. Taken from an earlier Morris design with background details by Dearle.*

now sit and see · nor ride nor haste

...aliant ...hat works earth   o happy year   the threat of winter year   and hangs aloft   from tree to tree   the banners of the spring to be

designed in 1890 for a dining room of Stanmore Hall are probably Morris & Co.'s best known tapestries today. Commissioned by William Knox D'Arcy – an Australian mining engineer who was later to hold the oil rights of Southern Persia – the tapestries formed part of a much larger overall scheme of decoration for the house. Having examined the rooms where the tapestries would hang, the height of the walls and positioning of windows, doors, and fireplace, it was decided to design six narrative panels depicting different incidents from the Arthurian legend of the 'Quest for the Holy Grail', with verdures to hang below describing the action of each upper panel. The commission has been fully described in several previous publications[42] and in an unpublished account written for D'Arcy by A.B.Bence-Jones in 1895.[43] In the latter document, many specific details of the designs are given, including the names of all the flowers included in Henry Dearle's background designs, identified for the author by Mr Tidy, the gardener at Stanmore Hall.

The tapestries are very fine and their design, decoration, and weaving establish them, beyond doubt, as the most significant tapestry series woven in the nineteenth century. Using the nineteenth-century device of splitting the wall into two, the design team of Burne-Jones, Morris, and Dearle, decided that the figurative tapestries would hang below the ceiling moulding and, because they were to be hung above eye level, should be designed somewhat distorted so that the scene would look normal from below. The wall dado – usually consisting of wood or plaster moulding – was to be supplied with inscriptions and on the lower wall would hang verdures of deer and trees, on to which would be placed shields of the various knights involved in the Quest. The six figurative panels portrayed the following scenes.

1 The Knights of the Round Table Summoned to the Quest by the Strange Damsel.
2 The Arming and Departure of the Knights (illus. p. 119).
3 The Failure of Sir Launcelot to enter the Chapel of the Holy Grail.
4 The Failure of Sir Gawaine.
5 The Ship (a small panel included to signify that the scene had passed to foreign lands).
6 The Attainment.

Six verdure panels were designed by Dearle, of which

Above: The dining room, Stanmore Hall showing the first HOLY GRAIL *panel and two verdures in situ.*
Top: The 'Attainment' tapestry from the HOLY GRAIL *series in situ. On the floor lay a version of* CLOUDS *carpet.*

two hung under each of the first and second panels. Because of the architecture of the room, and to heighten the drama of the scene, the last panel did not have an accompanying verdure nor did the small upright panel *The Ship*.

It is claimed that the tapestries influenced many contemporary designers. Versions were shown abroad, although the greatest influence was felt in Scotland, where Charles Rennie Macintosh and M.H.Baillie Scott were later to produce furniture in similar vein to that seen in the first tapestry panel. They, in turn, revolutionized British and continental twentieth-century design.

The Attainment was the first panel to be completed, and was exhibited at the Arts and Crafts Exhibition of 1893. *The Daily Chronicle* sent a reporter to interview Morris and the following information was gleaned:

It occupied three persons, as many as can comfortably sit across the warp, for two years. The people who made it, and this is by far the most interesting thing about it, are boys, at least they're grown up by this time, entirely trained in our own shop. It is really free hand work, remember, not slavishly copying a pattern, like the "basse lisse" method, and they came to us with no knowledge of drawing whatever, and have learnt every single thing they know under out training. And most beautifully they have done it! I don't think you could want a better example than this of the value of apprenticeship. Our superintendant Mr Dearle, has of course been closely watching the work all the time, and perhaps he has put in a few bits, like the hands and faces, with his own hands; but with this exception every bit has been done by these boys.[44]

Burne-Jones's studies for various parts of the tapestries (in the case of *The Ship* and the knight's armour, drawn from small models) are numerous and portrait heads of the knights, as well as figure and composition details still exist. Morris was responsible for the design of the heraldry and chose as his source two sixteenth-century books, which he studied in the British Museum, *Gyron le Courteois, avec la devise des armes des tous les Chevaliers de la table ronde*, published in Paris in 1520 and an undated leaflet, *La devise des armes des Chevaliers de la table ronde qui estoient du temps du tresrenome et vertueux Artus roy de la Grant Bretaique avec la description de leurs armoiries*. From these, Morris personally made the drawings for the tapestry workers,[45] Martin, Taylor, Sleath, Ellis, Knight, and Keach. The narrative panels, which were all eight feet high, were completed within four years of the original commission and the six verdure panels (all five feet high) were woven one year later by Taylor and Haines. The tapestry series remained at Stanmore Hall until D'Arcy's death in 1920, when they were sold[46] for £4,600 to the Duke of Westminster for Eaton Hall, Cheshire. Three of the narrative panels (the second, fourth and sixth) were subsequently put up for sale on 19 April 1978.[47]

Two further sets and three single designs were also woven from the Holy Grail cartoons. In 1895-6 Lawrence Hodson commissioned the second, fourth and sixth panel to be woven with one verdure for Compton Hall. These were sold back to Morris & Co. in 1906 when he moved to a smaller house and were purchased by subscription for Birmingham Museum and Art Gallery – Thomas Wardle had previously expressed interest in the panels and was ready to buy them should the museum fail. The third set of tapestries were woven for George McCulloch, an Australian friend of W.K.D'Arcy's, who owned a house at 184 Queen's Gate, London. Woven in 1898-9 the commission consisted of all the narrative panels as originally woven,[48] plus one verdure. The McCulloch panels were slightly larger than those woven before at eight feet six inches high, these tapestries were exhibited at the British Pavilion of the Paris International Exhibition of 1900, where they were awarded the Grand Prix. The panels changed hands in the early twentieth century, they were put up for sale by Mrs Coutts Mitchie in May 1927 and were bought by Lord Lee of Fareham for 880 guineas. The price had dropped considerably when the tapestries were next sold, at Christie's on 30 April 1953, when they fetched 370 guineas. An export licence was applied for in the same year and the tapestries were shipped to Italy. One panel has emerged since this time: *The Summons* which was put up for sale at Sotheby Belgravia on 24 September 1980 (lot 326), where it was bought on behalf of Birmingham Museum and Art Gallery for the record sum of £90,000.

A second series of tapestries was planned by Morris & Co. based on the Chaucer poem *Romaunt de la Rose* and the subjects chosen for illustration were those first used for the Rounton Grange embroidered panels of the 1870s. All the tapestries were based upon original designs by Burne-Jones but none of the three panels completed in this set were woven in his lifetime. On 30 June 1898, Philip Burne-Jones wrote to Henry Dearle, 'I am keeping back from the sale of my Father's works the Tapestry design he was at work at up to within a short time of his death – which I believe you intended to work out in tapestry . . . if you have enough to go upon or if the design is sufficient for your purposes'.[49] Of the three panels completed in the twentieth century – *The Pilgrim in the Garden* (also called *The Heart of the Rose*), *The Passing of Venus*, and *Love and the Pilgrim* – it is almost certainly the second panel which is referred to in this letter and it is clear that Dearle did use Burne-Jones's preparatory drawing but provided much of the design himself. The tapestry was woven between 1901 and 1907 but had a short life being destroyed by fire at the Brussels Exhibition of 1910. Fortunately a colour photograph was taken of the tapestry before destruction.[50] The tapestry was re-woven by Morris & Co. in 1922–3 for George Booth at an estimated price of £2,000 and Booth gave the tapestry to the Detroit Art Gallery. Certain modifications were made to this later weaving and Harry Currie Marillier, a director of the firm, wrote to Booth on 11 May 1922, 'We will try and design a more suitable border and will modify the arrangement of the "cage" and either make it less prominent or abolish it altogether as seems best.'[51] Possibly due to Marillier's constant reference to the tapestry being a Burne-Jones design, the normally modest and temperate Dearle wrote to Booth in December 1926:

> The Venus composition of figures and other conception of it is Burne-Jones's. He had partly executed – about half finished – a small sketching cartoon of the figures when he died so that I had to complete the designs from this roughly executed design – everything in the tapestry is mine – the background, the foreground, the pattern on the draperies and all the details were designed by me and as you know the borders designed especially for your panel.

He finished his letter regretting the necessary confidentiality of it but said he found 'things getting intollerable.' A roughly executed oil sketch of the scene and a trial weaving of one of the heads of the queen's attendants are now in the Metropolitan Museum, New York and a preparatory pencil sketch for the figure of the queen is in The Art Gallery of South Australia.

Reproduction tapestries

Despite Morris's abhorrence of the practice of copying oil paintings in tapestry, in 1896 a panel based on Botticelli's *Primavera* was woven for Wilfrid Blunt. It was a subject, Morris wrote, 'I have long wanted to do',[52] and the finished results met with moderate approval from Blunt. In his diary he wrote 'The new piece of tapestry . . . is up and is very decorative and brilliant in the drawing room,

'The Pilgrim in the Garden' or 'Heart of the Rose' from the ROMAUNT DE LA ROSE *tapestry series, woven in 1901.*

though the faces are hardly as good as they ought to be. It has been a great difficulty to execute it he [Morris] says and has turned out better than expected'. Blunt had inherited £1,000 from a close friend, Francis Currie, and earmarked this money specifically for two Morris & Co. tapestries.[53] *The Adoration* which was woven directly before the *Primavera* was hung in the hall at Newbuildings Place, his house in Horsham, Sussex, when it was finished and Merton Abbey weavers immediately started to weave the second commission. The *Primavera* cost £554, plus £1 2s 9d for lining, and was inscribed 'this tapestry from sandro botticelli's picture was done at merton abbey by william morris for wilfrid scawen blunt to commemorate the coming of age of his daughter judith'. It was claimed by Blunt that his daughter's likeness was represented in the tapestry.

A second version of this tapestry was woven with a more decorative border than the plain winding leaf design woven for Blunt, and showed a complex design of fruit and flowers. The second version was bought from Morris & Co. by Henry Arthur Jones.[54]

In the twentieth century a number of other reproduction tapestries were woven at Merton Abbey and in 1911 a copy of Filippo Lippi's *Annunciation*, a National Gallery painting, was woven by John Martin and Gordon Berry for St Mary's Convent, Chiswick. It

Above: 'The Arming and Departure of the Knights' from the HOLY GRAIL *tapestry series. First woven 1890–4.*
Top: Original colour photograph of THE PASSING OF VENUS *tapestry, destroyed by fire at Brussels in 1910.*

was not always easel paintings that were reproduced, however, and in 1910 Morris & Co. embarked on the weaving of a series of small tapestry panels designed by Professor E. W. Tristram and based on reconstructions of fourteenth-century painted panels in Westminster Abbey and Ranworth Church, Norfolk. These tapestries depict Edward Confessor (woven in 1910), Henry II, St Michael and St George (1911), and St John as Pilgrim (1914)[55] and they are probably the least attractive of any woven at Merton Abbey. The style is neither modern nor historically based and it is difficult to determine whether this can be attributed directly to the designer – who although an authority on medieval painting was not a professional artist – or to the weavers (Martin, Berry, Glassbrook and Fitzhenry) who may have encountered difficulty in following a type of design so different to that which they were accustomed. However, they had already achieved moderately successful results with a series of small reproduction tapestries woven for the Victoria and Albert Museum, including a number of small decorative strips copied from early Coptic panels and a copy of The Months, a South German fifteenth-century panel. The wisdom of the decision to weave such pieces specifically for purchase by the Victoria and Albert Museum must be questioned, as they add little to original works or to the appreciation of the skills of the Morris & Co. weavers. The Months reproduction – which took the form of a number of small panels – must have proved of some practical use for publicity purposes, being made on a loom set up in the firm's shop at 449 Oxford Street. The panels were woven by Mrs Orage with the assistance of apprentices.

Henry Dearle's tapestry designs

Morris was not a man to plume himself with feathers which did not belong to him; but neither was he one to bother himself about doing what someone else could do equally well for him; and it was only natural that he should depend more and more upon the assistance of a pupil who entered so entirely into his spirit, that he could be relied upon to do much what he himself might have done.

This description by Lewis F. Day[56] of Henry Dearle's role in Morris & Co. has not been bettered. It is clear that Morris did rely on Dearle a great deal, both for the

production of tapestry designs and for the supervision of the weavers and, from the date of his own first full design Fox and Pheasant,[57] woven in 1887, Dearle took some part in the weaving of every tapestry woven at Merton Abbey up to the year of his death in 1932. Unfortunately little is known about the man himself and although he was disliked by Burne-Jones, who found him humourless and at times badgering (it was Dearle's job to remind designers of the late arrival of commissioned designs), the weavers at Merton Abbey thought highly of him and respected his judgement at all times.

Dearle was always at his best when designing verdure panels and his finest piece Greenery, first woven in 1892, shows his ability to draw animals[58] and adapt them to a woodland scene. The effect is quite different from Morris's work, as seen in The Forest tapestry, and although Dearle's work shows none of the flamboyance or ingenuity of composition of Morris's early panel, the effect is entirely original. No conscious attempt by Dearle to modernize medieval verdure designs is apparent, but the results are much more sentimentally charged and thus in keeping with popular contemporary tastes. The original tapestry was bought by the Hon. Percy Wyndham for the hall at Clouds. At the house sale on 13 July 1933, Morris & Co. bought back the tapestry (lot 59) for £150 and sold it soon afterwards to Mrs Lucius Gubbins, a great patron of the firm, for £250. It is now on loan to the National Trust of Scotland and hangs in Crathes Castle, Banchory, Grampian and a second version, woven in 1915, is now in the Metropolitan Museum, New York.[59] The birds depicted in Greenery were used for two other small tapestry panels, Cock Pheasant and Hen Pheasant, which were both woven at the Arts and Crafts Exhibition of 1917. These panels are now in the collection of Birmingham Museum and Art Gallery. A similar verdure style but designed in the form of an upright picture, is Dearle's design The Brook, woven in 1916, and based on Alfred Tennyson's poem of the same name. This tapestry formed part of a significant collection of late Morris & Co. tapestries owned by James Fleming, a London restauranteur who lived at Aldwick Grange, Bognor.[60] The panel is now in the Whitworth Art Gallery, Manchester.

Dearle designed two figurative panels of religious subjects. A small panel of Christ and Mary in the Garden

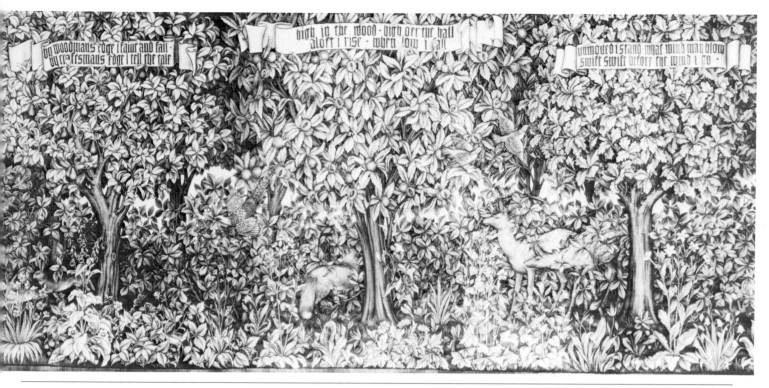

On woodmans edge it faire and fall · by craftsmans edge i tell the tale

high in the wood · high ore the hall aloft i rise · when low i fall

unmoved i stand · what wind may blow swift swift before the wind i go ·

GREENERY *tapestry, designed by Henry Dearle. Two versions were woven, the the first in 1892.*

was advertised in Morris & Co.'s catalogue of church furnishings as 'Arras tapestry Dossal £92'. This was woven in 1910 as an altar piece for Lillington Church in Warwickshire and by 1927 was being used in a private chapel at Middle Aston, Oxfordshire.[61] An earlier panel, *The Nativity* (illus. p. 122), is a much more attractive design and shows a definite Burne-Jones influence, with its sweetly pouting, guardian angels, dressed in classical drapery against a profusion of background lilies. Two tapestries were woven from this design, the first was bought by the Belgian Government and now forms part of the collection of the Musées Royaux d'Art et d'Histoire, Brussels. The second was woven in 1909 for Lord Spencer and was presented to his local church at Dallington near Northampton where it still can be seen.

The search by Morris & Co. in the early twentieth century for more commercial designs to encourage business has already been described in previous chapters. The tapestry workshop was not excluded from this general change in direction although the action taken was misjudged and badly timed. The tapestry side of the business had already survived one crisis, brought on through lack of orders in the mid 1890s, and it was clear

from this recovery that, with good management and publicity, they could continue for a considerable period simply re-weaving established designs, along with new tapestries created by Henry Dearle. It is probable that Dearle was of this opinion and, on the appointment of H. C. Marillier as a director in 1905, he was resentful not only of the interference in directing the workshops, but also of the choice of designs and, from this period, his own work began to deteriorate. Apart from the large tapestries already mentioned, Dearle designed a series of small decorative panels of indifferent design but of some commercial value. Some show scrolling acanthus leaves, much in the style of Morris, but without the subsidiary designs of small flowers to soften the effect, and others such as *Flowery Bough*[62] and *Vine*[63] incorporate flowers and bunches of grapes. These panels, which were used as wall-hangings and in some cases settee backs, were woven under Mrs Orage's supervision in the shop extension at 449 Oxford Street. Another derivative Dearle design of the period is *Floral and Tree Portiere*, woven by Berry and Glassbrook in 1909. This panel, which was bought by the Barr-Smiths for one of their homes in Australia, is a very similar design to Dearle's embroidered portiere, *Orange Tree*. A wider, more ornate

NATIVITY *tapestry designed by Henry Dearle, 1907. Woven by Taylor and Glassbrook for the Belgian government.*

border has been added and slight alterations made to the foreground flowers of the original design.[64]

Later designs

Most later changes in design and technique used at the Merton Abbey Tapestry Works must be attributed to H.C. Marillier as these follow closely on from the date of his appointment as one of four new directors of the firm. Whereas changes in the board continued throughout the twentieth century, Marillier stayed with the firm from 1905 until its demise in 1940, and was involved in the organization and clearance of the works prior to liquidation. Marillier had a great interest in historic tapestries and his publications, not only on the Merton Abbey Works, but on Teniers tapestries (published 1932), and the collection at Hampton Court Palace

(1931) are still used today. His own unpublished indexes of tapestry subjects, workshops and collections are now part of the collections of the Textiles and Dress Department at the Victoria and Albert Museum and have proved of invaluable assistance to scholars. It is understandable therefore that he was keen for Morris & Co. weavers to copy the historical works he admired so much. The friction that became evident between him as administrator and Dearle as controller of the works did, however, contribute towards a general lowering of morale in the tapestry sheds, although the weavers knew nothing of the dissent among management. By the 1920s, Percy Sheldrick described the tapestry section as a hot-bed of jealousy and disagreement, with weavers slashing each other's work to gain advancement for themselves.

Work produced at the looms began to decline and when Marillier wrote to the Victoria and Albert

ANGELI LAUDANTES *tapestry, woven in 1894. Taken from a Burne-Jones stained glass design for Salisbury cathedral.*

THE CHASE *tapestry, designed by Heywood Sumner in 1908. Woven by Martin, Taylor, Glassbrook and Berry.*

Museum in 1909 suggesting they acquire a new tapestry 'as the technical skills of the weavers has improved since the two examples in the Museum were made', the advice from A. F. Kendrick, then Keeper of the Department of Textiles, to his director, Cecil Harcourt-Smith was, 'In my opinion this increased skill has led them astray'.

Marillier was responsible for commissioning a number of designs from free lance designers and although this should have been a beneficial move, injecting fresh ideas into the now faultering section, his choice of designers appears to have been made on a social rather than an artistic basis. Three popular designers of the day were involved: Heywood Sumner (1853–1940), better known as a *sgraffito* designer, John Byam Shaw (1872–1919) an illustrator, and Mrs Adrian Stokes (1855–1927) a Royal Academician, all produced designs for tapestry and these panels were woven between 1908 and 1912. In *The Chase* woven in 1908, Heywood Sumner related his design, in subject matter at least, to the earlier Merton Abbey verdure panels, but the style is startlingly different,

producing an image much closer to children's book illustration than to a tapestry. The same criticism can also be levelled at Byam Shaw's 1909 tapestry *The Blindfolding of Truth*, in which the finished result – although based on a highly accomplished drawing, beautifully coloured and woven – is obscured by a proliferation of subsidiary groups of figures and the predominance of bold pattern. Marillier does not mention the ownership of this tapestry in his *History of the Merton Abbey Tapestry Works*, but it is known that it was purchased in 1927 from a sale by Asa Lingard of Scarborough. It is interesting to note that this tapestry was put up for sale in March 1981 but despite highly inflated prices at that time it did not reach its reserve and was withdrawn from the sale room. The third panel of this group was *Ehret die Frauen* by Mrs Adrian Stokes which depicts a group of female figures portraying womanhood in its many different aspects. It is surprisingly successful as a panel although its Germanic style of design and inscription makes it look very old fashioned to modern eyes.

Other commissions from outside designers included a very poor design from Ford Madox Brown of *Moses and the Burning Bush*, woven in 1912–13 for Captain Harvey and a modern, suitably patriotic 1914 design adopted from Sir Bernard Partridge's *Punch* magazine cartoon commemorating the coronation of King George V. A leaflet was published by Morris & Co. to accompany the exhibition of the panel in the Oxford Street shop, which received royal attention and some public acclaim and a large reproduction colour print, with a special war border, was also available from the firm. The Rev. E. Dorling who supplied the heraldic decoration for the tapestry also designed a screen panel of the royal arms which was woven in 1915.

By 1916, midway through the First World War, the tapestry works were forced to close having struggled on for two years with dwindling numbers of staff and materials becoming increasingly inaccessible. Mrs Orage continued to weave panels at 449 Oxford Street and Byam Shaw's second design produced for the firm, *Kings and Queens of England*, was woven under her instruction between 1915 and 1916. Continuing the patriotic themes of wartime, the tapestry takes the form of nine wallpanels depicting British monarchs from William the Conqueror to George V and the Prince of Wales. The figures are grouped in friezes with occasional strips of heraldic devices; they are of various lengths and each panel is twenty-two inches high (56 cm).[65] The tapestries are now in a private collection in New York.

After the war, the works did not open again until 1922 and immediately found itself in financial trouble, although two large commissions, for Eton College and for George Booth (the founder and benefactor of the Cranbrook community in Michigan) saved it from almost certain collapse. Weaving with vegetable-dyed wools was no longer possible and when Marillier wrote to Booth in April 1922 of the commission for the re-weaving of the *Passing of Venus* he explained why, 'It is the last great tapestry which we shall loom make in which the old vegetable dyes used by the Flemish weavers can be employed, because these dyes are no longer obtainable. Madder, which is the chief of them, has gone completely out of cultivation for dyeing; there seems no prospect of it ever being revived as few people other than ourselves were using it'. Staff were also a problem and

Marillier declared that he had not yet found enough competent weavers to cope with the two new commissions. 'We have some in training' he wrote (referring to Frederick Reed and Percy Sheldrick) and hope to get back one or more of our old hands'.[66] The problems were solved and both commissions completed, but the four panels ordered for Eton College Lower Chapel, based on the life of St George and designed by Lady Chilston,[67] took five years to weave.

An appeal on behalf of the firm was made in *The Times* on 27 December 1924, when yet another extended pause in work put its future in jeopardy. A number of influential figures, amongst them the tapestry historian W. G. Thompson and Alan Cole of the Victoria and Albert Museum wrote letters to the editor following this appeal. Alan Cole posed the question that as the only tapestry works that had existed for any length of time were those patronized by Royalty, or subsidized by the State, then should England not follow France's example at Gobelins. Marillier sent Booth the newspaper article and wrote, 'I am in hopes that it may bring in a client or two as we have nothing to look forward to at present after the next year or two and I should be sorry to have to close the Works, which would be a great hardship more over to the weavers'. This form of moral blackmail gained the desired results and Booth replied commissioning two tapestries for a proposed church to be built at Cranbrook.[68] He wished these to illustrate stories from the Old and New Testaments, to be called 'Old and New Dispensations'. He went on to suggest, 'Perhaps the best thing to do would be to move the Merton Abbey weavers to America to set up their looms here. I would not be surprised but it might be a profitable and happy enterprise for them. But whether the atmosphere of America would be as favourable to their best work as England I suppose there might be much doubt'. Booth was indeed a good friend to the firm as he could more easily have commissioned American weavers to carry out the works – Thomas Herter of New York in particular, whose work he admired. Excited that this additional work would 'keep the Works open and will mean taking on another weaver', Marillier wrote to Booth, in February 1925, with estimates for the work. Content for the fee simply to cover costs, 'we do not expect much profit', an estimate of £800 for each tapestry was made, Dearle, the chosen designer agreeing to give the designs free of charge. Warped up in 1926 the two large tapestries (each was twenty-two feet high) were woven on the large carpet loom now long out of use but suitable for adaptation to the purpose of tapestry weaving. The weavers involved in this commission were Frederick Reid and Percy Sheldrick, Edward Russell and Richard Carter (who died before they were completed) and Wallace Stevens, the most junior member of staff who was involved only in the later panel. The first tapestry was cut off the looms in July 1929. Marillier wrote to Booth, 'It is rather a fine piece of work, coarse of pitch because it hangs on a very high wall ... it hangs high and at a distance so the colours have been kept broad and free from small pattern'.

On the completion of the second panel in 1933 the firm received, almost immediately, another commission for tapestries, this time from Lancing College, near Worthing in Sussex. Lady Chilston had been asked to submit designs for banners for the bare walls of the apse in Lancing College Chapel and suggested to the headmaster, Mr C.H.Blakiston, that tapestries would be more appropriate. Three panels, thirty-five feet high and ten feet wide, were designed by Lady Chilston to form a reredos. The designs are, like the earlier St George series for Eton College, Renaissance in subject matter and style and are both quite unlike any previously worked at Merton Abbey. Each panel depicts a central throned figure surrounded by saints and shows Mary (left hand panel), Christ in Glory (centre), and St John the Baptist (to the right). In the borders of the tapestries are woven figurative and symbolic representations of saints. The panels took three years to weave and were supervized by Duncan Dearle (his father having died in 1932). Three extra weavers were employed to complete the task – Harry Carnegie, Sidney Mears and Arthur Wingate – and the firm's last apprentice, Douglas Griffiths, was taken on in 1934.[69]

During the weaving of the Lancing College tapestries, a number of other small commissions were undertaken. In 1934 a single panel, comprising a decorative map of South Africa, was woven for Sir Abe Bailey as a gift for the South African Government for its London Embassy in Trafalgar Square, where it still hangs in the foyer. It was designed by McDonald Gill (d. 1884), an architect and mural painter whose previous work had included the design of Bladen Estate in Dorset, murals in the House of Commons and poster designs for the London Underground. A second design by Gill was used for an armorial frieze woven for Coventry Corporation between 1935 and 1936. Gill's designs are more decorative and show more flair for the technique than Lady Chilston's and it is a pity that more orders for work of this kind were not forthcoming, for his modernistic and illustrative style suited the abilities of the weavers admirably.

Small reproduction panels continued to be made and the last known tapestry produced by the firm shows a design copied from an early sixteenth century Flemish *millefleurs* tapestry cushion cover which formed part of the Bock Collection, now in the Victoria and Albert Museum (a collection that Morris studied and listed many years before). Since this panel was decorative rather than figurative, it was woven by Morris & Co.'s least experienced weavers at the time, Mears, Stevens and Wingate, whilst Sheldrick was occupied weaving the Coventry armorial frieze.

Tapestry conservation

Introduced by Marillier in the early twentieth century, this side of the business survived despite a great deal of opposition from many small businesses set up both by ex-Morris & Co. weavers and by those from the now defunct Royal Windsor Works. In the 1920s the top floor of the firm's premises at 2B Granville Place, London were used, and the work, which was completed by women, was supervised by a French woman. According to Marillier in a letter written to the Victoria and Albert Museum in November 1929, 'she knows the feel of old wool which is much harder than modern ones', and was not only experienced in repairing tapestries but was of assistance to Marillier on his research into historical examples, since she was able to spot repairs without difficulty.

Although the firm's catalogues boasted that conservation by Morris & Co. involved the loom rather than the needle, most of the work completed was sewn. There is evidence that large missing areas of historical tapestries were replaced by sections woven at Merton Abbey however, an irreversible course of action which is no

Lunette tapestry MINSTREL FIGURE *designed by Morris in 1890, with background design by Dearle.*

longer adopted by conservators. The cleaning of tapestries was much less damaging and involved the use of bread, which was rubbed on to the tapestry until it had absorbed most of the dirt. Other sections of Morris & Co.'s workforce were involved in cleaning and rehanging after conservation and May Lea, an assistant in the upholstery and curtain making section, remembers working at Hampton Court Palace, Woburn Abbey, Beaulieu and other large houses.[71]

The technique of tapestry weaving is time-consuming and consequently expensive and, without subsidy, is unlikely to be financially viable for any length of time. The Merton Abbey Tapestry Works proved no exception to the rule, and although weathering a number of stormy periods, where lack of work, or workers, brought it near to closure, it was the war which closed it down. The demise was evident a few years beforehand and Marillier, attempting to raise some funds to help continue the weaving, offered designs and samples to the Victoria and Albert Museum, who were fortunate in acquiring a number of significant items at this period. On 21 March 1940, the business was placed in the hands of the receiver, Thomas Alfred Ryder of Throgmorton Avenue, London. In a fit of despondency, Marillier wrote to Eric Maglagen, then Director of the Victoria and Albert Museum, 'The war has killed Morris & Co. and at the age of 75 I find myself feeling like Tithonus with all his youth in ashes'.

Interior Design and the Retail Trade

It is not my intention in this chapter to evaluate Morris's (or subsequently Dearle's) use of textiles in commissions for house furnishings and decorative schemes or to describe in detail the contents of houses using Morris textiles as part of their decor. Instead, I hope by comparing such homes – the conventional with the avant-garde, the ostentatious with the understated – to demonstrate the true variety and versatility of Morris textiles as a fitting conclusion to this book.

A study of textiles in isolation from their purpose is always misleading and never more so than with Morris's own work. To admire Morris textiles simply as attractive flat patterns not only denies their success as furnishings, but underestimates Morris's genius as a designer. Morris never designed a textile without considering how it was to be used and the best technique to suit this purpose. He realized, from his experience of different techniques, that fabrics have different characteristics and that they look and perform differently depending on how they are used. Fabrics drape differently, for example, if made of different fibres, silks shimmer, wools give greater depth of colour, cotton and linen are hardwearing and mixtures of fibres – wool, silk, linen and cotton – can provide endless varieties of surface texture. It is this constant variety in types of cloth manufactured, quite as much as the design which makes William Morris the most original textile designer of the nineteenth century. The way in which he used these textiles in the home is equally important and it is due to his inclusion of printed textiles in most of his decorative schemes that these fabrics became, for the first time, as important as woven textiles and were never again classified for summer use only. Unlike many leading contemporary designers he never envisaged his textile designs as flat patterns and none of these were ever transferred to wallpaper blocks during his own lifetime, although one wallpaper design, *Larkspur*, was used later as a printed textile and two designs, *Marigold* and *Bird and Anemone*, were used contemporaneously as wallpaper and printed fabrics. For commercial reasons Morris & Co. printed a number of Morris's textile designs onto wallpaper after the designer's death but this clearly went against his intentions. This fact should be remembered particularly now when reproduction Morris textiles and carpets are seldom of original textile designs but usually adapted from other techniques.

Morris's own ideas on interior design are widely known today. Although he designed many outstanding wallpapers few found their way into his own home. He preferred the symplicity of white-washed walls or the draping or soft-pleating of printed cottons from picture rail to skirting board and the latter arrangement is probably his one most characteristic decorative scheme. The rest depended on the particular client and house to be decorated, and he avoided imposing his own very strong preferences upon them. In every commission he undertook, he did however, suggest a number of different textiles for each room believing that the natural tonal variety of vegetable dyes automatically blended one with another. These patterns provided a rather complicated juxtaposition of pattern and colour and he was in favour of simplifying the effect with an uncluttered arrangement of furniture, with little, if any ornamental knick-knackery. His advice on choosing patterns to live with, given in 'The Lesser Arts of Life' lecture (1882) is one of his most considered and eloquent passages and, thinly disguised, defined his own ambitions and philosophy of life. His advice on what qualities to look for particularly was as follows:

The Dutch suite, part of the first class accommodation on the liner Titantic. Wall-coverings were of UTRECHT VELVET.

1 Something that is possible for us to get.

2 Something that is beautiful.

3 Something that will not drive us either to unrest or into callousness.

4 Something that reminds us of life beyond itself, and which has the impress of human imagination strong on it.

5 Something which can be done by a great many people without too much difficulty and with pleasure.

Morris's moral attitudes to manufacture can be studied further. As a producer, he was keen to ensure:

that the workman shall take pleasure in his work, that decent conditions of light and breathing-space and cleanliness shall surround him, that he shall be made to feel himself not the brainless 'hand' but the intelligent cooperator, the *friend* of the man who directs his labor, that his honest toil shall inevitably win fair and comfortable wages, whatever be the low-water record of the market-price of men, that illness or trouble befalling him during his term of employment shall not mean dismissal or starvation.[1]

To the purchaser, he believed his public responsibility was, 'to revive a sense of beauty in home life, to restore the dignity of art to ordinary household decoration'.[2] He thought that every home, however modest, could benefit from such practical beginnings as choosing items that were beautiful and useful and the great difficulty was not starting with nothing, but having too much: 'I have never been in any rich man's home which would not have looked the better for having a bonfire made outside it of nine-tenths of all it held', as he said. He believed that it was only in the kitchens of the wealthy that one was likely to find objects of any use at all. 'By this accumulation of useless things not only are beautiful things kept out, but the very sense of beauty is perpetually dulled and ground away.'[3] He lectured against the acquisitiveness of the fortunate classes (which he called 'digesting machines') and even, at one point, turned on one of his best clients, Sir Lowthian Bell, 'like a mad animal', to announce that he was sick of 'ministering to the swinish luxury of the rich'. Because of these attitudes, it is likely that some later commissions, the decoration of Stanmore Hall, in particular, was left to Dearle to administer. Morris was not totally prejudiced in his choice of clients, however. Although he was probably happiest working with those who shared his politics as well as appreciating his artistry, he did not mind the banter and gentle teasing levelled at himself and Philip Webb (a man of the same socialist tendencies) when working for those of different beliefs; the aristocratic Wyndham family and the northern industrial, Sir Lowthian Bell, in particular.

Morris & Co. were commissioned by many fashionable families either to carry out the entire decoration and furnishing of their houses or, for those not wanting the whole effect, to supply embroideries, textiles or carpets. It became a fashionable imperative for all self-respecting London households to possess at least one item of Morris manufacture and through such mirrors of taste as *The Studio* (published in London from 1893), Alexander Koch's *Der Moderne Stil* (published in Darmstadt from 1897 to 1905) and, most notably of all, Hermann Muthesius's *Das Englische Haus* (Berlin, 1905) in which Morris interiors were frequently illustrated, this influence reached most parts of the world. Misconceptions did occur, however, especially in the US and at times the firm's name became associated with other modern fashion movements, whose designs, Morris believed, 'make our stuffy art stifling houses more truly savage than a Zulu's Kraal or an East Greenlander's snowhut'.[4]

By the 1890s, Morris had become a legend in his own lifetime. After his death, on 3 October 1896, he was remembered not as a poet, a philosopher or a radical Socialist however, but as a decorator. His obituary in *The Globe*, published the day of his death, described him as 'the head of a well-known firm of designers and producers to whose originality and energy were due the speedily-notable improvements in the adornment of our modern houses. Morris & Co. were . . . the pioneers of the real aestheticism as opposed to the unreal Aestheticism satirized by Mr Du Maurier in "Punch", Mr Burnard in "The Colonel" and Mr Gilbert in "Patience".' The *Daily Telegraph* (5 October 1896) went on, characteristically, to describe typical Morris clients, 'A good many University dons were under the spell of it [the firm's] influence; and when married tutors dawned upon the academic world, all their wives religiously clothed their walls in Norham Gardens and Bradmore Road with Morrisian designs of clustering pomegranates'. The decoration of such bourgeois dwellings had been described earlier in Moncure Conway's *Travels in South Kensington* (1882) in which, speaking of Bedford Park he said, 'The majority of residents have used the wallpapers and designs of Morris . . . whose decorative work has become so serious that a branch of the Bloomsbury establishment will probably become necessary in the vicinity.' Along with the contemporary aesthetic movement, Morris interiors were also satirized, notably through the pages of *Punch* magazine, and at times it was difficult to separate the two styles, but the magazines's two chief cartoonists, George Du Maurier and Linley Sambourne, both became clients of the firm. The use of Morris textiles in modest homes was seen only in London, however, and examples seen outside the capital were restricted to the large country houses of the wealthy. The considerable lack of Morris textiles in British provincial museum collections today is indicative of this somewhat exclusive use. European collections, on the other hand, are rich in examples, showing the firm's strong appeal abroad and it is interesting to note that many foreign museums were buying Morris textiles for their collections in the 1890s, earlier than any British collection, for even the South Kensington Museum had only a few isolated examples at this time. Bearing this in mind, it is amazing that Morris & Co. survived in such a conservative climate.

Fashionable novelists were not so shy in choosing 'Morris interiors' for their books. Mrs Humphrey Ward's novel *The Marriage of William Ashe* describes Lady Transmore's house as showing 'the rising worship of Morris and Burne-Jones', her walls covered with 'the well-known pomegranate or jessamine or sunflower pattern; her hangings were of a mystic greenish blue'.[5] In 1891, the firm was asked to provide stage settings for Henry Arthur Jones's play, *The Crusader*, at the Avenue Theatre, London, first performed on Monday, 2 November 1891. Unfortunately no photographs of this production survive although the programme gives some indication of the type of furnishings used, the action moving from 'Mrs Greenslade's Drawing Room in Mayfair' in Act One to 'The Rose Cottage and Rose Farm at Wimbledon' for the rest of the play. The subject of Act Three concerning, 'social reform and philanthropia', provided a fitting subject for the times, and the two different scenes allowed the advertisement of the firm's town and country styles of decoration. While criticizing the author for a poor production, the theatre critic of the *Illustrated London News* for 6 November said, 'He has mounted the play luxuriously and in excellent taste'. At what point Morris's style became considered good taste is interesting to discover, certainly by the end of the century many of Britain's leading designers and architects had accepted Morris textiles as part of their own interior designs. The designers Charles Ricketts and Charles Shannon used Morris printed textiles in their drawing room with its Hepplewhite furniture, and George Walton and Hugh Baillie Scott, two influential architects, used woven and printed textiles in a number of their design schemes.[6]

Morris interior decoration

Morris's own homes are probably the most obvious examples to study when attempting to pinpoint specific traits in his work, because in these he is likely to have used arrangements which appealed to him and his family. None of Morris's homes survive in their original condition although it is possible, through studying contemporary photographs, existing remnants of decoration and contemporary descriptions to get a clear idea of what they were like. As early as February 1862 Edward Burne-Jones wrote 'Top thrives ... and is slowly making Red House the beautifullest place on earth'.[7] In the Red House, his first home, it is likely that Morris tried out many of the ideas he was to develop later, and it is clear that the results were, to some eyes, weird. As Philip Webb's first domestic design, it is interesting to compare the house with later Webb designs, Clouds and Standen for instance, which were also decorated and furnished by Morris & Co. Whereas the Red House is characterized by small and intimate Gothicized architectural details, the overall effect is rather dark. The later designs have a lighter, larger sense of open spaces however. Morris's interior designs developed in much the same manner, and it is impossible to study Morris's interior designs without parallel reference to Webb's career. Not only were they close friends who worked together on many commissions, but their training and similar talents dictated a sympathetic development.

Financial difficulties and the inconvenience of long journeys from Bexleyheath to Queen Square caused the Morris family to sell the Red House (the only home Morris was ever to own) in 1865 and move to rooms over the firm's premises at 26 Queen Square. The disadvantages of, literally, living over the shop did not deter William and Janey from making the best of their new home, however, and George Wardle noted that the rooms were stylish and were admired and copied by many who visited the family.[8] The Morris family's third and last temporary home was at Horrington House, Chiswick Lane, where they lived from 1872–78. No record or comment has been found concerning the decoration of this house, but by the end of six years residence all members of the family were pleased to leave. Although 'easy to get at because of the omnibuses',[9] by November 1877 Morris was describing the place as 'doleful' saying he 'should be glad to be out'.

Kelmscott Manor at Lechlade, Oxfordshire was used as a holiday home by the Morris family. A joint tenancy was initially taken by Morris and Rossetti from 1872 to 1874, and then by Morris (until his death) with his publisher F.S.Ellis. As tenant he did very little to the house except minimal maintenance, replacing rotten floorboards with stone and wood-block for instance,[10] and as a holiday retreat it contained few possessions. Many of the original items of furniture and textiles remain at the manor to this day, and the numerous items sold at the manor sale of 19 and 20 July 1939 were brought from

The drawing room, Kelmscott House showing BIRD *wall-hangings,* TULIP AND LILY *carpeting and other textiles.*

Kelmscott House, London, by Janey after her husband's death, and from 8 Hammersmith Terrace by May Morris when she gave up the tenancy of her London house.[11] The importance of this action by Janey and May means that Morris's earliest textiles, embroideries from the Red House and the *Cabbage and Vine* tapestry are now available to the public.[12] May Morris wrote that whereas Kelmscott House in London was 'a place of sojourn on life's journey – this was "home"'.[13] Morris described the very strong atmosphere of the house as having 'a sadness about it, which is not gloom but the melancholy born of beauty I suppose, it is very stimulating to the

imagination', and it is clear to this day that, despite intensive redecoration and restoration, much of the soul of the man remains, 'the melancholy of the giant past' was how John Betjeman was to describe it some years later.[14]

Kelmscott House, Hammersmith, London was first described in a letter from Morris to Janey on 18 March 1878, the house was leased from April of the same year. It was in very bad repair but, Morris declared, 'there was no smell about'; it 'could easily be done up at a cost of money, and might be made very beautiful with a touch of my art . . . the situation is certainly the prettiest in London . . . I don't fancy going back to the bugs of

Bloomsbury'.[15] Looking over the River Thames the house had a long rambling garden with, in successive stages, a lawn, orchard and kitchen-garden. The house was much improved with Morris's 'art' and the long drawing room, on the first floor of the house, realized Morris's ambitions of creating one of the prettiest rooms in London. A visitor found it 'a most harmonious and peaceful house ... most exquisitely kept. In dirty Hammersmith, it was as clean as the cleanest country house and the beautiful blue tapestry hangings all round the big living room, with its four windows on the river, looked as if they had just been hung up ... the atmosphere was deliciously homely'.[16] The blue tapestry described was of *Bird* woven woollen fabric, arranged around the wall in folds. This use of fabric hung on walls was a system few were to copy, despite its practicality and good looks. Mackail wrote, 'People dressed themselves in his wall-hangings, covered books with them, did this or that with them according to their fancy, but hang walls with them they would not'. Kelmscott House was furnished with a mixture of antique items and those made by the firm. As well as *Bird*, other fabrics used included *Peacock and Dragon* and *Swivel*. Machine-made carpets were laid with oriental examples, the finest of which were displayed on the walls of the house.

Morris and Co. as decorators

In the official catalogue of the Boston Foreign Fair of 1883, Morris & Co. listed nine products of 'Decorative Art for Household Uses'. These were: 'Painted glass; Embroidery, and material for same; Arras tapestry; Hammersmith carpets; Axminster, Wilton and Kidderminster carpets; Damasks for wall-hangings, curtains and furniture in wool, wool and silk, cotton and silk, and all silk; Stamped velvets; Printed cloths for wall-hangings, curtains etc; Wallpapers.' These products, together with furniture and ceramic manufacture, made the firm the most self-contained retailers in Britain. Other shops, such as Liberty's of Regent Street, Morant's of Bond Street, Whiteley's and the Army and Navy Stores in Victoria also provided a similar range of products for sale but none could boast that most of these were manufactured in the firm's own workshops. Not only did Morris & Co's shop at 449 Oxford Street sell the firm's

objects but, from the end of the nineteenth century, followed the trend of other shops in selling oriental carpets and antique textiles. From 1905, under H.C.Marillier's direction, historical tapestries were sold.

With business expanding and many clients finding difficulty in locating the Queen Square showrooms, Morris & Co. moved in April 1877, to 264 Oxford Street (shortly afterwards re-numbered 449). Situated on the corner of Oxford Street and North Audley Street, the centre of London's most fashionable shopping area, it proved an ideal spot. It is likely that F. and R.Smith, (two brothers who were later to become Morris's partners in the firm) ran the shop from this early period and it is due to their good organization and management that business grew at this crucial stage. Products, drawings, pattern-books and photographs were all displayed in the shop and orders were taken here and transmitted to the workshops. After the move to Merton Abbey, clients

The Morris & Co. shop at 449 Oxford Street. From items in the window, the photograph dates from between 1896 and 1900.

were encouraged to visit the works, and orders were taken during visits. All commissions for interior designs were dealt with personally by Morris and, from 1890, by Henry Dearle, whereas small orders for individual pieces of fabric or items of upholstered furniture were dealt with by the shop managers.

Curtain-making and upholstery were carried out at 2B Granville Place, 'a large rambling old building, wooden from top to bottom and gas lit',[17] on the opposite side of Oxford Street, but close to the shop. The lower floor of the building was used for packing and storage, the first floor contained the workshop for making loose covers and upholstering chairs and the second floor was used for curtain making with pigeon-hole storage for rolls of fabric. The tapestry conservation workshop was run from the third, and top, floor.

Curtains had their own special 'Morris' headings, which were sewn by hand and had the appearance of modern rufflette tape. Linings, if not of specially designed fabrics (such as *Wreathnet, Borage,* or *Flowerpot*), were of toning cotton. Curtains of woven fabric were often trimmed with woollen braid and matching tie-backs and tassels were also available. It is unlikely that the firm made any of their own braids or tassels but got these from another manufacturer, probably A. Sindall (of 116–118 Middleton Road, East London), whose products resemble those on existing examples of Morris & Co.'s make-up. Not only woven fabrics were braided, however, and for the Holland Park set of embroidered hangings, matching braid and tasselled tie-backs have survived with the curtains (illus. p.24).

Many fabrics were available for use as loose covers, or

Page from the Morris & Co. catalogue Upholstered Furniture *c. 1915, showing a range of fabric upholstered chairs.*

as upholstery on the firm's chairs and couches, and the catalogue *Upholstered Furniture* (*c.* 1915), shows the great variety available. Although the items of furniture illustrated are shown covered in recommended fabrics (for example, the Hepplewhite settee in *Mohair Damask* and the Cecil armchair in *Strawberry Thief*), all could be bought cheaper if covered with less expensive fabric and prices for 2 shillings a yard printed cottons (the three lining fabrics) are quoted for each item also. A saving of £2 5s 6d could have been made on the Century easy chair by using one of the cheaper fabrics instead of *Trent* linen, which is illustrated at £11 2s 6d. A surprisingly large number of printed cottons were used for chair upholstery and this showed a definite movement away from conventional furnishings, where velvet pile and woven silk covers were more usual. Cottons had been used since the eighteenth century for loose over-covers, although the fabric was seldom used for upholstery. Morris's reasons for using printed cottons for upholstery were not purely aesthetic as he had realized that his hand-woven fabrics were less suited for this type of wear. He advised George Howard against using *Dove and Rose* fabric for chair upholstery because of the instability of the silk and wool weave, in which the silk was liable to wear more quickly than the wool. Other fabrics were equally vulnerable when sat upon, and the only woven fabrics recommended for upholstery were those power-loom woven by outside contractors.

It is not possible to ascertain who took over management of the Oxford Street shop in March 1890, when the Smith brothers were offered partnerships by Morris, although the names of three people – Lawrence Debney, G. Arnold and Miss (or Mr) Sheldon – appear on estimates and bills for the period 1890–1900. In the early twentieth century, Alfred Hewitt took over as shop manager and remained with the firm until 1940. An efficient man of charm and modesty, he helped maintain the good standing of the firm. After Morris's death the firm was left in the hands of his two partners and Henry Dearle who, by this time, was managing Merton Abbey. Dearle then became art director, probably the most crucial appointment in any commercial textile firm in the competitive world of British textile production at the end of the nineteenth century.

Without any official role in the business, May Morris

still kept an eye on things. Alfred Hewitt wrote:

> She always took a wide interest in her ... father's work, right up to the very end, and was always very critical that everything should be kept up to standard, especially the colourings, sometimes much to the despair of the Dyers, Printers and Weavers of the various work in question, and in fact, was a little inclined to think they were not quite as good as if supervised by her father, or that done in his lifetime ... having done spinning herself as well as dyeing, and knowing the texture of the material used, she was a very formidable critic.[18]

Before 1905 May was, however, guarding the interests of her mother and sister as Morris had empowered his trustees to either sell the business or form a limited company appointing themselves, or 'other fit persons' directors.[19] In 1905 the Smith brothers retired and the firm was registered as a private company under the title 'Morris & Company, Decorators Ltd' with a nominal capital of £45,000 divided into £1 shares. Eight directors were appointed: F. Smith, R. Smith, E. G. Morier Williams (who resigned after a year), W. A. S. Benson (at one time Morris's chief furniture designers), the Hon. Claud Lambton, H. C. Marillier, J. H. Dearle and the company's solicitor John J. Withers.[20] The differences felt by the firm and changes in design direction seen from this time have already been described in previous chapters. This had little effect on the side of the business concerning house decoration, however, and although few commissions concerning the decorating and furnishing of whole houses were forthcoming in the twentieth century many small jobs, involving single rooms or part houses, were received. A number of other interior decorating firms were already using Morris fabrics as part of their own furnishing schemes and examples of work by Cowtans of London, Howard & Son, and Heatons of Manchester and Liverpool all show examples.

In October 1917 the shop moved to 17 George Street, Hanover Square, an equally fashionable London shopping area equidistant between Oxford Street and Regent Street. These larger premises provided more display room than had been possible at Oxford Street and the wide staircase running from the ground to first floor showrooms, provided a long stretch of wall on which to display lengths of fabrics. The catalogue *A*

MORRIS & COMPANY

The new shop front at 17 George Street, Hanover Square, revamped c. 1925, a few years after the firm moved there.

View of the New Morris Showrooms (published after November 1925) illustrates displays and the new shop-front after modernization. In 1927 the curtain and upholstery making sections moved from Granville Place (which was scheduled for demolition) to premises at Chalk Farm in North London. This proved most inconvenient for staff and clients alike and undoubtedly contributed to a slackening off of this side of the business.

By 1920 Benson and the two Smith brothers had retired from the firm's board of directors, and on 26 November 1925 the firm's name was again changed in an attempt to keep up with modern trends. This time, it was named Morris & Company; Art Workers Ltd. A number of changes in directorship were made from this time until 1940, the year the firm closed, when, according to the firm's letterheading, just four directors remained: the Hon. Claud Lambton (Chairman), H.C.Marillier, Duncan W.Dearle and Lord Clonmore (who later became the Earl of Wicklow). A few years before the firm went into liquidation there is evidence[21] that the directors appointed two businessmen to try to put the business back on its feet. Only one of these men, A.C.Collins (who traded as a photographer under the name Keturah Collins), has been identified and it was he who was responsible for the publication of the firm's two last catalogues.

As well as selling directly to overseas clients, Morris & Co. were represented abroad, by a number of agents in different parts of the world. The first mention of such foreign trade was made by Morris in a letter to Thomas Wardle in 1876 when he wrote, 'I don't see why the German gentleman shouldn't try to sell our prints; I will write again about it'. By 1878 Messrs Cowtan and Tout Inc. of Madison Avenue, New York were the firm's main American agent. Walther of Frankfurt-am-Main and Hirchwald of Berlin both sold fabrics to European museums and private homes, and it is clear that the influential Siegfried Bing sold Morris fabrics from *Maison de l'Art Nouveau* in Paris. It was due to the sale and display of Morris's work in these shops that Morris designs became so popular throughout Europe, and that the influence of the 'Morris school' on the development of European decorative design is so great. Bing, who is credited with providing the name for this new style of design, sold Henry Dearle's textiles with equal enthusiasm and success as he did work by C.F.A.Voysey, Christopher Dresser, Lindsay Butterfield and Arthur Wilcox, now recognized as the chief British exponents of art nouveau. It was this readiness by French, German, Swiss and Scandinavian collectors to accept new designs that accounts for all of Henry Dearle's best work being found today in foreign collections.

Morris & Co. had a number of other European and American agents and one has recently been discovered in Philadelphia.[22] Miss Elizabeth Woodville, who owned Woodville & Co. at 1711 Walnut Street, Philadelphia (and from 1926 at 2052 Locust Street) travelled to London each summer and visited Morris & Co.'s shops on buying trips.

A selection of Morris & Co.'s most significant decorative schemes

Philip Webb's idea of architecture – that it was a common tradition of honest building[23] – matched Morris's views on the decoration and furnishing of interiors, and it is this common understanding that led to the successful completion of a number of commissions.

Although it is likely that Morris & Co. were involved, in some capacity, in the furnishing of earlier Webb-designed houses (for example Arisaig House, Near Fort William in Scotland, begun in 1863) the first large commission that the two firms worked on together was 1 Palace Green.

1 PALACE GREEN, LONDON   The home of George Howard, later ninth Earl of Carlisle and his family, built by Philip Webb between 1868 and 1872. Morris was involved to a considerable extent in the planning for the decoration of the house which started in 1872 and was completed ten years later. It is difficult to discover from existing photographs which textiles were actually used in the interior decoration and many of those shown are of the more conventional silk damask designs available in a number of shops at the time. Morris did, however, recommend a number of designs and was keen that fabric should be used around the walls in the boudoir. In December 1879, he wrote to Mrs Howard, 'Ned [Burne-Jones] and I duly went to Palace Green yesterday and our joint conclusion was that the best hanging for the walls … would be in the enclosed [sic] madder printed cotton, it brings out the greys of the picture better than anything else … and if you wanted drapery about it, we have beautiful stuffs and shades of red that would brighten all

up without fighting with the wall-hangings'. In 1881, Morris also suggested fabric wall-hangings for the drawing room and for curtains of *St James* silk, 'I suggest a dullish pink shot with amber like some of the chrysanthemums we see just now'. The focal point of interior decoration in the house was the dining room. This did not include textiles but was panelled in wood, with a frieze of painted panels based on the Cupid and Psyche legend, as related by Morris in *Earthly Paradise*. Designed and started by Burne-Jones, the panels were completed by Walter Crane. These are now in the Birmingham Museum and Art Gallery.

Morris & Co. supplied a number of carpets, tapestries and textiles for the Howards' two other homes, Castle Howard in York and Naworth Castle in Cumberland. Naworth, in particular, contained a number of specially designed items including a Hammersmith carpet of immense size for the library. Furnishing textiles and machine-made carpets from the firm's range were used in other rooms and passages.

ROUNTON   GRANGE,   NORTHALLERTON, YORKSHIRE   The home of the northern ironmaster Sir Isaac Lowthian Bell, his wife Margaret and daughters Florence and Ada Phoebe it was built between 1872 and 1876 in a late gothic style 'with Georgian motifs, kneaded

The drawing room, Rounton Grange, with early Morris carpet, FLOWER GARDEN *wall-coverings and* COMPTON *chair covers.*

The dining room, Rounton Grange showing the embroidery frieze designed by Morris and Burne-Jones.

by Webb into Northern sobriety'.[24] The decoration and furnishings were carried out soon after building completion. The two most decorative rooms were the dining room, for which Morris and Burne-Jones designed a frieze to be embroidered by Lady Bell and her daughters, and the drawing room, containing a Hammersmith carpet with stretched and battened wall-coverings of *Flower Garden* woven wool and silk fabric. Additions to the house, including a large common room, were made in 1890 by George Jack, Webb's assistant and, following these alterations, Morris & Co. supplied a number of further furnishings including loose-covers for most of the original upholstered furniture in *Compton* printed cotton.

Webb and Morris were also commissioned to build and decorate Smeaton Manor for Major A.P. and Mrs Ada Godman (*née* Bell) nearby. This resulted in another set of embroidered hangings, designed by Morris for Mrs Godman to embroider.

1 HOLLAND PARK, LONDON. In March 1880, Morris & Co. were commissioned to decorate and furnish the

Above: Antiquities room, 1 Holland Park, with CARBROOK *carpet,* FLOWER GARDEN *and* OAK *fabrics and Morris embroideries.*
Right: The hall, 18 Stafford Terrace, home of Linley Sambourne. The machine-woven Wilton carpet is a Dearle design, c. 1890.

The study, 1 Holland Park showing THE FOREST *tapestry as originally used. Other textiles and carpets are by Morris.*

home of Mr A.A.Ionides and family. Alexander Ionides was a member of a large and influential Greek émigré family who were cotton importers with interests in Manchester and London. The decoration of the house was completed on October 1888 and three sets of estimates and bills concerning the commission are now in the National Art Library, Victoria and Albert Museum. A complete set of photographs of the interior by Harry Bedford Lemere also survive. In Gleeson White's article, 'An Epoch-Making House', in The *Studio* magazine for 1898, he wrote, 'The real charm of the house is that it is a consistent example of the use of fabrics and patterns designed chiefly by Mr Morris, and that it represents the first flower of the "movement" in aesthetic furnishing which has now developed ... from a commonplace villa was gradually evolved a Victorian Interior.'

Morris provided far more positive schemes of decoration in this house than in either of the two earlier commissions and was clearly helped both by the strong personality of Ionides and by the fact that he did not consider that in this particular commission it was necessary for the interior decoration to be subordinate to the architectural details.

Textiles used included *The Forest* tapestry; *Holland Park, Carbrook, Little Tree* and *Little Flower* Hammersmith carpets with Axminsters carpets on the stairs

(illus. p. 84) and in the billiard room. *Flower Garden* woven silk was used on the walls of the drawing room and for upholstery, and *Oak* silk, *Bird* woven wool and *Utrecht velvet* were in other rooms. The total gross cost of the furnishings and decoration was £2,361 2s 10d, including the entire decoration of the house, supplying and fitting carpets, curtains and wall-hangings and the stuffing and re-upholstery of chairs. Included in this total was a bill for £27 11s 6d for 'making 11 journeys to Holland Park and advising on the decoration of Dining Room, Drawing Room, Antiquity Room, Staircase and Bed-room, superintending of same including patterns of paint'.

OLD SWAN HOUSE, CHELSEA EMBANKMENT, LONDON. The first decorative scheme completed for Wickham Flower, it was decorated and largely furnished by the firm from 1881. Two carpets, *The Large Swan House* and *Swan House* were designed specially for the house and many other textiles were used in the decoration. The drawing room walls were covered with *St James* silk and wool damask and *Utrecht Velvet* was used for upholstery.

Flower's country house Great Tangley Manor in Tangley, Surrey, to which he moved most of his London furniture in 1890, was also decorated by Morris & Co. Repairs and the second of two enlargements to this sixteenth-century house were carried out by Philip Webb in 1885. It is likely that Morris & Co.'s decoration followed Morris's visit to the manor in 1887. 'I have had one holiday this week: I went to see the Flowers (human) at Tangley Manor. It is a very beautiful old house',[25] he wrote. It is likely that the furnishings were added over a period of time, as the latest fabric used, *Daffodil* of 1891, can be seen in Bedford Lemere's 1895 photograph (illus. p. 81). The number of textiles used in the decoration of the house is great and as well as Wilton carpets included, *Flower Garden, Utrecht Velvet* (used for chair and footstool upholstery), *Windrush, Brother Rabbit* and *Large Stem*. The manor decorations epitomized Morris & Co.'s 'country cottage' style, one he was infinitely more at home with than when decorating town houses and country 'seats'! The interior arrangements were much admired by Hermann Muthesius in his study of architecture and interior decoration *Das Englische Haus* and, in translation,

The hall, Clouds *which housed the* GREENERY *tapestry and a* HOLLAND PARK *carpet. Loose covers are also by Morris.*

he wrote 'It is simply a house in which one wants to live ... it is without pomp or decoration, and has that natural decency which is so rare in our present culture'.

CLOUDS, SALISBURY, WILTSHIRE Philip Webb's 'magnum opus'[26] built for the Hon. Percy Wyndham, the younger son of Lord Leconfield, between November 1881 and the end of 1886. Decorations were completed before December 1889 when a great part of the inside was gutted by fire, caused by a maid leaving a lighted candle in a cupboard. Redecoration took three years and was paid for by the £27,000 insurance settlement. The chief colour employed in the house was white and in December 1886 Webb wrote to Wyndham 'when you decide on doing any white-washing as advised by William Morris, let me know, there is a way of doing even this properly'. The whiteness of the walls and ceiling were relieved only by the colour and patterns of Morris fabrics and unstained

wood. The house sets precedents not only in Webb's own career, and that of British interior design, but also 'set the style for a particular way of country house life',[27] and it became famous as a centre for entertaining leading political, artistic and literary figures. It was a great friend of the Wyndham family, Wilfrid Scawen Blunt, who wrote an article on the house for *Country Life* magazine on 19 November 1904.

Two large Hammersmith carpets were made for the house, *Clouds*, specially designed for the drawing room and a copy of the *Holland Park* design for the hall, which also contained the *Greenery* tapestry, *Peacock and Dragon* woven hangings and Morris upholstered chairs. Photographs of other rooms in the house show machine-woven *Tulip and Lily* Kidderminster carpeting in passages and loose covers of printed cotton – *Avon* and *Cray* – on furniture. The house and contents were sold in June 1933 and a number of items were bought by Morris & Co. and resold from 17 George Street.

WIGHTWICK MANOR, WOLVERHAMPTON, WEST MIDLANDS A black-and-white timber-decorated house built from 1887 by Edward Ould of the Liverpool and Chester firm of Grayson and Ould. The style of the house follows the mock-Elizabethan styles revived in the mid-nineteenth century in the city of Chester. In 1893 a larger extension was added to the property to enable the owner, Theodore Mander, a partner in a paint and varnish business, to entertain cricketing friends. Although it is difficult to estimate the date of Morris & Co.'s involvement in the decorations of the house it is unlikely that much work was done before the later extension was built, and only the use of printed linen in the Honeysuckle Room and *Dove and Rose* in the drawing room could be of an earlier date. The great parlour, part of the latter extension, is hung with *Diagonal Trail* and it is likely that this is the first time that this woven textile was used as part of a furnishing scheme. Theodore Mander was succeeded by his son Sir Geoffrey Mander, who was Member of Parliament for East Wolverhampton from 1929 to 1945. Many of the Morris textiles present in the house today were added by Sir Geoffrey and Lady Mander (Rosalie Glynn Grylls, herself a keen scholar and authority on nineteenth-century British art) and in 1937 the house was given to the

The great parlour, Wightwick Manor with wall-covering of DIAGONAL TRAIL *woven wool and chair covers also by Morris.*

National Trust. Sir Geoffrey Mander died in 1962 but Lady Mander still resides at the manor and has written a number of articles about it.[28]

BULLERSWOOD, CHISLEHURST, KENT A large house designed by Ernest Newton for the Sanderson family. Decoration by Morris & Co. began in 1889 and both Morris and Dearle were involved in the commission. *Trent* printed linen was used here for the first time and a specially designed Hammersmith carpet, named after the house, was woven for the drawing room. One bedroom and dressing room had 'walls hung with a sort of Arras', designed and printed by Morris',[29] although it is now difficult to discover which other

textiles, apart from those in the drawing room, were used in the house. Existing photographs of this room[30] show a highly decorated ceiling and cornice design dramatized by sparse furnishings. Only two Hammersmith carpets, the *Bullerswood* and another with a pleasing design of branching stylized floral forms (now in a private collection) provide any additional design and colour.

It is probable that this was the last commission that Morris concerned himself with. As a friend of the Sanderson family (Janey had travelled abroad with them on at least one occasion) he felt interested and concerned enough to supervise. In a letter to the Victoria and Albert Museum in 1921 offering items from the house which was to be sold, it was stated, 'it appears that the Drawing

The drawing room, Standen, which illustrates a partly reconstructed interior. The carpet, a recent addition to the house, is a Dearle design.

Room was decorated by William Morris under his personal supervision and nothing was allowed to be placed in it in addition to objects executed by himself except such as met with his approval'. Apart from the *Bullerswood* carpet, which was acquired by the museum, the rest of the contents of the house were sold on 18 September 1921, some items finding their way back into the Morris & Co. shop. The house is now a school.

STANMORE HALL, STANMORE, MIDDLESEX The house, a Victorian castle in the Tudor-Gothic style, was first built in 1847 with additions of a boudoir and other rooms by Brightwen Binyon *c.* 1888–90. Morris & Co. were commissioned by the owner, William Knox D'Arcy, to decorate the interior, a commission which took a number of years from 1888 until 1896, when the *Holy Grail* tapestries were completed for the dining room. Apart from planning the tapestry frieze, and designing the heraldry to be used on the panels, Morris took no further part in the commission, leaving the supervisory work and all new designs to be made by Dearle. It is clear that Morris felt the extravagance and flamboyance required by D'Arcy in the interior was not to his liking. New and old designs for carpets and textiles were used in the decoration. For the walls of the drawing room, Dearle designed the *Persian Brocatel* fabric and for a small alcove room, the *Golden Bough* was used for the first time. Carpets included

143

The drawing room, Stanmore Hall with wall-cover of Persian Brocatel *and other furnishings also by Morris & Co.*

re-weavings of the *Holland Park* and *Swan House* designs in the drawing room with an enlarged version of *Clouds* in the dining room. At least two new designs were woven as Hammersmith rugs, a small square panel with central petalled motif in the alcove and a design of stylized lotus flowers in the small drawing room. The commission did provide Dearle with an opportunity to decorate without financial stringency, and J.S.Gibson in his article, 'Artistic Houses' for the *Studio*, 1893, stated, 'Messrs William Morris [sic] have had a free hand, not merely in such matters as usually fall within the scope of the decorators but in the hangings, furniture, and carpets. Hence the work shows a curious instance of one very individual artist fettered by existing features'.

Stanmore Hall has had a chequered history since D'Arcy's death in 1920 when the house was first sold with Morris decorations. It changed hands three times before 1931 and eventually became used as the Royal National Orthopaedic Hospital. It is now empty, derelict and under a demolition order.

STANDEN, EAST GRINSTEAD, SUSSEX   A much

more fitting fate, as part of the National Trust, has saved this house. In 1891 Webb was commissioned by J.S. Beale, a solicitor, to build him a house on the Hollybush Farm Estate. The construction, which involved the moving of the original site, took from October 1892 to the summer of 1894. In London, Beale and his family, (wife and daughters) lived in Holland Park and were neighbours with the Ionides and Coronio families[31] and it is possible that they were introduced to Morris & Co.'s work through these friendships. Unlike Clouds and Rounton Grange, Webb was asked to build a weekend house and Halsey Ricardo, in his article 'A House in the Country' (*The Magazine of Art*, 1900) described the welcoming atmosphere of Standen, 'the human quality of the building lingers with one like a choice flavour'.

Although much redecoration and replacement of fabrics has been necessary since the house was first acquired by the National Trust in 1972, the original effect is beautifully maintained (illus. p. 143). Many original items of furniture, machine-made carpeting and embroideries have been retained and a set of Chippendale chairs and a settee upholstered with *Acorn* stamped plush are unique in their fine condition.

Joanna Barr-Smith at Auchendarroch. All furnishing textiles, including her workbag, came from Morris & Co.

TORRENS PARK, ADELAIDE, AUSTRALIA A town house on the outskirts of Adelaide with extensive grounds, Torrens Park was the home of Robert and Joanna Barr-Smith. Built in 1860. it was acquired by the Barr-Smiths in 1874 and extensively altered by Neville Ashbee, a London architect. Robert Barr-Smith a Scot, emigrated to Australia in 1854 and soon developed pastoral and mercantile interests in South Australia, founding the company Elder Smith with his brother-in-law, George Elder.[32] Auchendarroch was the Barr-Smith's Italianate villa 'hill station' in the surrounding Adelaide hills of Mount Barker about thirty miles from the city. Because of the heat of Adelaide in the summer the family spend much of their time at this house from the early 1890s. Joanna Barr-Smith, a friend of May Morris's was an extravagant shopper and although it is unlikely that Morris & Co. personally supervised the decoration of these two houses, all of the contents − wallpapers, fabrics, furnishings and carpets − were by Morris & Co. Having shopped in London for furnishings, local tradesmen were then employed to decorate the houses. The Barr-Smiths

were rich and influential and Joanna set the style for all fashionable Adelaide houses. Money was no object; when her husband died in 1915 his estate, when sworn for probate, was the largest that South Australia had ever known.

In 1904, the family left Torrens Park and moved to North Adelaide and their third home, Birksgate, which was also furnished from the Oxford Street shop. The Barr-Smiths were such good clients that amongst their possessions now in public collections in Adelaide is a printed swatch book, kept by the family for convenience in ordering. Joanna Barr-Smith bought a number of embroidery items from Morris & Co. which she completed herself at home, including the initialled workbag which appears in one photograph of her at home.

For all the richness of design and colour seen in the three Australian interiors the effect is strangely conventional and quite uncharacteristic of Morris's work for it is in simple arrangements and plain rooms that his textiles excel.

Catalogue of Repeating Textiles

*This chronological catalogue includes all known repeating designs
for woven and printed textiles produced by Morris & Co. and a small selection
of designs for machine-made carpets.
Unless otherwise stated, all items photographed are from the collection of the Victoria and Albert Museum, London.
Black and white illustrations, designs and small samples have been used
in the absence of more satisfactory samples. An arrow in the margin indicates the direction of the pattern.*

DATING OF TEXTILES Where available all registration of designs has been given. In all cases, the date of designing preceded this and when known this also has been quoted. References to books and exhibitions have only been given when this helps to clarify the date of the entry.

REPEAT SIZE Height is given first. 'Width' refers to the intended width of the finished fabric. All measurements vary from technique to technique and two samples of the same fabric can vary as much as half an inch in their repeat and up to two inches in fabric width. In most cases the measurements quoted refer to the sample illustrated, if this does not show a full repeat then a larger sample has been measured, if available.

PATTERN NUMBER This was Morris & Co.'s code for each pattern and colouring. In the case of printed cottons, random numbers are given to each colourway as it was adopted. For woven textiles the pattern number remained the same and a prefix was adopted for each colourway. e.g. 3/7124 is the third colouring adopted for design 7124.

UNKNOWN SAMPLES Five designs referred to in Morris & Co.'s catalogues have not been located, these are *Flower and Stripe, Jasmine Twill, Little Daisy, Trellis,* and a woven *Figured Rep.* In some cases the names of these designs are very similar to existing samples and may be misnomers, whereas *Figured Rep* is probably a plain fabric. There is a set of printing blocks for the design *Tudor Rose* at the William Morris Gallery, Walthamstow but, to date, no examples of the fabric have been found.

ABBREVIATIONS USED FOR PRINCIPAL COLLECTIONS
Berger Collection = Sanford and Helen Berger Collection, California.
Birmingham = City Museum and Art Gallery, Birmingham.
V&A = Victoria and Albert Museum, London.
Walthamstow = The William Morris Gallery, Walthamstow.

1 SMALL STEM printed onto wool and cotton. Copied Morris *c*. 1868 from a Bannister Hall printed cotton of the 1830s. Block-printed Thomas Clarkson, Bannister Hall. Repeat: $35\frac{1}{4} \times 36$ in (89.5×91.5 cm) Width of fabric: 36 in (91.5 cm) Pattern: 6417. *The illustrated sample, of printed wool, has a 'Queen Square' selvedge mark.*

2 LARGE STEM printed onto wool, cotton & linen. Copied Morris *c*. 1868 from a Bannister Hall printed cotton of the 1830s. Block-printed Clarkson. Repeat: 34×36 in (86.5×91.5 cm) Width: 36 in (91.5 cm) wool & cotton 54 in (137 cm) linen. Patterns: 6886 (wool), 6145 (cotton), 6150 (linen). Philadelphia Museum of Art.

3 COILING TRAIL printed cotton. Copied Morris *c*. 1868 from a Bannister Hall printed cotton of the 1830s. Block-printed Clarkson on cotton & possibly wool. Sample size: 6×4 in (15×10 cm) Width: 36 in (91.5 cm). Pattern: 6898, 1 colourway only. Part of a swatch sample book, William Morris Gallery, Walthamstow.

4 JASMINE TRAIL or JASMINE TRELLIS printed cotton. Designed Morris 1868–70. Block-printed Clarkson & later Thomas Wardle & Sons, Leek. Repeat: $17\frac{7}{8} \times 18$ in (45×45.5 cm) Width: 36 in (91.5 cm) Pattern: 966. *Morris's earliest known original design for textiles. Possibly also intended for wallpaper but never used.*

5 UTRECHT VELVET embossed mohair plush. 'Discovered and revived' Morris *c*. 1871. Probably adopted from range of J. Aldam Heaton, Manchester. Repeat: 26×24 in (66×61 cm) Width: 24 in (61 cm). Available from Morris & Co. in at least 14 colourways. *The design & technique of fabric inspired by 17th-century furnishing velvets.*

6 TULIP AND WILLOW printed linen. Designed Morris 1873. Block-printed in aniline dyes Clarkson's & registered by them 30 December 1873. After 1883 indigo-discharged at Merton Abbey. Repeat: $17\frac{1}{4} \times 17\frac{1}{4}$ in (44×44 cm). Width: 36 in (91.5 cm) Pattern: 1785. Original design: Birmingham. Blocks (22): Walthamstow.

7 TULIP printed cotton. Designed Morris, registered 15 April 1875. Block-printed Wardle. Repeat: $21\frac{1}{2} \times 9$ in (54.5 × 23 cm). Width: 36 in (91.5 cm) Patterns: 967, 987, 1033, 1059, 1087, 1164, 1368, 1382, 4107, 1626 & others. Original design & blocks (12): Walthamstow.

8 MARIGOLD printed onto silk, tusser silk, cotton & linen union. Designed Morris as a wallpaper, registerd 15 April 1875, used concurrently as a fabric. Block-printed Wardle. Repeat: 9×9 in (23 × 23 cm). Width: 36 in (91.5 cm) cotton & linen 19 in (48 cm) silk. Patterns: 960, 1609 (union), 2171.

◁ 9 LARKSPUR printed onto silk & cotton & woven as a silk damask. Designed Morris & registered as a textile 15 April 1875, used as a wallpaper from 1872. Block-printed Wardle. Power-loom jacquard woven by J.O.Nicholson of Macclesfield. Repeat: $12\frac{5}{8} \times 18$ in (32 × 45.5 cm). Width: 36 in (91.5 cm) printed cotton 19 in (48 cm) silk, 27 in (68.5 cm) woven silk. Patterns: 1203, 1138 (both printed).

10 CARNATION printed cotton. Probably designed Kate Faulkner. Registered 15 October 1875. Block-printed Wardle. Repeat $9\frac{1}{2} \times 18\frac{1}{4}$ in (24 × 46.5 cm). Width: 36 in (91.5 cm) Patterns: 449, 1026. *Designed some months before registration as this design is named in a letter from Morris to Wardle in September 1875.*

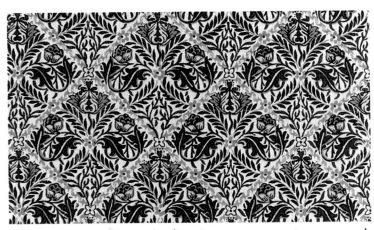

11 INDIAN DIAPER printed cotton, woven cotton & woven wool. Designed Morris before December 1875. Block-printed Wardle. Power-loom jacquard woven by contractors. Repeat (print: $4\frac{1}{2} \times 4\frac{1}{2}$ in (11.5 × 11.5 cm) Width: 36 in (91.5 cm) print. 50 in (127 cm) weave. Patterns: 1380 (print), 7521 (woven wool) in 3 colourways, 7635 (woven cotton) in 4 colours.

12 TULIP AND ROSE 3-ply carpeting & fabric, woven silk & linen & woven silk & cotton. Designed Morris, registered as a fabric 20 January 1876. 3-plys woven by Heckmondwike. Repeat: (3-ply) 35×17 in (89 × 43 cm). Width 36 in (91.5 cm) 3-ply, 54 in (137 cm) silk and linen. Patterns: 5117, 8819, 7640.

148

13 ANEMONE silk & wool fabric & silk damask. Designed Morris, registered 8 February 1876. Power-loom jacquard woven by H.C.McCrea. Repeat: $21\frac{1}{2} \times 10\frac{1}{4}$ in $(54.5 \times 26$ cm$)$. Width: 54 in $(137$ cm$)$ Pattern: 1739, 4 colourways. Design: Birmingham. *In the early 20th century a smaller version was power-loom woven in wool & silk.*

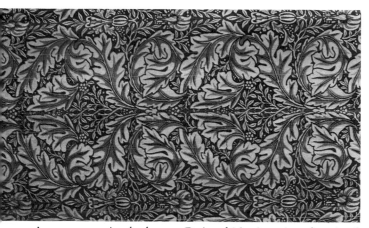

15 ACANTHUS printed velveteen. Designed Morris, registered 25 April 1876. Block-printed onto cotton velveteen Wardle. Repeat: 25×23 in $(63.5 \times 58.5$ cm$)$. Width: 24 in. Patterns: 1677, 1760, 1772. Contemporary photograph of design in Thomas Wardle album, V & A. *Printing trials did not start until September 1877.*

14 HONEYCOMB 3-ply carpeting & fabric, woven silk & wool, woven wool & cotton. Designed Morris, registered 11 February 1876. 3-plys woven Heckmondwike, silk & wool H.C.McCrea, later Merton Abbey. Repeat: $14\frac{3}{4} \times 8\frac{3}{4}$ in $(37 \times 22$ cm$)$. Width: 36 in $(91.5$ cm$)$ 3-ply, 54 in $(137$ cm$)$ other fabrics, later at 50 in $(127$ cm$)$. Patterns: 5124 (3-ply), 1771, 1912. Original design: Walthamstow. Private Collection.

16 IRIS printed cotton. Designed Morris, registered 25 April 1876. Block-printed Wardle. Repeat: $19\frac{1}{4} \times 9$ in $(49 \times 23$ cm$)$. Width: 36 in $(91.5$ cm$)$. Patterns: 6013, Preliminary design (for block-cutter): Berger Collection. *Trial in olive (1063) & curtain with 'Queen Square' selvedge in V & A. Morris called it 'Flower de luce'.*

17 BLUEBELL or COLUMBINE printed onto cotton and linen. Designed Morris, 1st printing trials 4 May 1876. Block-printed Wardle. Repeat: $18 \times 9\frac{1}{2}$ in $(45.5 \times 24$ cm$)$ Width: 36 in $(91.5$ cm$)$. Patterns: 2649, 4860, 6693. Design: V & A. *Original design labelled with both names but Bluebell crossed out.*

18 SNAKESHEAD printed cotton. Design Morris 1876. Block-printed Wardle. Repeat: $11\frac{5}{8} \times 9$ in (29.5×23 cm). Width: 36 in (91.5 cm) Patterns: 1573, 1837, 1840. Original design: Birmingham. Blocks (4): Walthamstow. *One length of fabric has 'Registered 1877' printed on it but no registration has been found.*

19 LITTLE CHINTZ printed onto cotton and linen. Designed Morris 1876. Block-printed Wardle. Repeat: $4\frac{3}{4} \times 4\frac{1}{2}$ in (12×11.5 cm). Width: 36 in (91.5 cm) Pattern: 1781. *Not as thought a small-scale version of 'Pomegranate'. Appears in early 1877 Wardle pattern book. V & A sample has 'Queen Square' selvedge denoting 1876 origin.*

20 AFRICAN MARIGOLD printed onto silk, tusser silk, cotton & challis. Designed Morris, registered 7 October 1876. Block-printed Wardle. Repeat: $17\frac{1}{2} \times 36$ in (44.5×91.5 cm). Width: 36 in (91.5 cm) cotton, challis, 19 in (48 cm) silk. Patterns: 1989, 1269, 1770, 4683 (all cottons). Original design: Walthamstow. *1st dye trials started 4 May 1876.*

21 HONEYSUCKLE printed onto linen, cotton, combed cotton, challis, silk, tusser silk & velveteen. Designed Morris, registered 11 October 1876. Block-printed Wardle. Repeat: 30×36 in (76×91.5 cm). Width: 36 in (91.5 cm) linen & cotton, silks vary $19 - 24$ in (48.5×61 cm). Patterns: 1479, 1793, 1794, 1795, 7415, 1592. Original design: Birmingham.

22 CROWN IMPERIAL woven cotton & MOHAIR DAMASK (smaller version) woven wool & mohair. Designed Morris, registered 18 November 1876. Power-loom jacquard woven, wool & mohair by Dixon, Bradford. Repeat: (*Crown Imperial*) $15\frac{3}{4} \times 10$ in (40×25.5 cm). Width: 36 in (91.5 cm), (*Mohair Damask*) 54 in (137 cm). Patterns: 495-8, 801, 1033 (*Crown Imperial*), 141, 234 (*Mohair Damask*).

23 SWIVEL woven cotton, woven cotton & silk, woven silk & wool. Designed Morris, 1877. Woven contractors, later at Merton Abbey. Repeat: 14×8 in (35.5×20.5 cm). Width: 50 in (127 cm) cotton, 36 in (91.5 cm) mixed fabrics. Woven in 2 scales. Patterns: 460, 1916. Original design: Walthamstow.

25 POMEGRANATE printed onto cotton and tusser silk. Designed Morris, registered 22 June 1877. Block-printed Wardle. Repeat: $13\frac{1}{2} \times 9\frac{1}{2}$ in (34.5×24 cm). Width: 36 in (91.5 cm) cotton, 19 in (48 cm) silk. Patterns 1686, 1826, both cotton. *Samples in silk, combed cotton, & cotton twill in Wardle pattern books.*

26 PEONY printed cotton. Designed Kate Faulkner, registered 22 June 1877. Block-printed Wardle. Repeat: $11\frac{1}{2} \times 12$ in (29×30.5 cm). Width: 36 in (91.5 cm) Patterns: 1659, 9406.

24 WILLOW woven silk. Adapted from an earlier wallpaper designed Morris 1874, 1st woven 1877. Hand-loom jacquard woven Queen Square, after at Merton Abbey. Sample size: $6\frac{7}{8} \times 13\frac{1}{2}$ in (17.5×34.5 cm). Width: unknown. Woven in at least 6 colourways. Collection of Sanford and Helen Berger.

27 VINE AND POMEGRANATE 3-ply carpeting & fabric. Designed Morris or Kate Faulkner *c.* 1877. Woven at Heckmondwike. Repeat: $16 \times 16\frac{1}{4}$ in (40.5×41 cm). Width: 36 in (91.5 cm). Pattern: 5134, in at least 7 colourways.

28 Pattern of sunflowers & acanthus leaves, printed onto silk, cotton & combed cotton. Designed Kate Faulkner or Morris, registered 13 January 1878. Repeat: $17\frac{1}{2} \times 18$ in (44.5×45.5 cm). Width: 36 in (91.5 cm) cottons, 19 in (48 cm) silk. Patterns: 1853, 1854, 1867, 1880, 1903, 1904. Public Record Office, Kew.

29 BIRD woven woollen double cloth. Designed Morris 1878. Hand-loom jacquard woven Queen Square, later Merton Abbey. Repeat: $28\frac{1}{2} \times 18\frac{1}{2}$ in (72.5 × 47 cm). Width: 54 in (137 cm). Patterns: 5148, 2828 (large scale, 3 colourways). Original design: Kelmscott House Collection. Private collection at Kelmscott Manor

30 PEACOCK AND DRAGON woven woollen fabric. Design Morris 1878. Hand-loom jacquard woven Queen Square, later Merton Abbey. Repeat: $43 \times 35\frac{1}{2}$ in (109 × 90 cm). Width: 72 in (183 cm), also 54 in (137 cm). Patterns: 200 (wider in 5 colourways) 5623 (2 colourways). Original design illustrated in L.F.Day (p. 4). Private Collection.

31 FLOWER GARDEN woven silk, woven silk and wool. Designed Morris 1879. Hand-loom jacquard woven Queen Square, later Merton Abbey. Repeat: $15\frac{3}{4} \times 13\frac{1}{2}$ (40 × 43.5 cm) silk, $19 \times 13\frac{1}{2}$ in (48 × 34.5 cm) silk & wool. Width: 27 in (68.5 cm), in silk in 4 colourways, 3 in silk & wool. *The colours were chosen to 'suggest the beauties of inlaid metal'.*

32 ACANTHUS woven silk damask, cotton & silk, woollen damask. Designed Morris, registered 15 May 1879. Hand-loom jacquard woven Queen Square, later Merton Abbey. From 1924 cotton and silk fabric by East Anglia Weaving Co. Repeat: $20 \times 13\frac{1}{2}$ in (51 × 34.5 cm). Width: 50 in (127 cm). Pattern: 1892, in at least 12 colourways.

33 BIRD AND VINE woven woollen fabric. Designed Morris, registered 15 May 1879. Hand-loom jacquard woven Queen Square, later Merton Abbey. Repeat: 27 × 15¼ in (68.5 × 38.5 cm). Width: 72 in (183 cm). Pattern: 5064, in 11 colourways. Working drawing: Illustrated L. F. Day (page 5). *Very popular for church furnishings.*

34 DOVE AND ROSE silk & wool double cloth. Designed Morris 1879. First woven by outworkers for Alexander Morton & Co. later Merton Abbey. Repeat: 20½ × 18 in (52 × 45.5 cm). Width: 36 in (91.5 cm). Point-paper: Walthamstow. Original design: Birmingham. In 5 colourways & 2 scales. *Small trial sample in V & A brocaded with gold.*

35 MADRAS MUSLIN woven silk & cotton leno. Designed Morris 1881. Woven on gauze loom Morton & Co. Repeat: 22½ × 6¾ in (57 × 17 cm). Width: 72 in (183 cm). In 3 colourways with pattern picked out in cream, pink or yellow.

37 OAK woven silk damask. Designed Morris 1881 Power-loom jacquard woven J. O. Nicholson, later hand woven Merton Abbey. Repeat: 32 × 20½ in (81.5 × 52 cm). Width: 63 in (160 cm). Pattern: 1540, in numerous colours. *Also used as a background silk for the firm's embroideries designed by May Morris and Henry Dearle.*

36 ST JAMES woven silk damask & figured silk. Designed Morris, registered August 1881. Power-loom jacquard woven J. O. Nicholson, later hand-woven Merton Abbey. Repeat: 39½ × 21 in (100.5 × 53.5 cm). Width: 63 in (160 cm). Available 'to order' in 6 colourways. Design: Kelmscott House Collection. William Morris Gallery, Walthamstow.

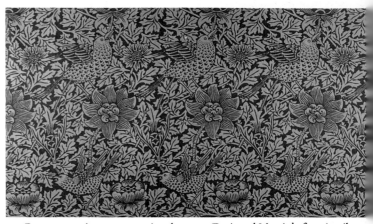

◁ 38 BRER RABBIT or BROTHER RABBIT printed cotton. Designed Morris, registered 20 May 1882. Indigo discharged & block-printed Merton Abbey. Repeat: $13\frac{1}{4} \times 9$ in (33.5×23 cm). Width: 36 in (91.5 cm). Patterns: 6, 51, 441, 988, 2286. Working drawing: Illustrated L.F.Day (p. 10). Blocks (2); Walthamstow.

39 BIRD AND ANEMONE printed cotton. Designed Morris before April 1881, registered 17 June 1882. Used as wallpaper & fabric. Indigo discharged & block-printed Merton Abbey. Repeat: $21\frac{1}{4} \times 9$ in (54×23 cm). Width: 36 in (91.5 cm). Patterns: 17, 31, 350, 413, 1351, 2037, 6157. Blocks (7): Walthamstow.

40 ROSE AND THISTLE printed cotton. Designed Morris before April 1881. Indigo discharged & block-printed Merton Abbey. Repeat: $23\frac{3}{4} \times 9$ in (60.5×23 cm). Width: 36 in (91.5 cm). Patterns: 10 (indigo discharged). 237, 1525, 1645, 3117. Original design: V & A. Blocks (4): Walthamstow.

41 WREATHNET printed cotton. Designed Morris 1882. Indigo discharged, madder vat dyed & block-printed Merton Abbey. Repeat: $5\frac{3}{4} \times 4\frac{3}{8}$ in (14.5×11.5 cm). Width: originally 27 in (68.5 cm) as lining fabric, later 36 in (91.5 cm). Pattern: 289. Working drawing: Birmingham. Original design: V & A.

42 BORAGE printed cotton. Designed Morris 1883. Indigo discharged & block-printed Merton Abbey. Repeat: $4\frac{3}{4} \times 4\frac{1}{2}$ in (12×11.5 cm). Width: 27 in (68.5 cm) later 36 in (91.5 cm). Printed in 2 scales; largest in red & yellow. Later samples indigo discharge printed. Block number I & paper fent: Walthamstow.

43 CORNCOCKLE printed cotton. Designed Morris, registered 22 February 1883. Block-printed Merton Abbey. Repeat: $22\frac{1}{4} \times 9$ in (56.5×23 cm). Width: 36 in (91.5 cm). Patterns: 383, 676, 1913. Blocks: (10) Walthamstow. *An example of Morris's designs where the title flower plays a small part.*

44 CAMPION woven wool, 3-ply carpeting & fabric. Designed Morris, registered 8 March 1883. Hand-loom jacquard woven Merton Abbey, 3-ply Heckmondwike. Repeat: 3-ply $33\frac{1}{2} \times 36$ in (85×91.5 cm). Width: 36 in (91.5 cm), fabric 72 in (183 cm). Patterns: 3-ply 2293, 3 colourways, 100 fabric, 6 colourways. *Used as a wall-covering in the drawing room at 28, Bruton St.* Cooper-Hewitt Museum, New York.

45 VIOLET AND COLUMBINE woven wool & mohair fabric. Designed Morris, registered 7 April 1883. Hand-loom jacquard woven Merton Abbey. Repeat: $41 \times 35\frac{3}{4}$ in (104×91 cm). Width: 72 in (183 cm). Pattern: 300, 4 colourways. Original design: V & A. *Shown for first time Boston Foreign Fair, 1883.*

46 STRAWBERRY THIEF printed cotton. Designed Morris, registered 11 May 1883. Indigo discharged Merton Abbey. Repeat: $20\frac{1}{2} \times 17\frac{1}{2}$ in (52×44.5 cm). Width: 36 in (91.5 cm). Pattern: 933, 1 colourway. Blocks (24): V & A. *These include original re-cut blues for surface prints.*

47 EVENLODE printed cotton. Designed Morris, registered 2 September 1883. Indigo discharged & block-printed Merton Abbey. Repeat: 21×9 in (53.5×22.5 cm). Width: 36 in (91.5 cm). Patterns: 1454, 6867, 1451. Original design: V & A. Blocks (33): Walthamstow. *The first Morris design named after a Thames tributary.*

48 WEY printed cotton & velveteen. Designed Morris c. 1883. Indigo discharged, block-printed cotton & surface block-printed velveteen Merton Abbey. Repeat: 9×12 in (23.5×30.5 cm). Width: cotton 36 in (91.5 cm), velveteen 27 in (68.5 cm). Patterns: cottons 1711, 1531, 1664, velveteen 5589. Original design: Birmingham.

49 KENNET printed cotton & velveteen & woven silk. Designed Morris, registered 18 October 1883. Indigo discharged, block-printed & woven Merton Abbey. Repeat: $27\frac{1}{2} \times 8\frac{3}{4}$ in (70×22 cm). Width: cotton 36 in (91.5 cm), velveteen & silk 27 in (68.5 cm). Patterns: 1828, 2007, 2031, 2094, 5982. Working drawing: Birmingham. Design & blocks (6): Walthamstow.

50 WINDRUSH printed onto cotton & linen. Designed Morris, registered 18 October 1883. Madder vat dyed & block-printed Merton Abbey. Repeat: $20\frac{1}{2} \times 17\frac{1}{2}$ in (52×44.5 cm). Width: 36 in (91.5 cm). Patterns: 1020, 1227, 1960, 1990, 2040, 5975, 4886. Design: Kelmscott House Collection. Blocks (17): Walthamstow.

51 FLOWERPOT printed cotton. Designed Morris, registered 18 October 1883. Indigo discharged Merton Abbey. Repeat: $4\frac{1}{2} \times 4\frac{1}{2}$ in (11.5×11.5 cm). Width: 27 in (68.5 cm), later 36 in (91.5 cm). Pattern: 1431, discharged colourway only. Working drawing (with instructions to block-cutter): Birmingham.

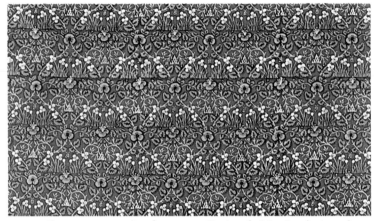

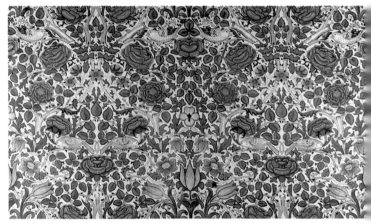

52 EYEBRIGHT printed cotton. Designed Morris, registered 23 November 1883. Indigo discharged Merton Abbey. Repeat: $5\frac{1}{4} \times 3\frac{1}{2}$ in (13.5×9 cm). Width: 27 in (68.5 cm) later 36 in (91.5 cm). Patterns: 1075, 1124. Original design: Birmingham.

53 ROSE printed onto cotton & linen. Designed Morris, registered 8 December 1883. Indigo discharged Merton Abbey. Repeat: 20×17 in (50.5×43.5 cm). Width: 36 in (91.5 cm). Patterns: 1050, 1494, 7283. Blocks: (19) Walthamstow. Design: illustrated L.F.Day (p. 25).

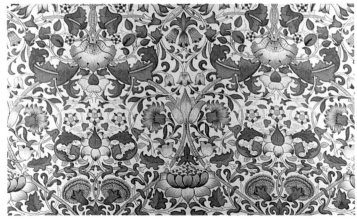

54 LODDEN printed onto cotton & linen. Designed Morris, 1884. Indigo discharged & block-printed Merton Abbey. Repeat: $24 \times 17\frac{1}{2}$ (61×44.5 cm). Width: 36 in (91.5 cm). Patterns: 1494 (discharged) 579,700,6561 (surface prints). Original design: illustrated L.F.Day (p. 17). *The 3 surface prints are catalogued by Morris & Co. as 'light colourings'*.

55 GRANADA woven silk velvet brocaded with gilt thread. Designed Morris, 1884. Woven, with blue areas block-printed Merton Abbey. Repeat: $15\frac{3}{4} \times 8\frac{3}{4}$ in (40×22 cm). Width: 27 in (68.5 cm). *The only velvet woven at Merton Abbey for which a special loom was set up. Only 20 yd (1829 cm) woven at a cost of £10 a yard.*

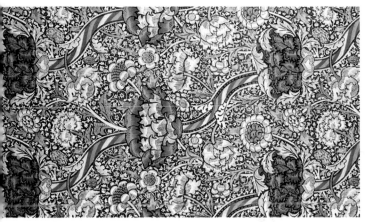

56 WANDLE printed cotton. Designed Morris, registered 28 July 1884. Indigo discharged Merton Abbey. Repeat: $38\frac{3}{4} \times 17\frac{1}{2}$ in (98.5×44.5 cm). Width: 36 in (91.5 cm). Pattern: 1899, discharged colourway only. Original design: illustrated L.F.Day (p. 11). Blocks (32): Walthamstow. *So entitled 'to honour the helpful stream'.*

57 CRAY printed onto cotton & linen. Designed Morris 1884. Block-printed Merton Abbey. Repeat: $36\frac{1}{4} \times 17\frac{3}{4}$ in (92×45 cm). Width: 36 in (91.5 cm). Patterns: 2015, 2109, 8245, 8171 (cottons) 3377 (linen). Blocks (34): Walthamstow. *Morris's most complex & expensive design requiring the most blocks.*

58 LEA printed cotton. Designed Morris, registered 2 February 1885. Indigo discharged & block-printed Merton Abbey. Repeat: $16 \times 9\frac{1}{2}$ in (40.5×24 cm). Width: 36 in (91.5 cm). Patterns: 2461, 2950, 3015, 3232, 3523, 3709. *A similar design to 'Wallflower' wallpaper.*

59 MEDWAY printed onto cotton & linen. Designed Morris, registered 21 September 1885. Indigo discharged & block-printed Merton Abbey. Repeat: $18\frac{1}{4} \times 12$ in (46.5×30.5 cm). Width: 36 in (91.5 cm). Patterns: 5741 (discharged) 7128 (surface printed). Original design: Birmingham. Working drawing for block-cutters: Walthamstow. *Used as 'Garden Tulip' wallpaper.*

60 AVON printed cotton. Possibly designed Dearle c. 1887. Block-printed Merton Abbey. Repeat: 29×35 in (73.5×89 cm). Width: 36 in (91.5 cm). Patterns: 6737, 7562. Design: Walthamstow.

61 CHERWELL printed onto velveteen & cotton. Designed Dearle, 1887. Block-printed Merton Abbey. Repeat: $39\frac{1}{3} \times 25\frac{3}{4}$ in (100×65.5 cm). Width: 27 in (68.5 cm) velveteen, 36 in (91.5 cm) cotton. Patterns: 3455, 5074, 6101 (velveteen) 9041, 9363 (cottons). *From 1891 used as 'Double Bough' wallpaper.*

62 SEVERN printed onto velveteen & cotton. Designed Dearle, 1887–90. Block-printed Merton Abbey. Repeat: $25\frac{1}{2} \times 27$ in (64.5×68.5 cm). Width: 27 in (68.5 cm) velveteen, later 36 in (91.5 cm) for cotton. Patterns: 7286 (velveteen) 9424, 9559, 9775, 9782 (cottons). Private collection at Kelmscott Manor.

63 TRENT printed linen. Designed Dearle, 1888. Block-printed Merton Abbey. Repeat: $55\frac{1}{4} \times 35$ in (140.5×89 cm). Width: 36 in (91.5 cm). Patterns: 6802, 7760, 7826, 9101, 9227. Original design: illustrated L.F.Day (p. 31). *The most expensive in the Morris & Co. range & the only pattern printed exclusively on linen. Used in 'Bullerswood' 1889.*

64 ISPAHAN woven woollen fabric. Designed Morris c. 1888. Hand-loom jacquard woven Merton Abbey. Repeat: 44×26 in (112×66 cm). Width: 54 in (137 cm). Pattern: 789 in 3 colourways. *Exhibited Arts & Crafts Exhibition 1889. A 4th sample in the V & A pattern book is marked '4/789-new scale.*

65 BROCATEL woven silk & woollen fabric. Designed Morris or Dearle c. 1888. Hand-loom jacquard woven Merton Abbey. Repeat: $28\frac{1}{2} \times 18$ in (72.5×45.5 cm). Width: 54 in (137 cm). Pattern: 525 in 2 colourways. *Exhibited Arts & Crafts Exhibition 1889.*

66 GOLDEN BOUGH woven silk & linen fabric. Designed Morris or Dearle *c.* 1888. Hand-loom jacquard woven Merton Abbey. Repeat: 27 × 18 in (68.5 × 45.5 cm). Width: 54 in (137 cm). Pattern: 1189 in 4 colourways. Original design: Birmingham. *A popular fabric for church furnishings. Used for Stanmore Hall.*

67 SMALL FIGURE or SILK DAMASK woven silk. Probably designed Dearle, 1888. Hand-loom jacquard woven possibly Merton Abbey. Repeat: 3 × 3¼ in (7.5 × 8 cm). Width: 24 in (61 cm). Pattern: 1500 in at least 4 colourways. *A substantial length of the silk was sold at the Kelmscott Manor sale, 1939 (lot 164).*

68 TULIP AND NET woven wool, woven wool & silk fabric. Designed Dearle 1888–9. Hand-loom jacquard woven Merton Abbey. Repeat: 26 × 17¼ in (66 × 44 cm). Width: 72 in (183 cm). Pattern: 812, 1 colour in woollen fabric, 2 in silk & wool. *A sample in V & A book is marked 'Mis-dyed, not a standard colour, Feb. 22. '89'.*

69 PERSIAN BROCATEL woven silk & wool, woven silk. Designed Dearle *c.* 1890. Woven in 2 weights on jacquard hand-loom Merton Abbey. Repeat: light-weight silk tissue 18½ × 13½ in (47 × 34.5 cm). Width: 27 in (69 cm), wool and silk, 54 in (137 cm). Pattern: 765, silk & wool in 1 colourway, tissue in 4.

70 FLORENCE printed velveteen. Designed Dearle *c.* 1890. Block-printed Merton Abbey. Repeat: 16½ × 12½ in (43 × 32 cm). Width: 27 in (68.5 cm). Patterns: 6536, 6590. *A sample in the V & A velveteen swatch book says 'Not kept in stock can only be made when 30 or more yards ordered'.* Musées Royaux d'Art et d'Histoire, Brussels.

71 VINE woven woollen fabric. Designed Dearle *c.* 1890. Hand-loom jacquard woven Merton Abbey. Repeat: 35 × 16 in (89 × 40.5 cm). Width: 54 in (137 cm). Pattern: 1901 in 3 colourways. Private collection.

72 GOLDEN STEM woven woollen fabric. Designed Dearle c. 1890.
Hand-loom jacquard woven Merton Abbey. Sample size (no full height
available): $37 \times 16\frac{3}{4}$ in (94×42.5 cm). Width: 54 in (137 cm). Pattern:
1092 in 4 colourways. Private collection at Kelmscott Manor.

73 SUNFLOWER woven woollen fabric. Designed Dearle c. 1890.
Hand-loom jacquard woven Merton Abbey. Sample size (no full height
available): $28\frac{3}{4} \times 15\frac{1}{2}$ in (73×39.5 cm). Width: 54 in (137 cm). Pattern:
1879 in 1 colourway. Private collection.

74 HELENA woven silk & wool double cloth. Designed Dearle c. 1890.
Power-loom jacquard woven Alexander Morton & Co. Sample size (no
full height available): $24\frac{1}{2} \times 16$ in (62×40.5 cm). Width: 52 in
(132 cm). Pattern: 3354, in 4 colourways. Original design: Waltham-
stow. Working drawing: Berger Collection.

75 TRAIL printed cotton. Designed Dearle as a wallpaper (*Flora*) in
1891, used soon after as a fabric. Block-printed Merton Abbey. Repeat:
14×9 in (35.5×23 cm). Width: 39 in (99 cm). Pattern: 7321. *May
Morris described this as 'an experiment in rather thin smallish pattern, not very
successful'.*

76 DAFFODIL printed cotton. Designed Dearle c. 1891. Block-printed
Merton Abbey. Repeat: 14×9 in (35.5×23 cm) Width: 36 in
(91.5 cm). Patterns: 6871, 8777, 9497. Original design & blocks (10):
Walthamstow. Illustrated in the *Art Journal* (1891) p. 109.

77 MOLE printed velveteen. Designed Dearle after 1892. Block-printed
Merton Abbey. Sample size: (no full repeat available) $10\frac{1}{2} \times 7\frac{1}{2}$ in
(27×19 cm). Width: 27 in (69 cm). Pattern: 6252. *Only known as small
samples in 2 swatch pattern books. Does not appear in Merton Abbey dye-book.*

78 YARE printed cotton. Designed Dearle, after 1892. Block-printed Merton Abbey. Repeat: in 2 sizes, 14 × 14 in (36.5 × 36.5 cm) and 7 × 12 in (18 × 30.5 cm). Width: 36 in (91.5 cm). Patterns: 4980, 5200. *A design labelled 'Yare' at Walthamstow is of a different pattern.* Private collection at Kelmscott Manor.

79 SHANNON printed cotton. Designed Dearle, after 1892. Block-printed Merton Abbey. Repeat size unknown. Width: 36 in (91.5 cm), There are 2 small samples of this textile in the V & A pattern book. Design illustrated, *Studio Yearbook*, 1917. *A similar design with different flowers in Berger Collection.*

80 Unidentified design, probably GRAVENEY. Designed Dearle after 1892. Block-printed Merton Abbey. Repeat: $17\frac{1}{8} \times 17\frac{7}{8}$ in (43.5 × 45.5 cm). Width: 36 in (91.5 cm). Patterns: 2978, 4372. There are 2 small samples of this pattern in the V & A pattern book. Norderfjeldske Kunstindustrimuseum, Trondheim.

81 Unidentified design, probably DERWENT or BROOK. Designed Dearle after 1892. Block-printed Merton Abbey. Sample size: $4 \times 5\frac{3}{4}$ in (10 × 14.5 cm) Width: 36 in (91.5 cm). Pattern: 256, 9147. *This is the only known sample of this textile.*

82 ROSE AND LILY woven silk & wool & woven silk tissue. Designed Dearle, 1893. Hand-loom jacquard woven Merton Abbey. Repeat: $24\frac{3}{4} \times 13\frac{3}{4}$ in (63 × 35 cm). Width: 27 in (68.5 cm). Available in 4 colourways: on white, blue, red or dark green grounds.

83 DIAGONAL TRAIL woven woollen fabric. Designed Dearle c. 1893. Hand-loom jacquard woven Merton Abbey. Repeat: $18\frac{1}{4} \times 16\frac{1}{2}$ in (46.5 × 42 cm). Width: 54 in (137 cm). Pattern: 1192, in 2 colourways. *Used on the walls of the great parlour at Wightwick Manor, part of the new extensions, c. 1893.*

84 WILLOW BOUGHS printed cotton. Designed Morris as a wallpaper in 1887, adapted for fabric *c.* 1895. Block-printed Merton Abbey. Sample size: 4 × 6 in (10 × 15 cm) Width: 36 in (91.5 cm). Pattern: 682. Part of a swatch pattern book. William Morris Gallery, Walthamstow.

85 SCROLL, LITTLE SCROLL or WILLOW printed cotton. Adapted *c.* 1895 from background pattern of *Powdered* wallpaper. Designed Morris, 1874. Indigo discharged & block-printed Merton Abbey. Repeat: 11½ × 11¾ in (29 × 30 cm). Patterns: 9419 at least 2 colourways. Block (1): Walthamstow. *This pattern is different from both the 'Willow' wallpaper and woven textile.* Private collection at Kelmscott Manor.

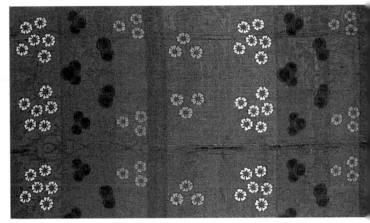

87 APPLE woven linen and silk fabric. Designed Dearle 1895–1900. Hand-loom jacquard woven Merton Abbey. Repeat: 24½ × 18¼ in (61.5 × 46.5 cm). Width: 54 in (137 cm). Pattern: 1902, in 3 colourways. Design: Berger Collection. *From 1915, in artificial silk it cost 18s 6d, in silk, 21s a yard.*

86 COMPTON printed cotton. Designed Dearle, registered as a wallpaper & textile. 27 February 1896. Block-printed Merton Abbey from wallpaper blocks. Repeat: 53¼ × 26½ in (136 × 67.5 cm). Width: 27 in (68.5 cm). Patterns: 502, 685. Working drawing & Blocks (34): Walthamstow. *Designed for Compton Hall, Wolverhampton.*

88 BLUEBELL 3-ply woven woollen carpeting & fabric. Designed Dearle, 1895–1900. Woven Heckmondwike. Design size: 14½ × 11⅞ (37 × 30 cm) Width: 36 in (91.5 cm). Pattern: 5140 in at least 2 colourways. Design: Berger Collection.

89 POPPY woven silk & linen. Designed Dearle 1895–1900. Hand-loom jacquard woven Merton Abbey. Repeat: $26\frac{1}{4} \times 26\frac{1}{2}$ in (66.5 × 67.5 cm) Width: 54 in. Pattern: 1905, available in 1 colourway. Museum Bellerive, Zurich.

90 TULIP woven woollen fabric. Designed Dearle, 1895–1900. Hand-loom jacquard woven Merton Abbey. Repeat: $16 \times 23\frac{3}{4}$ in (40.5 × 60.5 cm). Width: 54 in (137 cm). Pattern: 1986 available in 3 colourways.

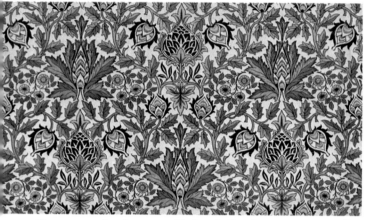

91 PERSIAN printed cotton. Designed Dearle 1895–1900. Indigo discharged Merton Abbey. Repeat: $18\frac{3}{4} \times 17\frac{1}{2}$ in (47.5 × 44.5 cm). Width: 36 in (91.5 cm). Pattern: 7958, in 1 colourway. Museum Bellerive, Zurich.

93 CROSS TWIGS woven silk & linen fabric. Designed Dearle c. 1898. Hand-loom jacquard woven Merton Abbey. Repeat: $26\frac{3}{4} \times 18$ in (68 × 45.5 cm). Width: 54 in (137 cm). Pattern: 592 in 2 colourways. *Exhibited at the Arts & Crafts Exhibition of 1899. A trial sample at the V & A shows it in various colourways.*

92 POMEGRANATE woven woollen fabric. Designed Dearle 1895–1900. Hand-loom woven jacquard woven Merton Abbey. Repeat: $27 \times 14\frac{1}{2}$ in (68.5 × 36.5 cm) Width: 54 in (137 cm). Pattern: 400 in 1 colourway only. Working drawing: Berger Collection. Private collection.

94 SQUIRREL or FOX AND GRAPE woven woollen fabric. Designed Dearle *c.* 1898. Hand-loom jacquard woven Merton Abbey. Repeat: $8\frac{1}{8} \times 17\frac{3}{4}$ in (20.5 × 45 cm). Width: 54 in (137 cm). Pattern: 3455 in 3 colourways. Original design & working tracing: Berger Collection. Design illustrated Berger Collection.

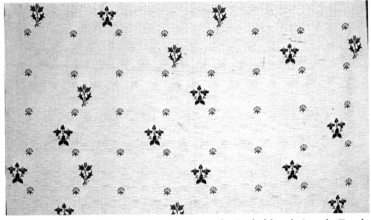

96 BROCADE woven cotton & wool. Probably designed Dearle 1900–1905. Jacquard loom woven possibly Merton Abbey. Repeat: $16\frac{1}{2} \times 19\frac{1}{2}$ in (41 × 49.5 cm). Width: 52 in (132 cm). *This is the only known sample & was bought from 449 Oxford Street, 1905.* Museum Bellerive, Zurich.

95 ELMCOTE woven wool & mohair fabric. Designed Dearle *c.* 1900. Hand-loom jacquard woven Merton Abbey. Repeat: 25 × 17 in (63.5 × 43 cm). Width: 54 in (137 cm). Pattern: 1899 in 3 colourways. Original design & working tracing: Berger Collection. Private collection at Kelmscott Manor.

97 POWDERED printed cotton. Designed Morris as a wallpaper, 1874, adapted for fabric *c.* 1902. Block-printed Merton Abbey. Repeat: 12 × 12 in (30.5 × 30.5 cm) wallpaper $10\frac{1}{2} \times 10\frac{1}{2}$ in (26.5 × 26.5 cm). Width: 36 in (91.5 cm). Blocks (8): Walthamstow. *Reprinted from the original blocks in 1952 by Stead McAlpin & Co. Ltd.* William Morris Gallery, Walthamstow.

98 RIBBLE printed cotton. Probably designed Kathleen Kersey, design registered Donald Brothers, 20 February 1904. Block-printed Donald Brothers, later Wardle. Size of sample: 9 × 6 in (23 × 15 cm) Width: 36 in (91.5 cm). Patterns: 209, 309, 408, 509. Wardle Pattern Book, Whitworth Art Gallery, University of Manchester.

99 COLNE printed cotton. Probably designed Kathleen Kersey as a wallpaper *c.* 1905. Indigo discharged & block-printed Merton Abbey. Repeat; 13 × 13¾ in (33 × 35 cm). Width: 27 in (68.5 cm). Patterns: 2613, 5654. *Although printed with wallpaper blocks no trace of this design as a wallpaper has been found.*

100 BOURNE printed cotton. Designed Dearle *c.* 1905 Block-printed Merton Abbey. Repeat: 14¼ × 17½ in (36 × 44.5 cm). Width: 36 in (91.5 cm). Pattern: 7775, 1 colourway. Design: Berger Collection. Illustrated in *The Studio*, 1906 (p. 184). William Morris Gallery, Walthamstow.

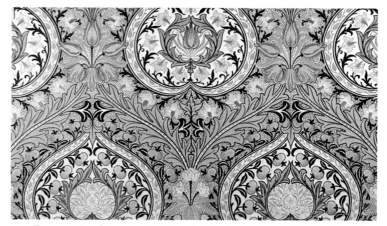

102 EDEN printed cotton. Designed Dearle *c.* 1905. Block-printed Merton Abbey, later Wardles. Repeat: 28 × 17½ in (71 × 44.5 cm). Width: 36 in (91.5 cm). Patterns: 9842, 9852. Preliminary design: Berger Collection. Blocks (13): Walthamstow. Illustrated in the *Art Journal*, 1905, & the *Studio Year Book*, 1906 (p. 184).

101 ROSEBUD printed cotton. Designed Dearle *c.* 1905. Block-printed Merton Abbey. Sample size (no full width available) 21½ × 9 in (54.5 × 23 cm). Width: 36 in (91.5 cm). Patterns: 4289, 4325. Original design: Berger Collection. Metropolitan Museum, New York.

103 CEDRIC woven wool & cotton fabric. Designed Dearle. *c.* 1905. Power-loom jacquard woven Merton Abbey. Size of design: approx. 11½ × 10 in (29 × 25.5 cm). Width: 52 in (132 cm). Pattern: 936 in 1 colourway.

105 LIVERPOOL printed silk. Designed Dearle *c.* 1905. Block-printed onto fine gossamer silk, probably Merton Abbey. Repeat: $14\frac{1}{2} \times 18\frac{1}{4}$ in (37×46.5 cm). Width: 27 in (68.5 cm) Pattern: 2047. Preparatory drawing: Berger Collection. *The nearest Morris & Co. came to manufacturing a dress fabric.* Private collection at Kelmscott Manor.

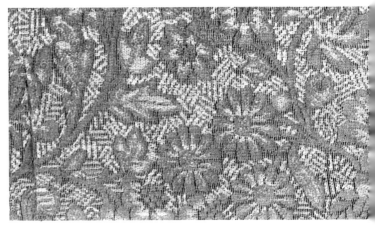

104 NEW PERSIAN woven silk & wool fabric. Designed Dearle *c.* 1905. Hand-loom jacquard woven Merton Abbey. Repeat size & width of finished fabric unknown. Design & small sample of fabric: Berger Collection. Design illustrated in the *Art Journal* 1906. *Pattern also used as 'Persian' wallpaper.* Illustrated from *Studio Year Book,* 1917.

106 MADRAS MUSLIN cotton & silk gauze. Designed Dearle 1905–10. Cotton gauze shot with silk woven on a jacquard loom Alexander Morton & Co. Size of sample (no full repeat available) $7 \times 8\frac{1}{2}$ in (17.5×21.5 cm). Width: 72 in (183 cm). In a number of colourways *Only known samples are in the V & A pattern book.*

107 BRIAR printed cotton. Designed Dearle *c.* 1906. Block-printed Merton Abbey. Repeat: $23\frac{1}{2} \times 17\frac{1}{2}$ in (59.5 cm × 44.5 cm). Width: 36 in (91.5 cm). Pattern: 8804 available in 1 colourway. Design: Berger Collection. Illustrated in the *Studio Year Book,* 1907

108 HUMMING BIRD or CRESTED BIRD printed cotton. Designed Dearle *c.* 1906. Block-printed Wardles. Sample size (no full height available) $25 \times 38\frac{1}{2}$ in (63.5×98 cm). Width: 36 in (91.5 cm). Patterns: 4939, 4941, 4986. Design: Berger Collection. *Another slightly different design illustrated in the 'Studio Year Book',* 1917. The Art Institute, Chicago.

109 STRIPE TWILL printed cotton. Designed Dearle or Kathleen Kersey *c.* 1906. Block-printed Merton Abbey. Repeat (height only): $6\frac{3}{4}$ in (17.1 cm). Width: 36 in (91.4 cm). Patterns: 6764, 6765, 6766. *Same cotton twill used as background fabric in 'Briar' and 'Humming Bird' or 'Crested Bird' (cat. nos. 107, 108).*

110 CARNATION woven wollen fabric Designed Dearle 1905–10. Hand-loom jacquard woven Merton Abbey. Repeat size unknown. Width: 54 in (137 cm). Pattern: 1895, in 3 colourways. A small sample of this fabric is in the Berger Collection. Illustrated from Morris & Co. catalogue.

111 IXIA woven wool & cotton fabric. Designed Dearle 1905–10. Power-loom jacquard woven possibly Merton Abbey. Size of design. $8\frac{7}{8} \times 13\frac{1}{2}$ in (22.5 × 34.5 cm). Width: 52 in (132 cm). Pattern: 982. Original design: Berger Collection. A small sample of this fabric is in the V & A pattern book. Design illustrated Berger Collection.

112 WREATH woven woollen fabric & silk damask. Designed Dearle 1905–10. Power-loom jacquard woven possibly Merton Abbey. Sample size: $7 \times 7\frac{3}{4}$ in (17.5 × 19.5 cm). Width: 50 in (127 cm). Pattern: 5012 (wool) in 6 colourways. Small samples of both fabrics in V & A pattern book. *Silk shows a larger-scale design than the wool. This design is different from both 'Wreath' wall paper and fabric.*

113 FLOWERING NET woven woollen fabric. Designed Dearle *c.* 1906. Power-loom jacquard woven probably by contractors. Repeat: 8 × 6 in (20.5 × 15 cm). Width: 50 in (127 cm). Pattern: 4493 in 3 colourways. Illustrated in the *Studio Year Book*, 1907 (p. 156). Illustrated from Morris & Co. catalogue.

114 CANTERBURY woven woollen fabric. Designed Dearle *c.* 1906. Power-loom jacquard woven probably by contractors. Repeat size unknown. Width: 50 ins (127 cm). Available 1 colourway only. Illustrated from *Studio Year Book*, 1907 (p. 156).

115 ALVA woven silk & wool fabric. Adapted from historical textile, 1905–10. Power-loom jacquard woven by contractors. Repeat size unknown. Width: 52 in (132 cm). Pattern: 7961 in 7 colours. Small samples in V & A pattern book. Illustrated from the Morris & Co. catalogue.

116 VENETIAN woven silk & linen & silk & wool fabric. Adapted from historical design & an earlier Morris & Co. wallpaper, 1905–10. Power-loom jacquard woven with jaspé (satin striped) ground by contractors. Repeat unknown. Width: 54 in (137 cm). Pattern: 4490 in 8 colours (silk & linen), 8818 in 3 (silk & wool). Illustrated from Morris & Co. catalogue.

117 PINEAPPLE woven woollen fabric. Adapted from 'XVI specimen in the South Kensington Museum'. c. 1910. Hand-loom jacquard woven Merton Abbey. Repeat size unknown. Width: 50 in (127 cm). Pattern: 1097 in 2 colourways. Small samples in the V & A pattern book. Illustrated from Morris & Co. catalogue.

118 MUSGROVE or GOTHIC PATTERN woven wool, Utrecht velvet, stamped silk velvet, woven silk damask. Adapted from historical design, before 1910. Hand-loom jacquard woven Merton Abbey. Repeat (wool): 23 × 11 in (58.5 × 28 cm). Width: (wool) 36 in (91.5 cm), (silk damask) 21 in (53.5 cm), (Utrecht) 24 in (61 cm). Pattern: 1910 (wool) in 3 colourways.

119 ANTIQUE CUT GENOA VELVET. Cut & uncut silk. Adapted from historical textile, before 1912. Woven for Morris & Co. by contractors. Repeat unknown. Width: 22 in (56 cm). Pattern: 512, in 2 colourways. Illustrated from Morris & Co. catalogue.

120 ANTIQUE CUT GENOA VELVET. Cut & uncut silk. Adapted from historical textile, before 1912. Probably woven for Morris & Co. by contractors. Repeat unknown. Width: 22 in (56 cm). Pattern: 513 in 3 colourways. Whitworth Art Gallery, University of Manchester.

121 CROWN printed onto cotton and linen. Adapted from 17th-century Italian brocade, before 1912. Block-printed Merton Abbey. Sample size: 4 × 5¾ in (10 × 14.5 cm) Width: 36 in (91.5 cm). Pattern: 9165, in 1 colourway. *An identical design was registered by Wardle, 6 March 1885. Small sample from V & A pattern book, only Morris piece known.*

122 ACORN embossed or stamped silk velvet. Adapted from historical design, before 1912. Either manufactured abroad or by Lister's of Halifax. Repeat: 15 × 12 in (38 × 30.5 cm). Width: 24 in (61 cm). Pattern: 293 in 3 colourways. *A label on this sample says 'to make price according to quality'.*

123 SISTINE woven silk & wool. Adapted from a '15th century design', before 1912. Power-loom jacquard woven by contractors. Repeat: 24 × 13 in (61 × 33 cm) Width: 50 in (127 cm). Pattern: 7679 in 4 colourways. *Popular for ecclesiastical use.*

124 TRINITAS woven wool & cotton fabric. Adapted from a historical design, 1912–14. Power-loom jacquard woven by contractors. Repeat: 49 × 12 in (124.5 × 30.5 cm). Width: 52 in (132 cm). Pattern: 1918 in at least 4 colourways. Small sample in the V & A pattern book. *Not listed in c. 1912 catalogue.* Private Collection at Kelmscott Manor.

125 MILLEFLEURS woven woollen fabric. Designed Dearle, 1912–14. Based on Flemish, *millefleurs* tapestries. Hand-loom jacquard woven Merton Abbey. Repeat: (Height unknown) width repeat: 17 in (43 cm). Width: 54 in (137 cm). Design illustrated in the *Studio Year Book*, 1917. Private Collection at Kelmscott Manor.

126 ST HILARY woven silk damask. Designed Dearle, 1912–14. Hand-loom jacquard woven Merton Abbey. Sample size (no full repeat available): 24½ × 28 in (61.5 × 71 cm). Width: 28 in (71 cm). Pattern: 5376 in at least 7 colourways. Small samples in V & A pattern book. *Not listed in the c. 1912 catalogue.* Private Collection at Kelmscott Manor.

127 HAMILTON woven silk & linen fabric. Designed Dearle, possibly based on historical design, 1912–14. Hand-loom jacquard woven Merton Abbey Sample size: $3\frac{3}{4} \times 6\frac{1}{4}$ in (9.5 × 15.5 cm). Probably woven to a width of 54 in (137 cm). Pattern: 1906 in at least 3 colourways. *V & A pattern book holds only known samples.*

128 SWEET BRIAR printed cotton. Designed Dearle as a wallpaper in 1912, used soon afterwards as a fabric. Block-printed Merton Abbey. Repeat: $23 \times 11\frac{7}{8}$ in (58.5 × 30 cm). Width: 36 in (91.5 cm). Pattern: 292, available with white or dark green ground. Illustrated in the *Studio Year Book*, 1913. Cooper-Hewitt Museum, New York.

129 BRENT or BRENTWOOD printed onto cotton & linen. Designed Dearle as a wallpaper *Brentwood* in 1913, used soon afterwards as a fabric. Block-printed Merton Abbey. Repeat: $8\frac{1}{4} \times 8\frac{1}{4}$ in (21 × 21 cm). Width: 36 in (91.5 cm). Small sample in the V & A pattern book. Illustrated in the *Studio Year Book*, 1917 Cooper-Hewitt Museum, New York.

130 RAMBLING ROSE printed cotton. Designed Dearle 1912–17. Block-printed Merton Abbey. Design size: $10\frac{3}{4} \times 13\frac{1}{4}$ in (26.5 × 33.5 cm). Width: 36 in (91.5 cm). Illustrated in the *Studio Year Book*, 1917. *No samples of this fabric have been found.* Original design illustrated: Sanford and Helen Berger Collection.

131 HATFIELD printed cotton. Adapted from an early 19th century textile, after 1915. Block-printed Merton Abbey. Sample size (no full repeat available) $9\frac{3}{4} \times 10\frac{3}{4}$ in (25 × 27.5 cm). Width: 36 in (91.5 cm). Pattern: 3274. *This sample originally formed part of a swatch pattern book.* Cooper-Hewitt Museum, New York.

132 HADDON printed cotton. Adapted from an early 19th century Indian textile design, after 1915. Block-printed Merton Abbey. Sample size (no full repeat available): 8 × 10 in (20.5 × 28 cm). Width: 32 in (81.5 cm). Pattern: 491. *Recommended for 'small windows and loose covers'.* William Morris Gallery, Walthamstow.

133 HOLKAM printed cotton. Adapted from an early 19th century textile, after 1915. Block-printed Merton Abbey. Sample size (no full repeat available): 8 × 10½ in (20.5 × 26.5 cm). Width: 36 in (91.5 cm). Pattern: 6320. *Part of a swatch pattern book*. William Morris Gallery, Walthamstow.

134 Unidentified floral design with Chinese-style birds, printed onto cotton after 1915. Possibly adopted from an earlier textile design. Block-printed Merton Abbey. Sample size: 4 × 5¾ in (10 × 14.5 cm). Width: 36 in (91.5 cm). *This is 1 of the only 2 known existing examples of this textiles, from the V & A pattern book.*

135 TANGLEY printed cotton. Adopted from an early 19th century textile design, after 1915. Block-printed Merton Abbey. Repeat: 35 × 17 in (89 × 43 cm). Width: 36 in (91.5 cm). Pattern: 6809. Private collection.

136 MERTON printed cotton. Designed Dearle, *c.* 1915–20. Block-printed Merton Abbey. Repeat: 9 × 8¾ in (23 × 22 cm). Width: 36 in (91.5 cm). Original design: Berger Collection. *Not the same as 'Merton' roller-printed wallpaper.* Private Collection at Kelmscott Manor.

137 INDIAN PINK printed cotton. Probably designed Dearle, after 1918. Block-printed Merton Abbey. Repeat: 8¾ × 9 in (22 × 23 cm). Width: 36 in (91.5 cm). Pattern: 6543. Small sample in the V & A pattern book. *The only large sample has a George Street label.* Private Collection at Kelmscott Manor.

138 Floral design, Jacobean revival style, printed cotton. Designer unknown, after 1918. Block-printed possibly Merton Abbey. Repeat: 10 × 6½ in (25.5 × 16.5 cm). Width: 36 in (91.5 cm). *Selvedge stamp 'Regd. Morris and Company'. This is the only known example of this textile.*

139 DAISY or GRASS carpet. Designed Morris 1870–75. Kidderminster carpeting made Heckmondwike, Brussels and Wilton pile made Wilton Royal Carpet Company. Repeat: $11\frac{1}{2} \times 9$ in (29 × 23 cm). Widths vary according to technique. Pattern: 5076, in various colourways, usually with blue or green backgrounds.

140 TULIP AND LILY carpet. Designed Morris c. 1875. Kidderminster carpeting woven Heckmondwike. Repeat: 14×9 in (35.5 × 23 cm). Width: 36 in (91.5 cm) & variations for staircarpets. Pattern: 5117 in various colourways, predominantly green, A special border was available with this design.

141 LILY carpet. Designed Morris c. 1875. Wilton pile carpet woven Wilton. Repeat: $9\frac{1}{2} \times 8\frac{3}{4}$ in (24 × 22 cm). Available in various widths. A sample at Walthamstow has a special border. Point-paper illustrated in Barbara Morris 'William Morris: His Designs for Carpets and Tapestries', *Handweaver and Craftsman*, Fall, 1961 (p. 18).

142 ROSE carpet. Designed Morris, registered 31 March 1876. Wilton pile carpet woven Wilton. Repeat: 12×9 in (30.5 × 23 cm). Available in various widths. Design: Walthamstow. Illustrated, with point-paper, in L.F.Day (p. 3). A carpet of this design in the V & A has a matching border.

143 BELLFLOWERS carpet. Designed Morris 1875–80. Wilton pile carpet woven Wilton. Repeat: $12\frac{3}{4} \times 13\frac{1}{2}$ in (32.4 × 34.3 cm) Available in various widths. A carpet of this design in the V & A has a matching border.

144 ARTICHOKE carpet. Designed Morris 1875–80. Kidderminster carpeting woven Heckmondwike. Repeat: $10\frac{3}{4} \times 8\frac{5}{8}$ in (27.3 × 21.9 cm). Width: 36 in (91.5 cm) & variations for stair carpet. Design: Wathamstow. A carpet of this design at Walthamstow has a matching border. William Morris Gallery, Walthamstow.

Catalogue Index

Catalogue References

PATTERN BOOKS

V&A pattern book Probably used for reference in Morris & Co.'s shops. This large book contains printed and woven textile samples sold by the firm. Although not comprehensive a number of late patterns are included. Given to the museum in 1940.

Wardle pattern books A set of Thomas Wardle's pattern books for the period 1875–1909 containing sample fents (trial samples) of all the Morris textiles printed at Leek. Whitworth Art Gallery, University of Manchester.

Merton Abbey Dye Book A ledger from Merton Abbey containing recipes for dyes used on printed cottons 1882 to 1891. Sanford and Helen Berger Collection, California.

Printed swatch books These show twentieth-century customer and shop sample swatches of Morris & Co.'s range of printed cottons and linens. The Victoria and Albert Museum and the William Morris Gallery, Walthamstow have complete books and the Cooper-Hewitt Museum, New York has samples removed from another.

BOOKS

G.H. Crow, 'William Morris, Designer', Special Winter Number of the *Studio*, 1934.

L.F. Day, 'William Morris and His Art', *The Art Journal*, Easter Art Annual, 1899.

J.W. Mackail, *The Life of William Morris* (London 1899).

May Morris, *William Morris – artist, writer, socialist* (London 1936).

Morris & Co. catalogues:

Church Decoration and Furniture (*c*.1936).

Printed Cottons and Linens (*c*.1912).

Silks, Woollen Tapestries, Brocades etc (*c*.1912).

The latter two were also printed together as:

Morris Chintzes, Silks, Tapestries (*c*.1912).

Specimens of Upholstered Furniture (*c*.1914).

A portrait of Janey Morris after Morris's death. The back-drop is ROSE *cotton.*

Dating Morris Textiles

There are various ways of identifying and dating Morris textiles other than by recognizing patterns and, in the case of printed textiles, carpets and tapestries, trade marks were used by the firm at different periods.

Printed Textiles

Identification marks were block-printed along the selvedges of all Morris & Co.'s printed cottons, wools and linens at yard intervals. The form of these changed and it is therefore possible to give them an approximate date.

This mark pre-dates the firm of Morris & Co. and is found on the earliest known sample of printed textile. It was probably used from 1868–1875, although slightly later samples have been found with this mark.

This mark was used after the foundation of Morris & Co. in 1875 but before the move to Oxford Street in spring 1877.

These are the most commonly found identification marks used for the period 1877–1917. Although the Oxford Street address was numbered 264 when the firm first moved there, no printed textiles have been found with this address, although one corrected label can be seen on a textile in the Victoria and Albert Museum. It is likely that the first form of address pre-dates the latter which is usually printed on a wavy line. One cotton has been found which has its registered number printed after the address.

The mark printed on a wavy line was used after the shop was moved from Oxford Street to 17 George Street, Hanover Square in October 1917 up until the firm's liquidation on 21 May 1940. A sample of cotton known to have been printed as later as 1937 has this mark.

This mark has been found on a surface-printed example of *Rose and Thistle* which is badly dyed and printed and is, almost certainly, a fake or late copy.

1905–1917	MORRIS & COMPANY DECORATORS Ltd., 449 OXFORD STREET, LONDON W.1.
1917–1925	MORRIS & COMPANY DECORATORS, LTD., 17 GEORGE STREET, HANOVER SQUARE, LONDON W.1.
1925–1940	MORRIS & COMPANY ART-WORKERS, LTD., 17 GEORGE STREET, HANOVER SQUARE, LONDON W.1.

(This sometimes appears without the address).

Labels

Printed paper labels are often still attached to small samples of fabric and pattern books and these can be useful in dating pieces. All those printed before 1905 follow the general format described for printed textiles. Later samples take a different form:

Carpets

Morris & Co. carpets were marked for only a short period, 1878–81, and then only on hand-knotted Hammersmith rugs. There are two variations of the mark used and these appear in the top right-hand corner of wall-rugs or corner edge of floor carpets.

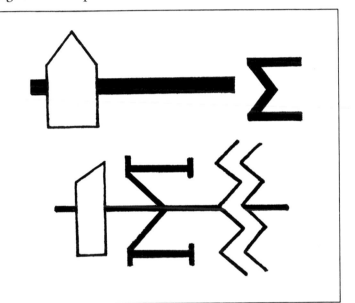

Tapestries

In contrast to carpets only late examples, those from 1912, were marked. This consists of a bishop's mitre, as shown here, and the weavers' initials. Initials have also been found on earlier examples. It is possible to give an approximate date for tapestries by discovering when the weavers involved were employed at Merton Abbey.

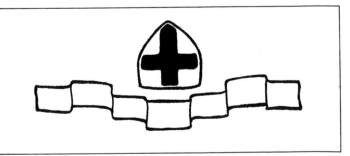

WEAVERS EMPLOYED BY MORRIS & CO. FOR EACH FIVE YEARS OF THE FIRMS'S HISTORY

1880 J.H.Dearle, William Knight, William Sleath.

1885 Knight, Sleath, John Martin (with Dearle supervising).

1890 Knight, Sleath, Martin, George Priestley, Robert Ellis, John Keech (or Keich).

1895 Knight, Sleath, Martin, Ellis, Keech, William Haines, William Eleman, Walter Taylor, George Merritt.

1900 Sleath, Martin, Taylor, Ellis, Keech, Merritt, John Glassbrook.

1905 Sleath, Martin, Taylor, Ellis, Merritt, Glassbrook, Gordon Berry.

1910 Sleath, Martin, Merritt, Glassbrook, Berry.

1915 Sleath, Martin, George Fitzhenry, Richard Carter, Mrs Orage, Miss Marillier.

1920 Sleath, Carter, H.Carnegie.

1925 Cater, Carnegie, Frederick Reed (or Reid), Percy Sheldrick, Edward Russell.

1930 Reed, Sheldrick, Russell, Duncan Dearle, Wallace Stevens (or Stevenson).

1935 Reed, Sheldrick, Russell, Stevens, Sidney Mears, Arthur Wingate, C.W. (unknown), Douglas Griffiths (with Duncan Dearle supervising).

(For further details of individual weavers see chapter 5.)

TEXTILE REPRODUCTIONS OF MORRIS DESIGNS SINCE 1940

Wallpaper designs used as textiles

In the early twentieth century Jeffrey & Co., who had always printed Morris & Co.'s wallpapers, were taken over by the Wallpaper Manufacturers' Association, which continued to print the designs for Morris & Co. until the firm went into liquidation in 1940. The blocks then became the property of the Wallpaper Manufacturers' Association and were allocated to their Arthur Sanderson & Sons factory; rightly regarded as the successor to Jeffrey & Co.

Sanderson have continued to produce both block-printed and machine-printed wallpapers from Morris designs since this time. They have also screen-printed a number of these wallpaper designs on to fabric and, more recently, have had them woven as machine-woven Axminster carpeting. Patterns sold include: (As furnishing fabrics) *Fruit, Jasmine, Pimpernel, Chrysanthemum, Bower, Blackthorn, Honeysuckle* (a May Morris wallpaper design), *Golden Lily* and *Willow Bough* (the only pattern used by Morris & Co. for fabric). (As carpeting) *Jasmine, Chrysanthemum, Poppy, Golden Lily, Granville, Blackthorn*

The reproduction of textile designs

In the last days of Morris & Co. a number of sets of wood blocks for printing fabrics were transferred to Stead McAlpin & Co. Ltd, of Cummerdale, Carlisle, who carried out printing for Morris & Co. on a commission basis (Stead McAlpin Ltd are commission printers who do not do their own marketing). When Morris & Co. went bankrupt, Stead McAlpin bought up all the blocks they held: all the other sets, which had become obsolete by this time, had already been disposed of.

After the 1939–45 war, Stead McAlpin arranged for the Old Bleach Linen Co., Belfast, to market a number of these and in the 1950s, Warner & Sons issued a set of machine-printed samples which included *Strawberry Thief, Compton* and *Corncockle*. In the last twenty years Stead McAlpin have been responsible for screen-printing a number of Morris designs for Liberty & Co. Ltd and the John Lewis Partnership (of which they are now a part). Morris fabrics currently available include *Windrush* (at John Lewis) and *Strawberry Thief, Daffodil, Willow, Honeysuckle, African Marigold, Snakeshead* and *Lodden* (at Liberty's). In America, Scalamandré Inc. sell *Lodden, Brother Rabbit, Daffodil, Strawberry Thief* and the only woven fabric available, *Bird.*

The John Lewis Partnership have recently given their collection of Morris & Co. blocks to the William Morris Gallery, Walthamstow and one set, *Strawberry Thief*, to the Victoria and Albert Museum.

It must be remembered that no Morris fabrics are still block-printed, indigo discharged or dyed with natural dye-stuffs and also, in many cases, not only colour-schemes but pattern scales too have been altered to fit in with modern manufacturing processes and new fabric widths.

Public Collections

Public collections containing Morris textiles

The number of Morris items in collections throughout the world vary greatly and although an indication of each museum's holdings has been given, where known, visitors would be wise to check on this and the availability of the exhibits beforehand to avoid disappointment. Opening hours should also be sought in advance. Standen, Wightwick Manor and Kelmscott Manor are all closed during the winter and open only on specific days during the summer months.

A number of collections containing Morris textiles have published details of their holdings. These catalogues follow their relevant museum entry. Publications concerning single items or part collections have not been included.

AUSTRALIA
MELBOURNE National Gallery of Victoria (Victorian Arts Centre): Catherine Holiday embroidery, one woven sample.

ADELAIDE Art Gallery of South Australia
One tapestry (*The Adoration*), swatch pattern book.

AUSTRIA
VIENNA Österreichisches Museum für Angewandte Kunst
Ten printed textiles.

BELGIUM
BRUSSELS Musées Royaux d'Art et d'Histoire
Printed textiles including five printed velveteens.
(see Marie-Francois Tilliet 'Tissus Anglais aux Musées Royaux d'Art et d'Histoire: De William Morris à l'Art Nouveau', *Bulletin des Musées Royaux d'Art et d'Histoire, Bruxelles*, 1978.)

CANADA
TORONTO Royal Ontario Museum: One printed textile.
MONTREAL McCord Museum, McGill University
One woven textile.

DENMARK
COPENHAGEN Dat Danske Kunstindustrimuseum
Nine woven textiles, twenty-three printed textiles.

FRANCE
MULHOUSE Musée de l'Impression sur Étoffes
Printed textiles only.

PARIS Musée des Arts Decoratifs: One printed textile.

GERMANY
BADEN-BADEN Staatliche Kunsthalle
One tapestry (first panel from the *Holy Grail* series, woven in 1932).

HAMBURG Museum für Kunst und Gewerbe
One tapestry (*The Adoration*), six printed textiles, one woven textile.

KARLSRUHE Badisches Landesmuseum
One tapestry (*Pilgrim in the Garden*).

KREFELD Textilmuseum: Printed textiles.
(See *Stoffe um 1900*, Textilmuseum, Krefeld, 1977 and *Stuttgart*, Württembergischen Landesmuseums.)
Printed and woven textiles.
(See *Textil-Dekor um 1900*, Württembergischen Landesmuseums, Stuttgart, 1980.)

STUTTGART Württembergischen Landesmuseums
One woven textile.

GREAT BRITAIN
BEDFORD Cecil Higgins Museum
Embroidered firescreen, embroidered fourfold screen.

BIRMINGHAM City Museum and Art Gallery
Nine tapestries, woven and printed textiles, two cushion covers designs.
(See Oliver Fairclough and Emmeline Leary *Textiles by William Morris and Morris & Co. 1861–1940 London 1981.*)

BRISTOL Museum and Art Gallery
Two pairs of woven curtains.

CAMBRIDGE Fitzwilliam Museum
One embroidered hanging, set of woven curtains.

CARDIFF Welsh Folk Museum
Embroidered hanging.

HARTLEBURY CASTLE Hereford and Worcester County Museum

Pair of woven curtains, printed textiles, one machine woven carpet.

LEICESTER County Museums, Art Gallery and Record Service School loans service; six printed textiles.
Decorative Arts Collection; Dress embroidered by May Morris, settee designed by Ernest Gimson, covered with Morris woven fabric, 1906.

LONDON Victoria and Albert Museum
Near comprehensive collection of printed and woven textiles. Machine and hand-knotted carpets, a number of large and small embroideries, designs, pattern-books, three large tapestries and a number of small panels.

LONDON William Morris Gallery, Walthamstow
Near comprehensive collection of printed and woven textiles. One tapestry and trial samples, embroideries, machine woven and hand-knotted carpets, a swatch pattern book and designs.
(See *Catalogue of the Morris Collection*, William Morris Gallery, Walthamstow, 1969.)

MANCHESTER Whitworth Art Gallery, University of Manchester
Tapestries, woven and printed textiles, Wardle pattern books.
(See exhibition catalogue, *Sources of Art Nouveau*, held at the museum, March–May 1969.)

NORWICH Castle Museum, Norfolk Museum Service
One tapestry (*The Adoration*).

NOTTINGHAM Museum of Costume and Textiles
Four prints given by Morris in 1890.

PRESTON Harris Museum and Art Gallery: Two tapestries.

WINCHESTER Chilcomb House, Hampshire County Museum Service: One tapestry (*The Chase*).

NATIONAL TRUST PROPERTIES
Standen, East Grinstead, East Sussex
(See *Standen, Sussex*, The National Trust, 1979.)
Wightwick Manor, Wolverhampton
(See *Wightwick Manor*, The National Trust.)

SOCIETY OF ANTIQUARIES London
Kelmscott Manor, Lechlade
(See A.R.Duffy *Kelmscott, An Illustrated Guide*, London Society of Antiquaries, 1977.)

WILLIAM MORRIS SOCIETY AND THE TRUSTEES OF KELMSCOTT HOUSE
Kelmscott House collection. This contains two Morris designs, printed and woven textiles and later embroidery designs. Collection not accessible at time of publication.
(See George Monk and Walter Gooch, *A Study and Catalog of Morris & Co. in the collection of the William Morris Center*, 1977–8. A typescript with photographs.) Available in the National Art Library and The William Morris Gallery, Walthamstow.

HUNGARY
BUDAPEST Iparművészeti Múseum
Ten printed textiles, one Hammersmith rug.

NEW ZEALAND
WELLINGTON Dominion Museum
Set of six embroidered panels by Lady Cory from designs by William Morris and Edward Burne-Jones, including *Pomona*.

NORWAY
TRONDHEIM Nordenfjeldske Kunstindustri Museum
Printed and woven textiles and a stool designed by J.S.Henry covered in Morris woven fabric. May Morris embroidered bag.
(See 'British Decorative Arts of the late 19th century in the Nordenfjeldske Kunstindustrimuseum', *Arbok 1961–2*.)

RUSSIA
LENINGRAD Hermitage Museum: One tapestry (*The Adoration*).

SWEDEN
STOCKHOLM Nordiska Museet: Two printed textiles.

SWITZERLAND
ZURICH Bellerive Museum (previously at the Kunstgewebemuseum, Zurich)
Printed and woven textiles, two machine-woven carpets, two embroidered cushion covers, two embroidered screens.
(See *Objekte des Jugendstils*, Museum Bellerive, 1975 and Exhibition catalogue *William Morris*, May–August 1978, Museum Bellerive.)

UNITED STATES OF AMERICA
BOSTON Museum of Fine Arts: Printed and woven textiles.

CHICAGO The Art Institute
Printed textiles (including a velveteen), woven textiles, machine-woven sample, One Hammersmith carpet.

CLEVELAND Museum of Art
Extension Services: five printed textiles, one woven.
Department of Textiles: three woven textiles.
(See David Whipple 'Textile Designs and Books by William Morris', *The Bulletin of the Cleveland Museum of Art*, September, 1978.)

CONNECTICUT Historical Society
May Morris embroidered panel.

CRANBROOK Academy of Art: Three tapestries.

CRANBROOK Cranbrook House
May Morris embroidered bed-hangings.

DETROIT Institute of Arts: One tapestry (*Passing of Venus*).

INDIANAPOLIS Museum of Art
Eight printed textiles, two machine-woven carpet samples.

LOS ANGELES County Museum: Two woven textiles.

NEW YORK Cooper-Hewitt
Large collection of printed and woven textiles, machine-made carpet samples and three embroidered cushion covers.

NEW YORK Metropolitan Museum of Art
Large collection of printed and woven textiles, one tapestry (*Greenery*) and tapestry fragment, Catherine Holiday embroidery.

PHILADELPHIA Museum of Art: Two printed textiles.

Acknowledgments

Unfortunately there is not enough room to thank all those who have guided, assisted and supported me while I researched and wrote this book. Although names are omitted, they are not forgotten, and I shall always be grateful for the generosity and, at times overwhelming, kindness I have been shown.

Before listing my contemporaries I would like to acknowledge the work of the late Peter Floud, a predecessor at the Victoria and Albert Museum whose untimely death denied me the privilege of meeting and knowing him. His writings have been a constant source of inspiration to me and his pioneering research in the 1950s and subsequent publications, always learned and often deliberately controversial, have provided the inspiration for my own work. At his death, Peter Floud was preparing for publication a book of similar context. I hope he would have found this book of interest.

On a more personal note, I would like to thank Suzanne Lodge, who first suggested that I would be interested in the subject. This book, imperfections and all, is the culmination of subsequent research, and during this time my colleagues, first at Birmingham Museum and Art Gallery and later at the Victoria and Albert Museum, have encouraged and supported me. Many colleagues at the Victoria and Albert Museum have assisted me and I would particularly like to thank Sally Chappell and Pip Barnard, who took many of the photographs, Frances Collard and Ann Buddle. All my friends in the Department of Textiles and Dress have provided invaluable assistance and encouragement and I would like to thank Natalie Rothstein, Santina Levey and Wendy Hefford for answering technical questions, reading my text and eradicating errors. Avril Hart and Valerie Mendes also provided moral support, Peter Giffin helped me to measure objects and Jennifer Wearden typed much of my draft.

Colleagues in British and foreign museums have been most helpful: Astri Aasen of Trondheim; Susan Anderson of Philadelphia; the director and staff of the Archives of American Art, New York; Mary J. Ballard of Detroit; Dr Sigrid Barden of Zurich; Ferenc Batari of Budapest; Adolph S. Cavallo of Philadelphia; Dr Guy Delmarcel of Brussels; Betsy G. Fryberger of Stanford University; Ruth Gasthaus of Krefeld; John Gerard of Cranbrook; the librarian and staff of Hammersmith Public Libraries; Peggy S. Gilfoy of Indianapolis; Dr Ruth Gronwoldt of Stuttgart; Emmeline Leary of Birmingham; Edward Maeder of Los Angeles; Gillian Moss of the Cooper-Hewitt Museum, New York; Charlotte Paludan of Copenhagen; Maritheres, Gräfin Preysing of Hamburg; the director and staff of the Public Record Office, Kew; Edith Standen of the Metropolitan Museum, New York; Naomi Tarrant of Edinburgh; Christa C.M. Thurman of Chicago: Dr Angela Volker of Vienna; S. Vsevolzhskaya of Leningrad; Maude Wallace of Manchester; Alice Zrebiec of the Metropolitan Museum, New York. I would particularly like to thank Norah Gillow and Peter Cormack of the William Morris Gallery, Walthamstow for arranging photography and supplying measurements of objects in their collections.

Many individuals have helped me: Joan Allgrove; Sanford and Helen Berger to whom I am particularly indebted for allowing me to study their collection; R.C.H. Briggs; Sue Charnock; Andrew Denham; Mrs Pauline Dower; A.R. Dufty; S. Francis; Mrs Cora Ginsburg; Geoffrey Green; Walter Gooch; the Hon. Janet Grant; Arthur Grogan; Rev. C.J. Hawthorn; James Joll; Mrs Alice Maclean; Lady Mander; Pauline Mason; Elizabeth Masterman; Mrs Margaret Masterson; George Monk; Barbara Morris (who has always been a great source of inspiration); Mrs Juliette Roddam; Jessie Serle; John Scott; Jean Wells; Michael Whiteway. I would also like to thank my publishers, particularly Russell Ash and Beatrice Phillpotts for their help and understanding.

My family have encouraged me throughout the time I have been writing and my sister, Vivien Lomax, has been very helpful in the last year driving me around England and America in search of Morris. Lastly, I would like to thank my husband Don, without whose constant support, care and understanding I would never have had the courage, energy or time to write this book.

Footnotes

Embroidery

1 J.W.Mackail, *The Life of William Morris*, (London 1899) p. 89.

2 G.B.J. (Georgiana Burne-Jones), *Memorials of Edward Burne-Jones* (London 1904) Vol. I p. 145.

3 Jane Morris mistakenly dates this to 1855 in her 'Red House Notes', British Museum Add. Ms. 45341. The inscription 'als ich kan' was first seen by Morris in Van Eyck's paintings during his 1856 holiday in the Low Countries and was later used by him in German, French and English translation.

4 Almost without colour now, Mackail described the piece in 1899 as 'of green trees with gaily coloured birds among them'.

5 G.B.J. op. cit. Vol. I p. 208.

6 A design for *Flamma Troie* is in the Victoria and Albert Museum and a colour sketch for *Venus* at Kelmscott Manor. The design for *Isoude* was still in Morris & Co.'s possession in 1940. A drawing for *Ariadne* possibly part of this scheme, or Burne-Jones's later plan of the same design, was lent by Sir Sydney Cockerell to the 1934 centenary exhibition at the Victoria and Albert Museum.

7 These three panels were finished by Bessie Burden, set into a Morris and Company screen and sold through the firm for £20 per panel in 1889. Letters between Miss Burden and the Earl of Carlisle concerning the sale are now in the Berger Collection.

8 This was originally in the possession of Edward and Georgiana Burne-Jones and can be seen hanging in the doorway of the dining room at The Grange, Fulham (the Burne-Jones's home from 1867) in T.M.Rooke's painting now at Batemans, Burwash in Sussex.

9 G.B.J. op. cit. Vol. I p. 273.

10 Birmingham Museum and Art Gallery (13/04).

11 A design for this is now in the Victoria and Albert Museum.

12 G.B.J. op. cit. Vol. I p. 213.

13 J.W.Mackail op. cit. Vol. I p. 154.

14 'Top' was Morris's nickname, originally derived at Oxford to describe his unruly hairstyle from the character in Harriet Beecher Stowe's novel *Uncle Tom's Cabin* newly published at that time.

15 Volume X, 8 May 1862 p. 241.

16 The Morris, Marshall, Faulkner & Co. day-book, now in the collection of Sanford and Helen Berger, mentions only one embroidery; 'Scarborough altar cloth £28' in the firm's quarterly accounts 'examined and allowed Xmas 1862.' The bill was not paid immediately and the following accounts, read at the partners' 20 May 1863 meeting, shows 'Scarborough altar cloth and hangings £42 9s 0d' This extra amount of £14 9s 0d almost certainly refers to the two riddel post hangings.

17 A water colour design for this altar frontal is now in the Victoria and Albert Museum.

18 Philip Webb, *Accounts with Morris & Co*, Birmingham Museum and Art Gallery.

19 Design registry no. 389703, 9 November 1882, Public Record Office. There are a number of embroidered border designs in Wardle's pattern book 14008, Whitworth Art Gallery, University of Manchester.

20 Minutes of evidence taken before the Royal Commission on Technical Instruction at the South Kensington Museum. Fifth day, Friday 17 March 1882.

21 Philip Webb's sketch-books from 1859 to 1861 show items from the South Kensington Museum collection and it is clear that Morris also visited at this time. From March 1885 to his death he sat on the Museum's Art Referees Committee advising on the acquisition of textiles, although it is clear that his expertise and advice had been sought much earlier than this, his earlier reports being written on a free lance basis. For further information on his association with the South Kensington Museum see 'William Morris and the South Kensington Museum' by Barbara Morris in *Victorian Poetry*, West Virginia University, Fall-Winter 1975.

22 A loan exhibition of embroideries at the South Kensington Museum in 1873 lists items from the collections of a number of noted artistic figures including Alfred (later Lord) Leighton, Val Prinsep and Matthew Digby Wyatt.

23 Now at the William Morris Gallery, Wathamstow (F. 140). A set of working drawings, presumably by George Wardle are now in the Victoria and Albert Museum. Photographs showing the embroideries *in situ* in Rounton Grange are now in the Trevelyan Archive at the University of Newcastle.

24 The *Musica* panel and a design for *Poesia* are now at the Birmingham Museum and Art Gallery. *The Musicians* is now in the Victoria and Albert Museum.

25 A tracing of the design in the Victoria and Albert Museum is marked 'Aglaia Coronia', she was an Ionides before marriage and a close friend of Morris. As early as April 1870 Morris wrote to her 'I will call on Tuesday, and bring you your worsteds'.

26 Photographs of Holland Park *c.* 1880–1888 do not show these embroideries in the house, which hints at an earlier date.

27 Harry Bedford Lemere photographs of the interior show a *Rose and Olive* fire-screen, one hanging and two covers of the same honeysuckle patterned design, embroidered pelmets and tablecloths (one taken from a registered design for a carpet border). A small embroidered table cover can even be seen in the bathroom. A bill for

May 1884 includes 'I traced table cover on green cloth £7, 15oz thick twist @ 5/6 (an ounce) £4.2.6.

28 British Museum Add. Ms. 45338, 8 March 1876.

29 Now in the Sanford and Helen Berger Collection.

30 British Museum Add. Ms. 45341, 21 March 1878.

31 Victoria and Albert Museum (Circ. 196–1961).

32 A sample in silk on linen is in the Welsh Folk Museum, Cardiff. Three others and the design are in the Victoria and Albert Museum.

33 Fortunately there are still a number of unfinished panels in public collections. Birmingham Museum and Art Gallery have two pounced backgrounds for cushion covers and the Victoria and Albert Museum own four small panels in which the embroidery has been started in the Morris & Co. workshops.

34 There are four *Flowerpot* panels in British public collections. An example embroidered by May Morris is in the William Morris Gallery, Walthamstow, another professional piece is in the Victoria and Albert Museum, an amateur work in Liverpool County Museums and a fourth pounced only, is in Birmingham Museum and Art Gallery.

35 An example, worked in silks on yellow linen now in the Victoria and Albert Museum is almost definitely the same as that exhibited in the Arts and Crafts Exhibition for 1890 (no. 112).

36 A typescript catalogue with slides, *A Study and Catalog of Morris & Co. in the collection of the William Morris Center, London* compiled by George Monk and Walter Gooch in 1977–8, can be studied in the National Art Library Victoria and Albert Museum and the William Morris Gallery, Walthamstow.

37 I am deeply indebted for much of the information published here concerning May Morris to Elizabeth Masterman. Not only did she allow me to read the fruits of her own intensive research but also taught me how to understand a modest and sympathetic artist a little better.

38 The marriage was dissolved in February 1898. Sparling had left London for Paris in 1893 'to better himself' and although returning for Morris's funeral in 1896 never lived with May again. Summary of the divorce proceedings *Daily Mail* newspaper, 8 February 1898.

39 For details of the day to day work of the embroidery workshop and May's teaching at the Central School of Arts and Crafts I am indebted to Mrs Margaret Masterson, niece of Ellen Mary Wright.

40 It is not known whether Mrs Jack worked as a professional or on a personal amateur basis with the firm; she was a highly accomplished needlewoman who regularly exhibited at the Arts and Crafts Exhibitions. The Victoria and Albert Museum own four panels embroidered by her. Three are from designs by her husband and the fourth is a copy of the intended engraved frontispiece to Rossetti's *The Early Italian Poets* (London 1861).

41 A comparison of wages of crafts women working in the late nineteenth century with other occupations is made in Anthea Callen's *Angel in the Studio: Women in the Arts and Crafts Movement 1870–1914* (London 1979).

42 Morris and Company Day Book 1892–6. National Art Library, Victoria and Albert Museum.

43 Several working drawings, pounced designs on greased paper for cushion covers and small panels are in the Victoria and Albert Museum. Among designs represented are *Rosebush*, *Olive and Rose*, *Bayleaf*, *Convolvulus*, *Autumn*, *Large Poppy* and *Apple Tree*.

44 Order 1544, Morris & Co. Day Book op. cit.

45 This binding and letters on the project are in the Norman H. Strouse Collection, California. Exhibited in *Morris & Co.*, Stanford University, March–May 1975 (no. 72).

46 Typescript of address by Una Fielding, written for the Kelmscott Fellowship Meeting planned for 24 March 1939 as a tribute to May Morris.

47 Miss Lobb first went to Kelmscott as a land girl in 1914.

48 Una Fielding op. cit.

49 See Morris & Co. catalogue, *The Coronation Thrones and other Furniture executed by Messrs Morris and Company*, 449 Oxford Street, c. 1912

50 Arts and Crafts lecture, 'Textiles', 1888.

Printed textiles

1 This was transferred in 1877 with the opening of the firm's first purpose-built shop at 449 Oxford Street.

2 The Morris family had four homes (one for holidays) in their thirty-seven year marriage. Horrington House, in which they lived between 1872 and 1878 was described by Janey as a 'good sort of house for one person to live in or perhaps two.' However it did prove convenient for transport for Morris travelling to and from Queen Square despite Janey's dislike. In 1878 they took a lease on The Retreat, the Mall, Hammersmith which they re-named Kelmscott House after Kelmscott Manor, Lechlade, Oxfordshire which they had previously leased with Rossetti in 1872. The family resided between Kelmscott House and Kelmscott Manor until Morris's death in 1896. A year later Janey disposed of the London house and went to live with Jenny. In 1913, the year before her death, she purchased Kelmscott Manor. Both Jenny and May lived there until their deaths in 1935 and 1938 respectively.

3 Founded in 1798, the Bannister Hall Print Works became the leading 'Furniture-printers' in the country. They were taken over by Thomas Clarkson in 1856, having previously been owned by Charles Swainson. In 1893 all the company's records, blocks, etc., were passed to Stead McAlpin & Company.

4 Although admiring early designs produced at the works and their present manufacturing techniques, Morris was less generous in his comments about the present firm's designs. 'The high class block printing works like Thomas Clarkson of Bannister Hall merely copy the latest fashions sent over from France.'

5 George Wardle, *Memorials of William Morris*, Christmas 1897. Add. Ms 45350. British Library.

6 May Morris, *William Morris artist, writer, socialist* (London 1936) Vol. I p. 43.

7 The wool is also stamped 'Morris and Company' but this pre-dates the foundation of the company. Morris used the title some years earlier (much to the annoyance of Rossetti) superceding the longer 'Morris, Marshall, Faulkner and Co.' J. W. Mackail, *The Life of William Morris* (London 1899) Vol I. p. 307.

8 Two other designs which probably date from this period are *Flower and Stripe* and *Jasmine Twill*. No identifiable samples of these have been found but both are described in a Morris & Co. catalogue as 'Old English "chintz" flower designs'.

9 Morris was content to have all his wallpapers printed with

chemical dyestuffs by Jeffrey and Co. under their excellent manager Metford Warner.

10 George Wardle op. cit.

11 Ibid.

12 An article on Morris's use of 'Blue and Red' written by Deryn O'Connor (lecturer in textile design) is in *William Morris and Kelmscott* (London 1981).

13 Some of Bannister Hall's printed cotton designs required as many as two hundred blocks.

14 William Morris, 'Of Dyeing as an Art,' Arts and Crafts lecture, 1889.

15 Typescript copies of Morris's letters to Wardle can be found in the National Art Library, Victoria and Albert Museum.

16 'M. Quarelles', Delormois, Scheffer, Koechlin, Persoz, Underwood and Napier. Of those not mentioned in the text the books used by Morris were: Delormois, *'L'art de faire l'indienne à l'instar d'Angleterre, et de composer toutes les couleurs, bon teint, propres à l'indienne'.* (Paris 1770).
Henrik Theophil Scheffer, *Essai sur l'art de la teinture.* (Paris 1787). Camille Koechlin, a French manufacturer from Toulouse in France was the originator of a refined system of turkey-red dyeing. No patents were taken out by him nor did he publish his work, but a British patent was taken out in the early nineteenth century by James Thompson of Clitheroe, Lancashire.

17 A survey of the natural dyestuffs used by Joshua Wardle has been published by F. Celoria in 'Fifty early 19th century dyestuffs', *Science and Archaeology* No. 7 July–September 1971.

18 Wardle was a founder member and for some time President of the Silk Association of Great Britain and Ireland (founded 1887).

19 Specimens of raw and spun silk produced under Wardle's direction are in the collections of the Victoria and Albert Museum.

20 Morris's initial contribution is considerably minimized in an article by Mabel Cox, 'Arts and Crafts Workers IV. Sir Thomas Wardle and the Art of Dyeing and Printing', *The Artist* 1897.

21 Wardle's costs were high and Morris complained about them. On 5 November 1875 he wrote, 'the prices are more than double Clarksons for block-printed cloths, and *his* prices are I am sure from the way we began business with him calculated above the usual scale.' Clarksons charged 1/5½d for cloths printed with two colours and 3/9d for nine colours.

22 Mackail op. cit. Vol. I p. 317.

23 The same system of pattern numbers was retained by Morris & Co. see catalogue.

24 Watts and Company, the leading ecclesiastical outfitters were turned down by Wardle. See Morris's letter of 25 March 1877.

25 The Wardle firm continued to print these designs throughout Morris and Company's history and in the twentieth century a few more patterns were added to this range.

26 This became Morris's 'party trick' for visitors. Fanny Wright, the embroideress, visited the Merton Abbey Works as a young girl with a number of her colleagues and remembered being upset at having her handkerchief whisked away from her by Morris and plunged irretrievably into the indigo vat to show the technique.

27 Emma Lazarus, 'A Day in Surrey with William Morris', *The Century Illustrated Magazine*, Vol. XXXII No. J. July 1886.

28 Much greater details of Morris's dyeing techniques can be found in an excellent unpublished thesis written by Peter Roberts, a copy of which was presented by the author to the William Morris Gallery, Walthamstow.

29 George Wardle op. cit.

30 These exhibits found their way into the South Kensington Museum through the Indian Section.

31 In 1919 Morris and Co. presented the Victoria and Albert Museum with a representative collection of Morris prints but *Carnation* was not amongst the first pieces delivered. H. C. Marillier, on behalf of the firm, wrote to the Museum, 'It was not one of William Morris's own designs, and for this reason I omitted it from the collection'. A sample of this pattern was subsequently sent.

32 Fiona Clark, *William Morris Wallpapers and Chintzes* (London 1973).

33 Introduction to the British India Section. Paris International Exhibition catalogue 1878.

34 'The Influence of South Kensington' in 'Dating Morris Patterns', *The Architectural Review*, July 1959.

35 Donald King, 'Textiles and the origins of printing in Europe', *Pantheon* International Zeitschrift für Kunst (Munich 1962) Vol. XX pp. 23–30.

36 *Textiles*, Arts and Crafts Lecture 1888.

37 A velveteen pattern book in the Victoria and Albert Museum contains samples of *Acanthus, Cherwell, Wey, Florence, Severn* and *Mole*.

38 Eighteen illustrations used by Morris for *Some Hints on Pattern Making*, a lecture given to the Working Men's College, London on 10 December 1881, are now in the William Morris Gallery, Walthamstow.

39 Patent Office Pattern Registers show a number of these Japanese cottons from 1873.

40 Aymer Vallance, *William Morris: His Art, His Writings and His Public Life* (London 1897).

41 George Wardle op. cit.

42 This thorough finishing may not always have been followed as a few samples of Morris printed cottons bled madder dye when tested in the Conservation Department of the Victoria and Albert Museum in preparation for an exhibition in 1978.

43 Red and yellow blocks for the design *Strawberry Thief*, now part of the set at the Victoria and Albert Museum are now impregnated with coloured dye.

44 The Merton Abbey dye-book had been exhibited in two exhibitions – *Morris & Co.*, Stanford Art Gallery, Stanford University, California 4 March – 4 May 1975 (catalogue no. 50). *The Pre-Raphaelite Era 1848–1914*, Delaware Art Museum, 12 April – 6 June 1976 (catalogue 4–56).

45 J. W. Mackail op. cit. Vol. II p. 59

46 George Wardle op. cit.

47 *Campion* and *Violet and Columbine* registered in March and April 1883 and *Granada*, an experimental piece.

48 By 1889 two other printers were also on the staff. The Arts and Crafts Exhibition catalogue for that year mentions George Hill, Harry Hill and F. Townsend.

49 John Brandon-Jones, 'The Importance of Philip Webb' in *William Morris & Kelmscott* (London 1981).

50 The period was also marked with a change in pattern names.

All of these 'flowing' designs are named after tributaries of the Thames, a subject of great interest to Morris. In the Summer of 1880 he set out with friends to trace by boat the Thames from Hammersmith to Lechlade (Kelmscott House to Kelmscott Manor). The journey is described in his *News from Nowhere* published as a book in 1891.

51 Victoria and Albert Museum number 442–1883

52 Mackail op. cit. Vol. II p. 35

53 George Wardle op. cit.

54 Ibid.

55 William Morris Gallery, Walthamstow, BL A479.

Woven Textiles

1 Eight of these designs were reproductions, three were adapted from other media and one, referred to in the firm's printed catalogue as 'figured rep' has not been identified. This is likely to have been a plain or slightly patterned fabric.

2 Morris & Co. catalogues *Morris Chintzes, Silks, Tapestries, Etc, c.* 1912.

3 Aymer Vallance, *William Morris: His Art, His Writings and His Public Life*, (London 1897).

4 Both of these designs were rewoven by the East Anglia Weaving Company for Sanderson's in the 1950s but were not commercially successful. The weaving firm closed in 1971 when the factory was demolished to make way for a new road.

5 The only textile manufacturers exhibiting at this time with these initials were Bennett and Adams fine linen weavers in Coleraine, Ireland and Bradwell and Adams of Ardwick, Manchester who were manufacturers of commemorative printed velveteens.

6 Lucie Armstrong, 'Silks and Satins', *Art Journal* (1891) p. 19.

7 'The Lesser Arts of Life'. Part of 'Hopes and Fears for Art', a series of five lectures published in 1882, given by Morris in Birmingham, London and Nottingham.

8 *The Commonweal* (paper of the Social Democratic Federation) for 6 August 1887

9 May Morris, *William Morris artist, writer, socialist* (London 1936) Vol. I p. 48.

10 Now in the City Museum and Art Gallery, Birmingham.

11 Letter from Morris to Thomas Wardle, 17 November 1876. Part of a set of typescript copies in the National Art Library, Victoria and Albert Museum.

12 Letter dated 13 April 1877 op. cit.

13 Peter Floud 'Dating Morris Patterns', the *Architectural Review* (July 1959).

14 An essay on the subject of Morris's bird designs has been written by Jacqueline Herald 'On Designing Textiles with Birds' in *William Morris and Kelmscott* (London 1981).

15 Jacqueline Herald op. cit.

16 J. W. Mackail, *The Life of William Morris* (London 1899) I.

17 Jocelyn Morton, *Three Generations in a Family Textile Firm* (London 1971).

18 Exhibited in 'The Mortons' exhibition held at the Victoria and Albert Museum, 1973.

19 'Weighting' means passing silk through a solution of tin.

20 Estimates and bills now in the National Art Library, Victoria and Albert Museum.

21 A sample of *Whittingaeme* is now in the Victoria and Albert Museum and the later weaving of *St James* can be studied in the archives of Warner & Sons at Braintree in Essex.

22 A Bedford Lemere photograph of this room is now in the National Monument Record. Illustrated in Nicholas Cooper, *The Opulent Eye* (London 1976) plate 133.

23 The gold thread was made of gilt paper wound around a silk core.

24 The textile was exhibited in Paris and was sold to the Museum through a French dealer, M. Brucciani. A member of the Rothschild family saw the textile on exhibition and offered the dealer far in excess of what had already been agreed but the original deal was honoured.

25 Catalogue numbers 403 called *Ispalian*, 410 and 438 both 'silk brocatelle' and 422 'silk and linen damask'.

26 In the archive at the William Morris Gallery, Walthamstow.

27 Quoted in Philip Henderson, *William Morris: his life, work and friends* (London 1967) p. 192.

28 Emma Lazarus, 'A Day in Surrey with William Morris,' *The Country Illustrated Magazine* July 1886 Vol XXXII No. J.

29 The Museum of Decorative Art, Copenhagen, bought this from the dealer Hirchwald in Berlin in 1894; the Nordenfjeldske Kunstindustrimuseum, Trondheim, from Bing in Paris in 1897, and the Bellerive Museum from Morris & Co., London in 1905.

30 Samples of *Apple* in the Morris & Co. pattern book, Victoria and Albert Museum are in artificial silk.

31 Morris & Co. catalogue, *Morris Chintzes, Silks Tapestries Etc, c.* 1912.

32 *Handweaver and Craftsman* magazine, 1930.

33 Edward Payne, 'Memories of Morris & Co.', *The Journal of the William Morris Society*, Vol. IV No. 3, Summer 1981.

34 Morris & Co.'s last catalogue published between 1917 and 1925.

Carpets

1 There were three Orient Line boats launched between 1886–8 and it is likely that these were carpeted by Morris. Existing illustrations of the interior of the liners take the form of advertising drawings, which give no detail of furnishing patterns.

2 Patent Office carpet registers for the period show as many designs for linoleum as for carpets.

3 The catalogue was published after 1925 as the term 'Morris and Company Art Workers Ltd' is used.

4 'Textiles', Arts and Crafts Lecture, 1888.

5 A description of Morris's aims from the Morris and Company brochure for the Boston Foreign Fair of 1883, quoted in Ray Wilkinson's *William Morris as Designer* (London 1967).

6 'Some Hints on Pattern Designing', a lecture delivered at the Working Men's College, London, 10 December 1881.

7 Ibid.

8 Philip Henderson, *Letters of William Morris* (London 1950) p. 71.

9 Called *Poppy* and used as a table-cloth border for 1 Holland Park. Illustrated in Day (p. 18).

10 Design is illustrated in 'The Art of William Morris', by Lewis F. Day, Easter Art Annual, *Art Journal Extra Number*, 1899.

11 Carpet designs are transferred on to graph or point-paper of squares to signify to the jacquard card puncher, or the hand weaver where a particular colour (and subsequently the pattern) is needed.

12 The Heckmondwike Manufacturing Co. Ltd. were, at the time, one of the few carpet manufacturers to complete all manufacturing processes from the treatment of raw materials to spinning, dyeing, weaving and finishing, all at their own premises.

13 Letter to Thomas Wardle. Typescript in the National Art Library, Victoria and Albert Museum.

14 In the Morris & Co. catalogue *Embroidery Work* (c. 1912) 6 designs, available in 16 colourings for 3-ply carpeting, are mentioned and one design in 2-ply (available in 3 colourings).

15 *Tulip and Rose, Vine and Pomegranate, Campion, Honeycomb, Wreath, Artichoke, Daisy, Bluebell, Tulip and Lily*, Unidentified design (William Morris Gallery, number F29).

16 'Textiles', Arts and Crafts Lecture, 1888.

17 Public Record Office, registered number 317781.

18 Public Record Office, registered number 330645. Morris found out that the Heckmondwike firm were selling this pattern to other retailers, chiefly to one of his greatest competitors, Maples. Morris and George Wardle went to see Sir John Maple to complain but Maple saw no harm in the venture believing that he too should be able to benefit. George Wardle *Memorials of William Morris*, 1897 British Library, Add. Ms.

19 J. W. Mackail, *The Life of William Morris* (London 1899) Vol. I p. 355.

20 An ex-Morris worker, Mr W. C. Powell, stated in a letter of July 1952 to the Victoria and Albert Museum that 'The Wilton Royal Carpet Co. Ltd. were the only people who made all the carpets sold by Morris & Company whilst I was in their employ'. Mr Powell started work there in 1928.

21 Brochure for the Boston Foreign Fair, 1883 op. cit.

22 J. W. Mackail op. cit. p. 357

23 *Daisy* was also woven as Brussels carpeting. A sample of this has been used to cover a footstool, now at Kelmscott Manor.

24 Lewis F. Day op. cit. p. 3.

25 Sample in the Victoria and Albert Museum.

26 Designs for these two carpets are illustrated in 'A Disciple of William Morris' by Lewis F. Day in *The Art Journal*, 1905. Two other designs for these carpets are in the Berger Collection.

27 Carpets at the Victoria and Albert Museum, The William Morris Gallery, Walthamstow and Kelmscott Manor.

28 Although advertised as 'in preparation' in 1912, Morris & Co. never published a carpet catalogue.

29 Lewis F. Day 1899 op. cit. (opposite p. 8).

30 Estimates and bills for 1 Holland Park are now in the National Art Library, Victoria and Albert Museum.

31 C. E. C. Tattersall, *A History of British Carpets* (London 1934).

32 Letter from Jack Smith, Marketing Manager of Brintons, written to the Victoria and Albert Museum, 4 February 1954.

33 Museum number 719–1897. Purchased from Janey in 1897 for £200. This carpet hung on the wall of the dining room at Kelmscott House. At least one other carpet from Morris's collection was known to the museum; a seventeenth-century Ushak from Asia Minor lent by May Morris during the twentieth century.

34 See Barbara Morris, 'William Morris and the South Kensington Museum' in *Victorian Poetry*, West Virginia University, Fall/Winter 1975.

35 Letter dated 13 March 1893 to Thomas Armstrong, Director of the Art Division of the Department of Science and Art, Morris first met Armstrong in 1864 through Edward and Georgiana Burne-Jones who were next door neighbours.

36 'Textiles', Arts and Crafts Lecture, 1888.

37 Christopher Dresser, 'Principles of Decorative Design', first published as part of a series of articles in Cassell's *Technical Educator* are issued, revised in book form, in 1873.

38 'Some Hints on Pattern Designing'. Lecture to the Working Men's College, London, 10 December 1881.

39 *The Hammersmith Carpets*, Morris and Co. brochure, October 1882.

40 Letter dated 13 April 1877, quoted in Philip Henderson, *The Letters of William Morris* (London 1950).

41 Although never stated, it is likely that the weaver was from the Glasgow firm of John Lyle & Company Ltd. who produced hand-woven carpets before turning to Brussels, Wilton and Axminster machine techniques.

42 In 1889, entries list weavers 'The Misses E. & M. Merritt and L. & M Phipps'.

43 Quoted in Paul Thompson, *The Work of William Morris* (London 1967).

44 One rug at the William Morris Gallery, Walthamstow (a design is in the Victoria and Albert Museum) shows a border of pairs of facing birds, almost identical to some of her own embroideries.

45 Letter to Georgiana Burne-Jones, August 1880, quoted in Henderson op. cit. p. 138.

46 All in the Victoria and Albert Museum.

47 Henderson op. cit. p. 153.

48 Mackail and other biographers wrongly date this 1880.

49 Oliver Fairclough and Emeline Leary, *Textiles by William Morris and Morris & Co. 1861–1940* (London 1981) p. 53.

50 The inscription on C. 16, Kelmscott House Collection (which is a design for St James's Palace) infers that Carbrook was being decorated at the same time.

51 A popular design, Morris gave examples of this rug to his sister Henrietta and as a present to Margaret Burne-Jones on her marriage to J. W. Mackail. The latter is now in the Victoria and Albert Museum. Another is in the collection of the William Morris Gallery, Walthamstow and at least one other is in private hands.

52 Exhibited in the Arts and Crafts Exhibition of 1899.

53 *Morris & Company in Cambridge*, Fitzwilliam Museum, Cambridge, exhibition held September-November 1980 (no. III).

54 'Morris. Walter Crane. Ashbee. Voysey. Und die Englische Abterlung in Turin 1902' in *Deutsche Kunst und Dekoration* Vol. XI, February 1903.

55 Lent to the Victoria and Albert Museum for photography in the 1950s.

56 Douglas Griffiths 'Reminiscences of a tapestry weaver', Notes in the William Morris Gallery, Walthamstow.

57 Exhibited at the *Victorian and Edwardian Decorative Arts*

Tapestry

1 'Some Hints on Pattern Designing', lecture to the Working Men's College, 10 December 1881.

2 Letter from William Morris to Thomas Wardle, 13 April 1877.

3 Letter to Thomas Wardle, 14 November 1877.

4 E.B.Bence-Jones, *The Holy Grail Tapestries* unpublished typescript. National Art Library, Victoria and Albert Museum.

5 'Lesser Arts of Life' op. cit.

6 Aymer Vallance, 'The Revival of Tapestry Weaving, an interview with William Morris' in *Studio*, Vol. III, 1894.

7 Both recommendations were backed by other advisers, Burne-Jones for the *Troy* tapestries and George Howard, Earl of Carlisle, for the other. See 'Morris and the South Kensington Museum' in *Victorian Poetry*, West Virginia University, Fall-Winter 1975.

8 Linda L.A.Parry, 'The Tapestries of Edward Burne-Jones' in *Apollo*, November 1975.

9 J.W.Mackail, *The Life of William Morris*, Vol. I p. 230.

10 Linda L.A.Parry op. cit.

11 Morris Socialist diary for 26 January 1887.

12 Lecture to Birmingham School of Art, 1894.

13 Museum number E. 1–1955.

14 A number of these panels survive in private and public collections. Examples at the William Morris Gallery, Walthamstow depict heads, hands and feet as well as panels of floral details. The Sanford and Helen Berger Collection has two small floral panels and a small horizontal design, of flowers and a bramble against a wooden fence, is at Kelmscott Manor.

15 Aymer Vallance op. cit.

16 E.B.Bence-Jones op. cit.

17 Ibid.

18 The Royal Windsor Tapestry Works utilized the *basse lisse* method and both men found it difficult at first to adapt to the upright looms.

19 Information gained by the author from an interview with Percy Sheldrick.

20 Now at the William Morris Gallery, Walthamstow.

21 'Tributes to Walter Taylor', *The Weavers Journal* 1966, pp. 827–8.

22 A number of William Haines panels, and his indentures for the Royal Windsor Tapestry Works were given to the Victoria and Albert Museum in 1980 by his son Victor.

23 H.C.Marillier, *History of the Merton Abbey Tapestry Works* (London 1927).

24 The cartoon was bought by the Victoria and Albert Museum for £70 in 1898.

25 A set acquired by the Victoria and Albert Museum in 1896 were shown to Morris who greatly admired them.

26 A design of Dearle's new background for *Flora* inscribed 'Baroda Museum' is in William Morris Gallery, Walthamstow.

27 Marillier lists ten small *Flora* tapestries of which two were woven in 1896 three in 1898, and two in 1900. Single tapestries were woven in 1904, 1915 and 1920. Another version not listed by Marillier was woven by Arthur Wingate and Wallace Stevens in 1938 and presented to Lady Chilston. Marillier lists six small *Pomona* tapestries, woven in 1898, 1899, 1900, 1903, 1904, 1920. All of these tapestries are still in private hands except for one set of the two designs at Exeter College, Oxford, a *Pomona* panel at the Harris Art Gallery, Preston, also at the Victoria and Albert Museum and at the Art Institute of Chicago and a *Flora* panel in the collection of the Walker Art Gallery, Liverpool.

28 All of the inscriptions on Morris & Co. tapestries were embroidered under the direction of May Morris by the firm's embroidery section.

29 This sample of tapestry was acquired by the museum from a London dealer.

30 Plate 147, Nicholas Cooper, *The Opulent Eye* (London 1976).

31 Aymer Vallance op. cit.

32 Duncan Robinson and Stephen Wildman, *Morris & Company in Cambridge* 1980 no. 53 p. 37.

33 This tapestry was also referred to as *The Seasons*.

34 Marillier published this as *St Cecilia*, 1887, although his own unpublished catalogue in the Victoria and Albert Museum attributes this correctly.

35 *St Cecilia* was designed in 1875 for the East window of St George's Chapel, Christchurch Cathedral, Oxford. It was used with the *St Agnes* design as part of the windows of the 1877 commission for St Helen's church, Welton near Brough in Yorkshire. (see A.Charles Sewter, *The Stained Glass of William Morris and His Circle*, Yale 1974).

36 The stained glass cartoon, worked in 1880, is in the City Museum and Art Gallery, Carlisle.

37 Illustrated in Marillier op. cit. p. 10.

38 *Angeli Laudantes* was repeated in 1898 and 1902. In 1904 one single angel with the inscription 'Alelulia' was woven. This is now in the Harris Art Gallery, Preston. In the same year a pair of single angels with harps were woven as a private memorial. In 1905 two large tapestries with the angel figures but altered backgrounds, extended to include verdures of shields, were woven for Eton College chapel, as memorials of those who died in the Boer War. These are probably the first panels to bear the weavers' initials.

39 Mackail Vol. II p. 226.

40 Repeated in 1894 (for Wilfrid Blunt), 1895 (Eton College), 1900, 1901, 1902, 1904, 1906 (for Carrow Abbey) and 1907 (Roker Church).

41 Invoice now in the National Art Library, Victoria and Albert Museum.

42 'The Arras Tapestries of the San Graal at Stanmore Hall', in *Studio*, Vol. XV, 1899, Linda Parry, 'The Stanmore Hall Tapestries' in *Art at Auction*, 1978.

43 E.B.Bence-Jones op. cit.

44 'Art, Craft and Life, a chat with Mr William Morris', *The Daily Chronicle*, Monday 9 October 1893.

45 E.B.Bence-Jones op. cit.

46 Sotheby's, 16 July 1920, lot 130.

47 Lots 91 to 93, the tapestries fetched £36,000, £28,000 and £40,000 respectively.

48 According to Marillier the fifth and sixth tapestries were woven together although later sales catalogues contradict this.

49 Photocopy of a letter, DD/235/29. Hammersmith Public

Libraries.

50 The Victoria and Albert Museum owns the colour negative.

51 Correspondence between Booth and Morris & Co. is held in the Archive of American Art, New York. A wood and metal cage containing a moulded figure of Venus was made for Burne-Jones to copy in his studio. See 'Notes on some unfinished works of Sir Edward Burne-Jones by his son'. *The Magazine of Art*, 1900, p. 162.

52 Letter in the National Art Library, Victoria and Albert Museum.

53 Elizabeth Longford, *A Pilgrimage of Passion, the life of Wilfrid Scawen Blunt* (London 1979) p. 283

54 An embroidered copy was made of this tapestry, the size reduced from 8ft 11 in × 19 ft 3 in to 5 ft 6 in × 8 ft 8 in.

55 Edward Confessor, Henry II and St John as Pilgrim are owned by Westminster Abbey and two of these, the first and third panels, were exhibited in Birmingham Museum and Art Gallery, 1980 (exhibition numbers T. 26, 27).

56 'A disciple of William Morris', *The Art Journal*, 1905, pp. 85–89.

57 Now in Whitworth Art Gallery, University of Manchester.

58 There are a number of Dearle tapestry designs in the Sanford and Helen Berger Collection including a small detailed study of *Fox and Pheasant* and two drawings for *Greenery*. Also in the collection is a small notebook marked 'JHDearle Oct. 20/76 which shows drawings of foxes, deer etc.

59 *Metropolitan Museum Bulletin*, Vol 5, 1947.

60 Fleming owned '*The Chase* (woven in 1908), *Ehret die Frauen* (1912), *The Brook* (1916), two late versions of the small *Flora* and *Pomona* tapestries (1920) and the second weaving of *Love and the Pilgrim*. The *Flora* and *Pomona* panels were sold by Lindsay Fleming on 12 February 1965 and the other panels were sold at Sotheby Belgravia on 7 June 1972.

61 Marillier op. cit.

62 The Victoria and Albert Museum owns a scroll panel and *Flowery Bough*.

63 Illustrated in *Studio Yearbook*, 1910, p. 130.

64 Illustrated in *Studio Yearbook*, 1910, p. 131.

65 The second, fifth, fourth and sixth panel are illustrated in *Studio Yearbook of Decorative Art*, 1917, p. 80. (illustrated in this order.)

66 28 June 1922. Letter in Archive of American Art, New York.

67 As the Hon. Mrs Akers Douglas, Lady Chilston wrote a number of articles on tapestry for *Country Life* in the 1930s.

68 *David Instructing Solomon in the Building of the Temple* was hung at the back of the clergy's marquee at the laying of the cornerstone of the church in 1926.

69 Douglas Griffiths' reminiscences are documented at the William Morris Gallery, Walthamstow.

70 G.F.Wingfield Digby and Wendy Hefford, *Victoria and Albert Museum – The Tapestry Collection*, Medieval and Renaissance, 1980, cat. no. 39, illus. 59B.

71 May Lea (*née* Harris) *Memories of Working for Morris & Company* Typewritten document in the author's possession.

Morris textiles, interior design and the retail trade

1 Emma Lazarus, 'A Day in Surrey with William Morris', *The Country Illustrated Magazine*, July 1886 V X X X II No. J.

2 Ibid.

3 J.W.Mackail, *The Life of William Morris* Vol. II p. 63.

4 Emma Lazarus op. cit.

5 Quoted in Jack Lindsay, *William Morris* (London 1975) p. 149.

6 H. Muthesius, *Das Englische Haus* (Berlin 1905) illus. 62, 160, 161, 162, 169.

7 Mackail op. cit. Vol. I p. 164.

8 George Wardle, *Memorials of William Morris, Christmas 1897*, Add Ms. 45350, British Library.

9 Mackail op. cit. Vol. I p. 289.

10 A.R.Dufty, *Kelmscott, An Illustrated Guide* London Society of Antiquaries, 1977.

11 A.R.Dufty 'Kelmscott' in *William Morris and Kelmscott* (London 1981).

12 Many objects have been added since the house was taken over by the Society of Antiquaries in 1962.

13 May Morris, *A Visit of the Workers' Educational Association to Kelmscott Manor, 15th July 1916*. A specially printed essay.

14 Quoted from an unpublished letter written to the Women's Guild of Art on 14 October 1939 paying tribute to May Morris.

15 British Library Add. Ms. 45338.

16 Unpublished letter from Helena Maria Sickert to the Women's Guild of Art, 7 June 1939.

17 May Lea (*née* Harris.) *Memories of Working for Morris and Company* A typewritten document in the author's possession.

18 Letter written 7 March 1940 to the Women's Guild of Art.

19 Report of William Morris's will in the *Daily News* (Thursday, 17 December 1896). Morris left £55,069 and apart from life annuities for Bessie Burden (£150) and Jenny's nurse, Emma Oldham, (£100), Janey was left all leasehold property contents, up to £500 worth of books and at least £1,000 a year in order to keep herself and Jenny. May was willed an annuity during her mother's lifetime of £250; the estate transferring to her on her mother's death.

20 Catalogue for the exhibition *Morris & Company 1861–1940*, Arts Council 1961.

21 From incomplete correspondence on file at the Victoria and Albert Museum.

22 For this information the author thanks Mr Adolph S. Cavallo and Susan Anderson of the Textiles department, Philadelphia Museum of Art.

23 W.R.Lethaby, 'Philip Webb and His Work', *The Builder*, 1925.

24 Mark Girouard, *The Victorian Country House* (London 1979).

25 Mackail op. cit. Vol. II.

26 Girouard op. cit.

27 Ibid.

28 See articles in *The Connoisseur* (January 1962) and in *The Antique Collector* (June 1975).

29 From an inventory of part of the house made by a member of staff of the Victoria and Albert Museum, 1921.

30 In 'The Work of Ernest Newton' *The Studio* 1898 pp. 170–178.

31 *Standen, Sussex*, the National Trust, 1979

32 For information concerning the Barr-Smiths I would like to thank Mrs Jessie Serle.

INDEX